Street-Level Bureaucracy

STREET-LEVEL BUREAUCRACY

Dilemmas of the Individual in Public Services

M I C H A E L   L I P S K Y

Russell Sage Foundation

NEW YORK

The Russell Sage Foundation

The Russell Sage Foundation, one of the oldest of America's general purpose foundations, was established in 1907 by Mrs. Margaret Olivia Sage for "the improvement of social and living conditions in the United States." The Foundation seeks to fulfill this mandate by fostering the development and dissemination of knowledge about the country's political, social, and economic problems. While the Foundation endeavors to assure the accuracy and objectivity of each book it publishes, the conclusions and interpretations in Russell Sage Foundation publications are those of the authors and not of the Foundation, its Trustees, or its staff. Publication by Russell Sage, therefore, does not imply Foundation endorsement.

Library of Congress Cataloging-in-Publication Data

Lipsky, Michael.
   Streel-level democracy : dilemmas of the individual in public services /
   Michael Lipsky.—Updated ed.
   p. cm.
   Includes bibliographical references and index.
   ISBN 978-0-87154-544-2 (alk. paper)
   1. Social workers.   2. Social policy.   I. Title.
   HV41.L53 2010
   361.301--dc22   2010003955

The paper used in this publication meets the minimum requirements of American National Standard for Information Sciences—Permanence of Paper for Printed Library Materials. ANSI Z39.48-1992.

RUSSELL SAGE FOUNDATION
112 East 64th Street, New York, New York 10065
10 9 8 7 6 5 4 3 2 1

For Joshua and Jacob

CONTENTS

Contents

Contents

PREFACE

Dilemmas of the Individual in Public Services

Prepared For The Thirtieth Anniversary, Expanded Edition Of Street-Level Bureaucracy

This book is in part a search for the place of the individual in those public services I call street-level bureaucracies. These are the schools, police and welfare departments, lower courts, legal services offices, and other agencies whose workers interact with and have wide discretion over the dispensation of benefits or the allocation of public sanctions.

It is also an inquiry into the structure of one of those resonant moments in civic life. Like driving on interstate highways, playing in a public park, voting, dining in a smoke-free restaurant, paying taxes, and listening to National Public Radio, interactions with street-level bureaucracies are places where citizens experience directly the government they have implicitly constructed. Unlike these other experiences, however, citizen encounters with street-level bureaucracies are not straightforward; instead, they involve complex interactions with public workers that may deeply affect the benefits and sanctions they receive.

Street-Level Bureaucracy was originally published in 1980 and made two distinctive claims. The first was that the exercise of discretion was a critical dimension of much of the work of teachers, social workers, police officers, and other public workers who regularly interact with citizens in the course of their jobs. Further, the jobs typically could not be performed according to the highest standards of decision making in the various fields because street-level workers lacked the time, information, or other resources necessary to respond properly to the individual case. Instead, street-level bureaucrats manage their difficult jobs by developing routines of practice and psychologically simplifying their clientele and environment in ways that strongly influence the outcomes of their efforts. Mass processing of clients is the norm, and has important implications for the quality of treatment and services.

These observations are instructive in themselves, and have profound implications for public policy. They suggest that understanding public policies in street-level bureaucracies requires analysis of how the unsanctioned work responses of street-level bureaucrats combine with rules and agency pronouncements to add up to what the public ultimately experiences as agency performance.

The second claim was that work as diverse and apparently unrelated as that of guidance counselors, judges, police officers, and social workers to a degree is structurally similar, so that one could compare these work settings with each other. Describing front-line public service delivery in terms of a small number of analytic characteristics made possible a new way of seeing these very familiar public roles, and how they were like and different from one another.

However diverse these occupations otherwise are, they could now be seen as embodying an essential paradox that plays out in a variety of ways. On the one hand, the work is often highly scripted to achieve policy objectives that have their origins in the political process. On the other hand, the work requires improvisation and responsiveness to the individual case. Not only that, but generally the public wants administrators of public services to be at least open to the possibility that a special case is presenting itself, or that extraordinary efforts of one sort or another are called for.

Essentially all the great reform efforts of the last thirty years to improve performance or accountability in street-level public services may be understood as attempts to manage this apparently paradoxical reality: how to treat all citizens alike in their claims on government, and how at the same time to be responsive to the individual case when appropriate. The phrase "street-level bureaucracy" hints at this paradox. "Bureaucracy" implies a set of rules and structures of authority; "street-level" implies a distance from the center where authority presumably resides.

In *Street-Level Bureaucracy*, I show how people experience public policies in realms that are critical to our welfare and sense of community. Too often we read about education, policing, social work, and other vital public services without realizing or being given concrete understanding of how these public policies result from the aggregation of the separate actions of many individuals, or how and why the actions in question are consistently reproduced by the behavior of individuals.

The book is grounded in observations of the collective behavior of public service organizations and advances a theory of the work of street-level bureaucracies as individual workers experience it. I argue that the decisions of street-level bureaucrats, the routines they establish, and the devices they invent to cope with uncertainties and work pressures, effectively *become* the public policies they carry out. I maintain that public policy is not best understood as made in legislatures or top-floor suites of high-ranking administrators. These decision-making arenas are important, of course, but they do not represent the complete picture. To the mix of places where policies are made, one must add the crowded offices and daily encounters of street-level workers. Further, I point out that policy conflict is not only expressed as the contention of interest groups, as we have come to expect. It is also located in the struggles between individual workers and citizens who challenge or submit to client-processing.

For example, many people are convinced that police officers disproportionately single out African Americans for scrutiny and wrongly use skin color and racial characteristics to target blacks for attention. Police officials invariably deny that they engage in racial profiling, and suggest that if blacks are stopped disproportionately it is because they act in ways that legitimately trigger police inquiry. It is evident that, to the extent racial profiling exists, it arises not from official policy or direct racial orientations but out of the ways police officers draw on social stereotypes in exercising the discretion sanctioned by their departments.

Similarly, we know that service bureaucracies consistently favor some clients over others, despite official policies designed to treat people alike. To understand how and why these organizations sometimes perform contrary to their own rules and goals, we need to know how the rules are experienced by workers in the organization, what latitude workers have in acting on their preferences, and what other pressures they experience.

Few callings deserve greater respect than those involving public service. As citizens we are grateful to those people who teach our children, protect life and property, manage our natural resources, and help people in need to access social services. These functions have evolved as hallmarks of inclusive, prosperous societies throughout the world. Some street-level occupations are highly respected and well-paid. Others, such as some social workers, have a more contested position in society. Some operate in relative obscurity, whereas others, such as police officers and child protection workers, are among those who are often in the news for regrettable developments. If a child dies while in protective care, or a person is badly treated while in custody, everyone in those agencies experiences the resulting public criticism.

One important way in which street-level bureaucrats experience their work is in their struggle to make it more consistent with their strong commitments to public service and the high expectations they have for their chosen careers. People often enter public employment with a commitment to serving the community. Teachers, social workers, public defenders, and police officers partly seek out these occupations because they offer socially useful roles. Yet the very nature of these occupations can prevent recruits to street-level bureaucracies from coming even close to the ideal conception of their jobs. Large classes, huge caseloads, and other challenging workload pressures combine with the contagious distress of clients who have few resources and multiple problems to defeat their aspirations as service workers.

Ideally and by training, street-level bureaucrats should respond to the individual needs or characteristics of the people they serve or confront. In practice, they must deal with clients collectively, because work requirements prohibit individualized responses. Teachers should respond to the needs of the individual child; in practice, they must develop techniques to manage a classroom of children. Police officers should respond to the presenting case; in reality, they must develop techniques to recognize and respond to various types of confrontations, particularly those that threaten their authority or may pose danger. At best, street-level bureaucrats invent modes of mass processing that more or less permit them to deal with the public fairly, appropriately, and thoughtfully. At worst, they give in to favoritism, stereotyping, convenience, and routinizing—all of which serve their own or agency purposes.

Compromises in work practices and attitudes are often rationalized as reflecting workers' greater experience on the job, their appreciation of practical and political realities, or their more realistic assessment of the nature of the work. But these rationalizations only summarize the prevailing structural constraints on human service bureaucracies. They are not "true" in an absolute sense. The teacher who psychologically abandons her commitment to help every child to read may succumb to a private assessment of the status quo in education. But this compromise says nothing about the potential of individual children to learn or the capacity of the teacher to instruct. This potential remains intact. It is the system of schooling, the organization of the schooling bureaucracy, that teaches that children are developmentally "'slow'" or unmotivated, and that teachers must abandon their early commitments to be an excellent teacher to every child.

In the same way, the criminal justice system allows police recruits to presume that they can approach with impunity young people hanging out in certain neighborhoods to see whether they are in possession of guns or drugs, even if they have no evident cause for suspicion other than the coincidence of age, race, and neighborhood. Young police officers learn that judges will back them up if the young people claim that the officers planted evidence or made up their own descriptions of the encounters. Court officers, judges, prosecutors, and public defenders collaborate in the mass processing of a great many new and repeat juvenile offenders each year yet retain the ideal that each may have his or her fair and full "day in court."

Some street-level bureaucrats drop out or burn out relatively early in their careers. Those who stay on, to be sure, often grow in the jobs and perfect treatment and client-processing techniques that provide an acceptable balance between public aspirations for the work and the coping requirements of the job. These adjustments of work habits and attitudes may reflect lower expectations for themselves, their clients, and the potential of public policy. Ultimately, these adjustments permit acceptance of the view that clients receive the best that can be provided under prevailing circumstances.

Street-level bureaucrats often spend their work lives in these corrupted worlds of service. They believe themselves to be doing the best they can under adverse circumstances, and they develop techniques to salvage service and decision-making values within the limits imposed on them by the structure of the work. They develop conceptions of their work and of their clients that narrow the gap between their personal and work limitations and the service ideal. These work practices and orientations are maintained even as they contribute to the distortion of the service ideal or put the worker in the position of manipulating citizens on behalf of the agencies from which citizens seek help or expect fair treatment.

Should teachers, police officers, or social workers look for other work rather than participate in practices that seem far from ideal? This would mean leaving clients to others who have even fewer concerns and less interest in clients than they do. It would mean not only starting over in a new career, but also abandoning the satisfactory aspects of the work they have managed to carve out.

Should they stay in their jobs and dedicate themselves to changing client-processing conditions from within their agencies? This approach is problematic as well, though it is the career path taken by many who leave direct service for management. In their new positions, some will be reformers striving for change to the limit of their capacity and what the times will bear. Others will settle for the status quo.

The structure of street-level bureaucracy also confronts clients with dilemmas bearing on action. Consumers of public services, for the most part, cannot choose the public services to which they will be subject. They must accept the schools, courts, and police forces of their communities. If they are poor, they must also accept the community's arrangements for health care, income support, housing subsidies and other benefit programs. In approaching the institutions that administer these policies, they must strike a balance between asserting their rights as citizens and conforming to the behaviors public agencies seek to place on them as clients. As citizens, they should seek all to which they are entitled. As bureaucratic subjects, they must temper their demands in accord with their assessment of the limitations of the public agencies which control benefits and sanctions. Although it is apparent that exceptions are often made and additional resources often found, clients also recognize the potential costs of unsuccessfully asserting their rights.

On matters of the greatest urgency and moment, such as health care, education, justice, housing, and income, clients passively seek support and fair treatment from public agencies when evidence and experience suggest that their hopes may go unrewarded. The dilemmas of action may be particularly acute if clients are poor, are immigrants, or are of a different racial or ethnic background than the public employees with whom they interact. Should I wait my turn and submit to the procedures of the agency, despite reservations? I risk being unable to gain attention to my particular needs and concerns. Should I speak out forcefully and demand my rights? I risk antagonizing the workers by disrupting office procedures.

It is no small thing to adjust successfully to the rigors of the street-level workplace. Virtually all jobs involve adjustments to routines of practice, challenges to keeping a fresh outlook despite repetitive tasks, and compromises between personal needs and vocational requirements. Despite the many barriers to effective practice described in these pages, street-level bureaucrats frequently manage to find a satisfactory balance between the realities of the job and personal fulfillment. The society is all the better for their capacity to find a satisfactory balance in their work life.

When I originally wrote this book, I was intent on elaborating on the coping behaviors of street-level bureaucrats. In doing so I emphasized the gap between the realities of practice and service ideals. This approach had its value, to judge from the reception the book has enjoyed over the years. But it led to neglect of an important reality: vast numbers of people in public service on a daily basis go to work at rewarding and fulfilling jobs. They meet their classes, carry out their assignments, and manage their caseloads without much complaint. Work goes on in these public service organizations to general satisfaction. Partly this is because workers, clients, and the general public have more modest expectations than they might have. But it also goes on because frontline workers have figured out how to do what they regard as a reasonable job with resources at their disposal.

How does one reconcile a clear-eyed assessment of the dilemmas of street-level bureaucracy with the reality that many if not most teachers, police officers, and social workers like what they do and do their jobs relatively well by community standards?

There are two ways to understand the term "street-level bureaucrat." One is to equate it with the public services with which citizens typically interact. In this sense, all teachers, police officers, and social workers in public agencies are street-level bureaucrats without further qualification. This is the way the term has commonly come to be used.

Another way—the one I originally intended—was to define street-level bureaucracy as public service employment of a certain sort, performed under certain conditions. In this second approach, street-level bureaucrats interact with citizens in the course of the job and have discretion in exercising authority; in addition, they cannot do the job according to ideal conceptions of the practice because of the limitations of the work structure.

When I first wrote the book, I did not mean to suggest that every frontline worker experienced stressful working conditions. I know teachers who with little effort are able to pay attention to every child in their small school. I know art teachers who experience little stress in leading their classrooms through exercises. I know National Park rangers whose daily routines require coping with boredom as much as anything else.

In this second conception of the term, in other words, not every teacher, police officer, or public social worker experiences the pressures that I stated street-level bureaucrats face by definition. Frontline workers whose jobs are relatively free of restrictive structural constraints will still develop routines in response to their work requirements. But the routines will not be developed primarily to cope with a difficult work environment. If we adopt the second perspective, we can see that not every frontline worker experiences the pressures this book analyzes.

Additionally, although many street-level coping behaviors may widen the gap between policy as written and policy as performed, other coping behaviors reflect acceptable compromises between the goals of enacted policy and the needs of the street-level workers. Not every coping mechanism distances the worker from the goals of the organization. Indeed, the best workers are the ones who bridge the gap.

Perhaps it is best to imagine a continuum of work experiences ranging from those that are deeply stressful and the processing of clients is severely underresourced, to those that provide a reasonable balance between job requirements and successful practice. Workers' places on that continuum might change over time as they gain experience, as caseloads and assignments vary, or as the workplace itself adopts new approaches or engages new clienteles. All street-level bureaucrats potentially confront circumstances that lead them to coping mechanisms representing departures from the service ideal. But all frontline workers do not cope with these issues all the time.

Still another reason that many street-level bureaucrats can successfully negotiate the gap between the ways they cope with their jobs and public expectations is that those expectations are undoubtedly considerably lower than the ideal. Public expectations may replicate on a societal basis the compromises street-level bureaucrats adopt in coping with their clients person by person.

This can be explained partly by the fact that the work of street-level bureaucrats is mostly hidden from public view, so even attentive citizens do not necessarily know what is going on agency by agency. Also, to the extent that general expectations of public services go beyond demands for efficiency and honest administration, they are likely to focus on incremental improvement. That is, the hopes of the public for improved agency performance are likely to focus on marginal changes in client or administrative outcomes, and are likely to be based on limited indicators. Reformers who hold out for prospects of radically better services and client outcomes tend to be dismissed as excessively idealistic.

A final set of dilemmas confronts citizens who are continuously, if implicitly, asked to evaluate public services. This occurs in focused forums such as a referendum on a school budget or a revolt against high property taxes. It also occurs in diffuse expressions of dissatisfaction with the public sector, such as Colorado's famous Taxpayers' Bill of Rights (TABOR), which set in motion a drastic decline in public services until TABOR was suspended by voters in 2005. Indeed, the many initiatives to limit state and local spending in recent decades have largely been understood as attacks on the value of government.

What are the policy alternatives? When all the "fat" has been trimmed from agency budgets and all the "waste" eliminated, the basic choices remain: to further automate, systematize, and regulate the interactions between government employees and citizens seeking help; to drift with the current turmoil that favors reduced services and greater standardization in the name of cost effectiveness and budgetary controls; or to secure or restore the importance of human interactions in services that require discretionary intervention or involvement.

How much can human intervention be eliminated from teaching, nursing, policing, and judging? The fact is that we must have people making decisions and treating other citizens in the public services. We are not prepared as a society to abandon decisions about people and discretionary intervention to machines and programmed formats. Yet how can one advocate greater attention to the intervening and discretionary roles of street-level bureaucrats in the face of the enormous and often well-deserved popular discontent with the effectiveness and quality of their work?

I try to address these questions in this book. I do not exonerate street-level bureaucracies, excuse their deficiencies, or urge their support as currently structured. Rather, I locate the problem of street-level bureaucrats in the structure of their work, and attempt to identify conditions that would better support a reconstituted public sector dedicated to appropriate service and respect for clients—one that would be more likely to produce effective service providers. In developing the street-level bureaucracy framework, I identify the common elements of occupations as apparently disparate as, say, police officer and social worker. The analysis of street-level bureaucracy helps us identify which features of people-processing are common, and which are unique, to the different occupational milieux in which they arise.

Moreover, this essentially comparative approach permits us to raise questions systematically about apparent differences in various service areas. For example, recognition that all street-level bureaucracies need to control clients gives perspective to police officer shows of force and raises questions about precisely what in the work context of police officers makes client control so dominant a theme.

Just as one of the most important contributions of the concept of "professionalism" is to facilitate understanding of the differences between, say, doctors and nurses, in the same way the concept of street-level bureaucracy should encourage exploration of important differences in public services as well as contribute to an understanding of central tendencies that they share.

Street-level bureaucrats are major recipients of public expenditures and represent a significant portion of public activity at the local level. Citizens directly experience government through them, and their actions *are* the

Preface

policies provided by government in important respects. I start by summarizing the importance of street-level bureaucrats in contemporary political life and explain the sense in which these low-level workers may be understood to "make" the policies they are otherwise charged with implementing (part I). Then I treat the common features of street-level work and explore the implications of these conclusions for client outcomes, organizational control, and worker satisfaction (part II).

The utility of the street-level bureaucracy approach can be tested only in efforts to understand whether common features of the framework lead to common behavioral outcomes. I explore this general question with reference to street-level tendencies to ration and restrict services, control clients and the work situation, and develop psychological dispositions that reduce the dissonance between worker expectations and actual service outcomes (part III). In the next section, I provide an assessment of the effect of fiscal crisis on street-level bureaucrats, and a discussion of the potential for reform and reconstruction of these critical public functions (part IV).

These latter chapters may be of particular interest to readers of this new edition for the insight they may provide on developments over the last thirty years. On the one hand, the implications that reform movements within the professions might play a restorative role today seem more farfetched than they did thirty years ago. On the other hand, the choices available to the society for managing street-level bureaucracies toward greater responsiveness and democratic accountability remain reasonably intact. It is also noteworthy that the theme of fiscal crisis, which dominated discussions of cutbacks in public services as a result of tax revolts of the late 1970s, are still with us today. These themes are reviewed and account taken of recent developments in public services in the final chapter, which was written especially for this edition.

ACKNOWLEDGMENTS

2010

For more than thirty years I have been privileged to track the development of street-level bureaucracy as the ideas embodied in this book have rolled out, been used and evaluated, and deployed in new ways. They serve some simply to designate classes of actors in the policy process. In other hands they have been adopted and the framework modified to guide extensive inquiries into very specific lines of work. Researchers have organized their research based on the street-level bureaucracy perspective in the study of customs inspectors in Senegal, employment counselors in Australia, and labor inspectors in the Dominican Republic. It has been extremely gratifying to have been able to observe closely this swirl of ideas.

Of all the comments and critiques I have received during this long period, two have remained particularly memorable. The first is a set of accounts of many current and former public sector workers who have read the book, usually on the occasion of having returned to graduate school after a few years in the field. They say that in reading the book they recognize themselves and their struggles at work. They report that the book helped them feel better about the way they adapted to life in the organization. The difficulties they were having at work, they now understood, were not necessarily attributable to their personal failings, but instead at least in part were the result of the structure of their jobs. I particularly appreciate these comments because a first step in empowerment of the individual is recognizing the systemic basis of one's condition or circumstances.

As to the second, a few years after the book was published I agreed to be interviewed by telephone from my office at MIT by students in North Dakota who were studying to be social workers. One student thought the book was very persuasive but, she said essentially, "You paint such a grim picture—after reading your book I don't know whether I want to go into the field!" I was taken aback, but she was right. Whatever the value of the book

Acknowledgments

for researchers and policy analysts, I understood that for people considering careers in public service the book might well be discouraging.

I have tried to address this concern here, in the new preface to the book, but the topic deserves much greater attention. Literally millions of people choose to go into the public sector because of the rewards and challenges of working with and for other people. They deserve much more public approval and respect (and usually higher pay) than they generally receive. In support of these choices, it would be good to know, from systematic research conducted from a street-level bureaucracy perspective, how police officers, teachers, and social workers find that satisfactory balance between the expectations of the job and what they are able to accomplish.

I thank the Russell Sage Foundation for keeping the book in print over all these years, and inviting me to revise the preface and write a new chapter for this edition. I am very grateful to Robert Behn, Evelyn Brodkin, Carolyn Hill, Deborah Stone, Steven Rathgeb Smith, and Soeren Winter, friends and distinguished scholars, who offered comments on a draft of the new chapter on painfully short notice. I owe special thanks and recognition to my colleagues at Demos, who provide a remarkable home for researchers and activists committed to striving for an inclusive democracy and shared prosperity, supported by an effective and responsive public sector.

1980

My interest in the common work characteristics of street-level bureaucrats was first prompted in 1969 while writing a review of a book on the police. That year I wrote a paper (and later published), "Toward a Theory of Street-Level Bureaucracy," recording my initial thoughts and speculations on the importance of work structure in establishing the relationship between citizens and these public employees.

This book presents the theory toward which I was pointing in the original essay. The book partially reformulates and greatly expands my earlier statement and takes up many new considerations, such as the implications of the fiscal crisis for street-level bureaucracy, that were not contemplated earlier.

I have been greatly aided in this work by a grant from the Russell Sage Foundation to the M.I.T.-Harvard Joint Center for Urban Studies, and by the hospitality at different times of the Institute for Research on Poverty at the University of Wisconsin, and the Department of Political Science and the Graduate School of Public Affairs of the University of Washington. Graduate students at the University of Washington, students at the College of Public and Community Service of the University of Massachusetts, Boston, as well as graduate students at M.I.T. have taught me a great deal about street-level bureaucracy over this period.

Many friends and colleagues have contributed to this work in conversation, in their writings, or through expressions of personal interest and support. I am particularly grateful in various measures to Robert Alford, Gary Bellow, Murray Edelman, Willis Hawley, Ira Katznelson, Jeanne Kettleson, Margaret Levi, Hannah Lipsky, David J. Olson, Jeffrey Pressman, Martin Rein, Charles Sabel, and Aaron Wildavsky. My debt to many other writers who have written usefully on public services that function as street-level bureaucracy is recognized in the notes. I am pleased to acknowledge my double debt to Martha Wagner Weinberg, first as tireless and inventive research assistant, and second (many years later) as valued colleague at M.I.T.

Many of the ideas that comprise this book were developed in collaboration with Carl Hosticka, Jeffrey Prottas, and Richard Weatherley when they served as research assistants under the Russell Sage grant. I am proud of that association and deeply appreciate their many insights and contributions to our common enterprise.

This book has been greatly influenced by Suzanne Lipsky. Among her many contributions has been her recognition and analysis of the potential of people to sustain and recover their humanity despite contributing to or being subjects of oppressive social systems.

PART I

INTRODUCTION

CHAPTER 1

The Critical Role of

Street-Level Bureaucrats

Public service workers currently occupy a critical position in American society. Although they are normally regarded as low-level employees, the actions of most public service workers actually constitute the services "delivered" by government. Moreover, when taken together the individual decisions of these workers become, or add up to, agency policy. Whether government policy is to deliver "goods"—such as welfare or public housing—or to confer status—such as "criminal" or "mentally ill"—the discretionary actions of public employees are the benefits and sanctions of government programs or determine access to government rights and benefits.

Most citizens encounter government (if they encounter it at all) not through letters to congressmen or by attendance at school board meetings but through their teachers and their children's teachers and through the policeman on the corner or in the patrol car. Each encounter of this kind represents an instance of policy delivery.

Public service workers who interact directly with citizens in the course of their jobs, and who have substantial discretion in the execution of their work are called *street-level bureaucrats* in this study. Public service agencies that employ a significant number of street-level bureaucrats in proportion to their work force are called *street-level bureaucracies*. Typical street-level bureaucrats are teachers, police officers and other law enforcement personnel, social workers, judges, public lawyers and other court officers, health workers, and many other public employees who grant access to government programs and provide services within them. People who work in these jobs tend

3

to have much in common because they experience analytically similar work conditions.[1]

The ways in which street-level bureaucrats deliver benefits and sanctions structure and delimit people's lives and opportunities. These ways orient and provide the social (and political) contexts in which people act. Thus every extension of service benefits is accompanied by an extension of state influence and control. As providers of public benefits and keepers of public order, street-level bureaucrats are the focus of political controversy. They are constantly torn by the demands of service recipients to improve effectiveness and responsiveness and by the demands of citizen groups to improve the efficacy and efficiency of government services. Since the salaries of street-level bureaucrats comprise a significant proportion of nondefense governmental expenditures, any doubts about the size of government budgets quickly translate into concerns for the scope and content of these public services. Moreover, public service workers have expanded and increasingly consolidated their collective strength so that in disputes over the scope of public services they have become a substantial independent force in the resolution of controversy affecting their status and position.

Street-level bureaucrats dominate political controversies over public services for two general reasons. First, debates about the proper scope and focus of governmental services are essentially debates over the scope and function of these public employees. Second, street-level bureaucrats have considerable impact on peoples' lives. This impact may be of several kinds. They socialize citizens to expectations of government services and a place in the political community. They determine the eligibility of citizens for government benefits and sanctions. They oversee the treatment (the service) citizens receive in those programs. Thus, in a sense street-level bureaucrats implicitly mediate aspects of the constitutional relationship of citizens to the state. In short, they hold the keys to a dimension of citizenship.

Conflict over the Scope and Substance of Public Services

In the world of experience we perceive teachers, welfare workers, and police officers as members of separately organized and motivated public agencies. And so they are from many points of view. But if we divide public employees according to whether they interact with citizens directly and have discretion over significant aspects of citizens' lives, we see that a high proportion and enormous number of public workers share these job characteristics. They comprise a great portion of all public employees working in domestic affairs. State and local governments employ approximately 3.7 million people in local schools, more than 500,000 people in police operations, and over 300,000 people in public welfare. Public school employees represent more than half of all workers employed in local governments. Instructional jobs represent about two-thirds of the educational personnel, and many of the rest are former teachers engaged in administration, or social workers, psychologists, and librarians who provide direct services in the schools. Of the 3.2 million local government public employees not engaged in education, approximately 14 percent work as police officers. One of every sixteen jobs in state and local government outside of education is held by a public welfare worker.[2] In this and other areas the majority of jobs are held by people with responsibility for involvement with citizens.

Other street-level bureaucrats comprise an important part of the remainder of local government personnel rolls. Although the U.S. Census Bureau does not provide breakdowns of other job classifications suitable for our purposes, we can assume that many of the 1.1 million health workers,[3] most of the 5,000 public service lawyers,[4] many of the employees of the various court systems, and other public employees also perform as street-level bureaucrats. Some of the nation's larger cities employ a staggering number of street-level bureaucrats. For example, the 26,680 school teachers in Chicago are more numerous than the populations of many of the Chicago suburbs.[5]

Another measure of the significance of street-level bureaucrats in public sector employment is the amount of public funds allocated to pay them. Of all local government salaries, more than half went to public education in 1973. Almost 80 percent of these monies was used to pay instructional personnel. Police salaries comprised approximately one-sixth of local public salaries not assigned to education.[6]

Much of the growth in public employment in the past 25 years has occurred in the ranks of street-level bureaucrats. From 1955 to 1975 government employment more than doubled, largely because the baby boom of the postwar years and the growing number of elderly, dependent citizens increased state and local activity in education, health, and public welfare.[7]

Street-level bureaucracies are labor-intensive in the extreme. Their business is providing service through people, and the operating costs of such agencies reflect their dependence upon salaried workers. Thus most of whatever is spent by government on education, police, or other social services (aside, of course, from income maintenance, or in the case of jails and prisons, inmate upkeep) goes directly to pay street-level bureaucrats. For example, in large cities over 90 percent of police expenditures is used to pay for salaries.[8]

Not only do the salaries of street-level bureaucrats constitute a major portion of the cost of public services, but also the scope of public services employing street-level bureaucrats has increased over time. Charity was once the responsibility of private agencies. The federal government now provides for the income needs of the poor. The public sector has absorbed responsibilities previously discharged by private organizations in such diverse and critical areas as policing, education, and health. Moreover, in all these fields government not only has supplanted private organizations but also has expanded the scope of responsibility of public ones. This is evident in increased public expectations for security and public safety, the extension of responsibilities in the schools to concerns with infant as well as post-adolescent development, and public demands for affordable health care services.[9]

Public safety, public health, and public education *may* still be elusive social objectives, but in the past century they have been transformed into areas for which there is active governmental responsibility. The transformation of public responsibility in the area of social welfare has led some to recognize that what people "have" in modern American society often may consist primarily of their claims on government "largesse," and that claims to this "new property" should be protected as a right of citizens.[10] Street-level bureaucrats play a critical role in these citizen entitlements. Either they directly provide public benefits through services, or they mediate between citizens and their new but by no means secure estates.

The poorer people are, the greater the influence street-level bureaucrats tend to have over them. Indeed, these public workers are so situated that they may well be taken to be part of the problem of being poor. Consider the welfare recipient who lives in public housing and seeks the assistance of a legal services lawyer in order to reinstate her son in school. He has been suspended because of frequent encounters with the police. She is caught in a net of street-level bureaucrats with conflicting orientations toward her, all acting in what they call her "interest" and "the public interest."[11]

People who are not able to purchase services in the private sector must seek them from government if they are to receive them at all. Indeed, it is taken as a sign of social progress that poor people are granted access to services if they are too poor to pay for them.

Thus, when social reformers seek to ameliorate the problems of the poor, they often end up discussing the status of street-level bureaucrats. Welfare reformers move to separate service provision from decisions about support payments, or they design a negative income tax system that would eliminate social workers in allocating welfare. Problems of backlog in the courts are met with proposals to increase the number of judges. Recognition that early-childhood development largely establishes the potential for later achievement results in the development of new programs (such as Head Start) in and out of established institutions, to provide enriched early-childhood experiences.

In the 1960s and early 1970s the modal governmental response to social problems was to commission a corps of street-level bureaucrats to attend to them. Are poor people deprived of equal access to the courts? Provide them with lawyers. Equal access to health care? Establish neighborhood clinics. Educational opportunity? Develop preschool enrichment programs. It is far easier and less disruptive to develop employment for street-level bureaucrats than to reduce income inequalities.

In recent years public employees have benefitted considerably from the growth of public spending on street-level bureaucracies.[12] Salaries have increased from inadequate to respectable and even desirable. Meanwhile, public employees, with street-level bureaucrats in the lead, have secured unprecedented control over their work environments through the development of unions and union-like associations.[13] For example, teachers and other instructional personnel have often been able to maintain their positions and even increase in number, although schools are more frequently under attack for their cost to taxpayers. The ratio of instructional personnel in schools has continued to rise despite the decline in the number of school-age children.[14] This development supplements general public support for the view that some street-level bureaucrats, such as teachers and police officers, are necessary for a healthy society.[15]

The fiscal crisis that has affected many cities, notably New York and more recently Cleveland and Newark, has provided an opportunity to assess the capacity of public service workers to hold onto their jobs in the face of enormous pressures. Since so much of municipal budgets consists of inflexible, mandated costs—for debt service, pension plans and other personnel benefits, contractually obligated salary increases, capital expenditure commitments, energy purchases, and so on—the place to find "fat" to eliminate from municipal budgets is in the service sector, where most expenditures tend to be for salaries. While many public employees have been fired during this crisis period, it is significant that public service workers often have been able to lobby, bargain, and cajole to minimize this attrition.[16] They are supported in their claims by a public fearful of a reduced police force on the street and resentful of dirtier streets resulting from fewer garbage pickups. They are supported by families whose children will receive less instruction from fewer specialists than in the past if teachers are fired. And it does not hurt their arguments that many public employees and their relatives vote in the city considering force reductions.[17]

The growth of the service sector represents the furthest reaches of the welfare state. The service sector penetrates every area of human needs as they are recognized and defined, and it grows within each recognized area. This is not to say that the need is met, but only that the service state breaches the barriers between public responsibility and private affairs.

The fiscal crisis of the cities focuses on the service sector, fundamentally challenging the priorities of the service state under current perceptions of scarcity. Liberals have now joined fiscal conservatives in challenging service provision. They do not do so directly, by questioning whether public services and responsibilities developed in this century are appropriate. Instead, they do it backhandedly, arguing that the accretion of public employees and their apparently irreversible demands upon revenues threaten the autonomy, flexibility, and prosperity of the political order. Debates over the proper scope of services face the threat of being overwhelmed by challenges to the entire social service structure as seen from the perspective of unbalanced public budgets.

Conflict over Interactions with Citizens

I have argued that street-level bureaucrats engender controversy because they must be dealt with if policy is to change. A second reason street-level bureaucrats tend to be the focus of public controversy is the immediacy of their interactions with citizens and their impact on peoples' lives. The policy delivered by street-level bureaucrats is most often immediate and personal. They usually make decisions on the spot (although sometimes they try not to) and their determinations are focused entirely on the individual. In contrast, an urban renewal program might destroy a neighborhood and replace and substitute new housing and different people, but the policy was prolonged, had many different stages, and was usually played out in arenas far removed from the daily life of neighborhood residents.

The decisions of street-level bureaucrats tend to be redistributive as well as allocative. By determining eligibility for benefits they enhance the claims of some citizens to governmental goods and services at the expense of general taxpayers and those whose claims are denied. By increasing or decreasing benefits availability to low-income recipient populations they implicitly regulate the degree of redistribution that will be paid for by more affluent sectors.

In another sense, in delivering policy street-level bureaucrats make decisions about people that affect their life chances. To designate or treat someone as a welfare recipient, a juvenile delinquent, or a high achiever affects the relationships of others to that person and also affects the person's self-evaluation. Thus begins (or continues) the social process that we infer accounts for so many self-fulfilling prophecies. The child judged to be a juvenile delinquent develops such a self-image and is grouped with other "delinquents," increasing the chances that he or she will adopt the behavior thought to have been incipient in the first place. Children thought by their teacher to be richly endowed in learning ability learn more than peers of equal intelligence who were not thought to be superior.[18] Welfare recipients find or accept housing inferior to those with equal disposable incomes who are not recipients.[19]

A defining facet of the working environment of street-level bureaucrats is that they must deal with clients' personal reactions to their decisions, however they cope with their implications. To say that people's self-evaluation is affected by the actions of street-level bureaucrats is to say that people are reactive to the policy. This is not exclusively confined to subconscious processes. Clients of street-level bureaucracies respond angrily to real or perceived injustices, develop strategies to ingratiate themselves with workers, act grateful and elated or sullen and passive in reaction to street-level bureaucrats' decisions. It is one thing to be treated neglectfully and routinely by the telephone company, the motor vehicle bureau, or other government agencies whose agents know nothing of the personal circumstances surrounding a claim or request. It is quite another thing to be shuffled, categorized, and treated "bureaucratically," (in the pejorative sense), by someone to whom one is directly talking and from whom one expects at least an open and sympathetic hearing. In short, the reality of the work of street-level bureaucrats could hardly be farther from the bureaucratic ideal of impersonal detachment in decision making.[20] On the contrary, in street-level bureaucracies the objects of critical decisions—*people*—actually change as a result of the decisions.

Street-level bureaucrats are also the focus of citizen reactions because their discretion opens up the possibility that they will respond favorably on behalf of people. Their general and diffuse obligation to the "public interest" permits hope to flourish that the individual worker will adopt a benign or favorable orientation toward the client. Thus, in a world of large and impersonal agencies that apparently hold the keys to important benefits, sanctions, and opportunities, the ambiguity of work definitions sustains hope for a friend in court.

This discussion helps explain continued controversy over street-level bureaucracies at the level of individual service provision. At the same time, the peculiar nature of government service delivery through street-level bureaucrats helps explain why street-level bureaucracies are apparently the primary focus of community conflict in the current period, and why they are likely to remain the focus of such conflict in the foreseeable future. It is no accident that the most heated community conflicts since 1964 have focused on schools and police departments, and on the responsiveness of health and welfare agencies and institutions.[21] These are the sites of the provision of public benefits and sanctions. They are the locus of individual decisions about and treatment of citizens, and thus are primary targets of protest. As Frances Fox Piven and Richard Cloward explain:

. . . people experience deprivation and oppression within a concrete setting, not as the end product of large and abstract processes, and it is the concrete experience that molds their discontent into specific grievances against specific targets. . . . People on relief [for example] experience the shabby waiting rooms, the overseer or the case-worker, and the dole. They do not experience American social welfare policy. . . . In other words, it is the daily experience of people that shapes their grievances, establishes the measure of their demands, and points out the targets of their anger.[22]

While people may experience these bureaucracies as individuals, schools, precinct houses, or neighborhood clinics are places where policy about individuals is organized collectively. These administrative arrangements suggest to citizens the possibility that controlling, or at least affecting, their structures will influence the quality of individual treatment. Thus we have two preconditions for successful community organization efforts: the hope and plausibility that individual benefits may accrue to those taking part in group action and a visible, accessible, and blamable collective target.[23]

Community action focused on street-level bureaucracies is also apparently motivated by concerns for community character. The dominant institutions in communities help shape community identity. They may be responsive to the dominant community group (this has been the traditional role of high schools in Boston) or they may be unresponsive and opposed to conceptions of community and identity favored by residents, as in the case of schools that neglect the Spanish heritage of a significant minority. Whether people are motivated by specific grievances or more diffuse concerns that become directed at community institutions, their focus in protesting the actions of street-level bureaucracies may be attributed to the familiarity of the agency, its critical role in community welfare, and a perception at some level that these institutions are not sufficiently accountable to the people they serve.

Finally, street-level bureaucrats play a critical role in regulating the degree of contemporary conflict by virtue of their role as agents of social control. Citizens who receive public benefits interact with public agents who require certain behaviors of them. They must anticipate the requirements of these public agents and claimants must tailor their actions and develop "suitable" attitudes both toward the services they receive and toward the street-level bureaucrats themselves. Teachers convey and enforce expectations of proper attitudes toward schooling, self, and efficacy in other interactions. Policemen convey expectations about public behavior and authority. Social workers convey expectations about public benefits and the status of recipients.

The social control function of street-level bureaucrats requires comment in a discussion of the place of public service workers in the larger society. The public service sector plays a critical part in softening the impact of the economic system on those who are not its primary beneficiaries and inducing people to accept the neglect or inadequacy of primary economic and social institutions. Police, courts, and prisons obviously play such a role in processing the junkies, petty thieves, muggers, and others whose behavior toward society is associated with their economic position. It is a role equally played by schools in socializing the population to the economic order and the likely opportunities for different strata of the population. Public support and employment programs expand to ameliorate the impact of unemployment or reduce the incidence of discontent; they contract when employment opportunities improve. Moreover, they are designed and implemented to convey the message that welfare status is to be avoided and that work, however poorly rewarded, is preferable to public assistance. One can also see the two edges of public policy in the "war on poverty" where the public benefits of social service and community action invested neighborhood institutions with benefits for which potential dissidents could compete and ordinary citizens could develop dependency.[24]

What to some are the highest reaches of the welfare state are to others the furthest extension of social control. Street-level bureaucrats are partly the focus of controversy because they play this dual role. Welfare reform founders on disagreements over whether to eliminate close scrutiny of welfare applications in order to reduce administrative costs and harassment of recipients, or to increase the scrutiny in the name of controlling abuses and preventing welfare recipients from taking advantage. Juvenile corrections and mental health policy founder on disputes over the desirability of dismantling large institutions in the name of cost effectiveness and rehabilitation, or retaining close supervision in an effort to avoid the costs of letting unreconstructed "deviants" loose. In short, street-level bureaucrats are also at the center of controversy because a divided public perceives that social control in the name of public order and acceptance of the status quo are social objectives with which proposals to reduce the role of street-level bureaucrats (eliminating welfare checkups, reducing parole personnel, decriminalizing marijuana) would interfere.

Public controversy also focuses on the proper kind of social control. Current debates in corrections policy, concerning automatic sentencing and a "hard-nosed" view of punishment or more rehabilitative orientations, reflect conflict over the degree of harshness in managing prison populations. In educational practice the public is also divided as to the advisability of liberal disciplinary policies and more flexible instruction or punitive discipline and more rigid, traditional approaches. The "medicalization" of deviance, in which disruptive behavior is presumed cause for intervention by a doctor rather than a disciplinarian, is another area in which there is controversy over the appropriate kind of social control.

From the citizen's viewpoint, the roles of street-level bureaucrats are as extensive as the functions of government and intensively experienced as daily routines require them to interact with the street ministers of education, dispute settlement, and health services. Collectively, street-level bureaucrats absorb a high share of public resources and become the focus of society's hopes for a healthy balance between provision of public services and a reasonable burden of public expenditures. As individuals, street-level bureaucrats represent the hopes of citizens for fair and effective treatment by government even as they are positioned to see clearly the limitations on effective intervention and the constraints on responsiveness engendered by mass processing.

CHAPTER 2

Street-Level Bureaucrats

as Policy Makers

Street-level bureaucrats make policy in two related respects. They exercise wide discretion in decisions about citizens with whom they interact. Then, when taken in concert, their individual actions add up to agency behavior. The task in this chapter is to demonstrate that the position of street-level bureaucrats regularly permits them to make policy with respect to significant aspects of their interactions with citizens. Later chapters will explore the implications of making policy at the street level.

The policy-making roles of street-level bureaucrats are built upon two interrelated facets of their positions: relatively high degrees of discretion and relative autonomy from organizational authority.

Discretion

Unlike lower-level workers in most organizations, street-level bureaucrats have considerable discretion in determining the nature, amount, and quality of benefits and sanctions provided by their agencies.[1] Policemen decide who to arrest and whose behavior to overlook. Judges decide who shall receive a suspended sentence and who shall receive maximum punishment. Teachers decide who will be suspended and who will remain in school, and they make subtle determinations of who is teachable. Perhaps the most highly refined example of street-level bureaucratic discretion comes from the field of cor-

13

rections. Prison guards conventionally file injurious reports on inmates whom they judge to be guilty of "silent insolence." Clearly what does or does not constitute a dirty look is a matter of some subjectivity.[2]

This is not to say that street-level workers are unrestrained by rules, regulations, and directives from above, or by the norms and practices of their occupational group. On the contrary, the major dimensions of public policy—levels of benefits, categories of eligibility, nature of rules, regulations and services—are shaped by policy elites and political and administrative officials. Administrators and occupational and community norms also structure policy choices of street-level bureaucrats. These influences establish the major dimensions of street-level policy and account for the degree of standardization that exists in public programs from place to place as well as in local programs.

To the extent that street-level bureaucrats are professionals, the assertion that they exercise considerable discretion is fairly obvious. Professionals are expected to exercise discretionary judgment in their field. They are regularly deferred to in their specialized areas of work and are relatively free from supervision by superiors or scrutiny by clients.[3] Yet even public employees who do not have claims to professional status exercise considerable discretion. Clerks in welfare and public housing agencies, for example, may exercise discretion in determining client access to benefits, even though their discretion is formally circumscribed by rules and relatively close supervision.

Rules may actually be an impediment to supervision. They may be so voluminous and contradictory that they can only be enforced or invoked selectively. In most public welfare departments, regulations are encyclopedic, yet at the same time, they are constantly being changed. With such rules adherence to anything but the most basic and fundamental precepts of eligibility cannot be expected. Police behavior is so highly specified by statutes and regulations that policemen are expected to invoke the law selectively. They could not possibly make arrests for all the infractions they observe during their working day.[4] (Like doctors and clergymen in many jurisdictions, they are required to be on-duty and ready to intervene even during their off-duty hours.) Similarly, federal civil-rights compliance officers have so many mandated responsibilities in comparison to their resources that they have been free to determine their own priorities.[5] It would seem that the proliferation of rules and responsibilities is only problematically related to the degree of discretion street-level bureaucrats enjoy.[6]

Although the case for the pervasive existence of discretion in street-level work is fairly easy to make it is important to remember that in public services some interactions take place with citizens that involve relatively little bureaucratic discretion. Patrolmen assigned to traffic duty or gun permit applications, for example, may interact with the public but exercise little discretion in performing these tasks. Discretion is a relative concept. It follows that the greater the degree of discretion the more salient this analysis in understanding the character of workers' behavior.

Since many of the problems discussed here would theoretically disappear if workers' discretion were eliminated, one may wonder why discretion remains characteristic of their jobs. The answer is that certain characteristics of the jobs of street-level bureaucrats make it difficult, if not impossible, to severely reduce discretion. They involve complex tasks for which elaboration of rules, guidelines, or instructions cannot circumscribe the alternatives. This may be the case for one of at least two reasons.

First, street-level bureaucrats often work in situations too complicated to reduce to programmatic formats. Policemen cannot carry around instructions on how to intervene with citizens, particularly in potentially hostile encounters. Indeed, they would probably not go out on the street if such instructions were promulgated, or they would refuse to intervene in potentially dangerous situations.[7] Similarly, contemporary views of education mitigate against detailed instructions to teachers on how and what to teach, since the philosophy prevails that to a point every child requires a response appropriate to the specific learning context.

Second, street-level bureaucrats work in situations that often require responses to the human dimensions of situations. They have discretion because the accepted definitions of their tasks call for sensitive observation and judgment, which are not reducible to programmed formats. It may be that uniform sentencing would reduce inequities in the criminal justice system. But we also want the law to be responsive to the unique circumstances of individual transgressions.[8] We want teachers to perceive the unique potential of children. In short, to a degree the society seeks not only impartiality from its public agencies but also compassion for special circumstances and flexibility in dealing with them.[9]

A third reason discretion is not likely to be eliminated bears more on the function of lower-level workers who interact with citizens than with the nature of the tasks. Street-level discretion promotes workers' self-regard and encourages clients to believe that workers hold the key to their well-being. For both workers and clients, maintenance of discretion contributes to the legitimacy of the welfare-service state, although street-level bureaucrats by no means establish the boundaries of state intervention.

The search for the correct balance between compassion and flexibility on the one hand, and impartiality and rigid rule-application on the other hand presents a dialectic of public service reform. Reformers attempt to limit worker discretion at one time, and increase it at another. In order to make ambulance dispatch by untrained personnel more efficient, health planners work to rationalize emergency dispatch procedures by developing a programmed format to aid in identifying health emergencies.[10] Meanwhile, other health planners seek to replace untrained admission clerks with health professionals in order to insure greater sensitivity to the health problems of prospective patients.[11] Programmed learning materials are introduced to release teachers for more intensive work with some students, while all students benefit from these motivational and self-paced features. Later this innovation is found wanting because it eliminated teachers' feedback to students and encouraged regimentation rather than individualized learning.[12] To the extent that tasks remain complex and human intervention is considered necessary for effective service, discretion will remain characteristic of many public service jobs.

Relative Autonomy from Organizational Authority

Most analysts take for granted that the work of lower-level participants will more or less conform to what is expected of them. Organizational theorists recognize that there will always be some slippage between orders and the carrying out of orders, but this slippage is usually attributed to poor communication or workers' residual, and not terribly important, disagreement with organizational goals. In any event, such difficulties are usually considered unimportant enough that organizations can overcome them.

This observation is partly derived from the recognition that lower level workers' behavior in organizations, including public agencies, appears to be cooperative. Workers for the most part accept the legitimacy of the formal structure of authority, and they are not in a position to dissent successfully.

But what if workers do not share the objectives of their superiors? Lower-level participants in organizations often do not share the perspectives and preferences of their superiors and hence in some respects cannot be thought to be working toward stated agency goals. At least this is the case when workers are not recruited with an affinity for the organization's goals; workers do not consider orders from "above" legitimate; or the incentives available to supervisors are matched by countermeasures available to lower-level participants. One can expect a distinct degree of noncompliance if lower-level workers' *interests* differ from the interests of those at higher levels, and the incentives and sanctions available to higher levels are not sufficient to prevail.[13]

Sometimes different levels of organizations are more appropriately conceived as intrinsically in conflict with each other rather than mutually responsive and supportive.[14] At times it is more useful to view lower-level workers as having distinctly different interests and the resources to pursue those interests. Here discrepancies between policy declarations and actual policy would be expected and predictable. And explanations for the discrepancies would be searched for not in the breakdown or inadequacy of the compliance system but in the structure of the work situation from which workers' "antagonistic" interests arise.

In such organizations policy may be carried out consistent with the interests of higher levels, but this should be understood as resulting from the mutual adjustment of antagonistic perspectives as well as the result of shared interests. In such cases the latent conflict in the interests of different levels is suppressed or is a matter of indifference to one or both parties. This approach takes as problematic the mutuality of interests, and it searches instead for the mechanisms by which essentially antagonistic or divergent interests are adjusted.[15]

Some of the ways lower-level workers can withhold cooperation within their organizations include such personal strategies as not working (excessive absenteeism, quitting), aggression toward the organization (stealing, cheating, deliberate wasting), and negative attitudes with implications for work (alienation, apathy).[16] Workers may take advantage of collective resources to act noncooperatively by forming trade unions or by exercising rights under collective bargaining agreements or civil service regulations. These collective strategies for noncooperation contribute to workers' willingness to display lack of motivation and to perform at only minimal levels.[17]

These forms of noncooperation injure organizations' abilities to achieve their objectives because workers perform at less than full capacity. The management challenge perceived to be at the heart of the problem is how to make workers' needs for personal, material, or psychological gratification mesh with the organization's needs. Thus the management problem regarding worker absenteeism becomes how to improve job satisfaction while retaining productivity.

However, there is another class of conflicts between lower-level workers and the organizations that arise not from the personal needs of the workers alone but also from their positions within their organizations. The role of street-level bureaucrats, like other roles, may be conceived as a set of expected interests[18] as well as expected behaviors. Street-level bureaucrats may be shown to have distinctly different interests from the interests of others in the agencies for which they work. Moreover, certain features of their role make it possible for them to make these differences manifest. Differences in interests, and the possibility of surfacing the differences, permit analysis of the structural position of street-level bureaucrats from a conflict perspective.[19]

In the following brief discussion, the nature of the conflict between the objectives and orientations of street-level bureaucrats and those in higher authority roles is considered first. Then the capacity of street-level bureaucrats' ability to resist organizational directives is treated.[20]

Differences between Street-Level Bureaucrats and Managers

In general lower-level workers have different job priorities than managers. At the very least, workers have an interest in minimizing the danger and discomforts of the job and maximizing income and personal gratification. These priorities are of interest to management for the most part only as they relate to productivity and effectiveness. In street-level bureaucracies lower-level workers are likely to have considerably more than minimal differences with management. Earlier it was suggested that worker compliance is affected by the extent to which managers' orders are considered legitimate. Street-level bureaucrats may consider legitimate the right of managers to provide directives, but they may consider their managers' policy objectives illegitimate. Teachers asked to participate in compensatory education programs in which they do not believe, or policemen no longer able to arrest derelicts for alcoholism, may resist these policy objectives in various ways.

One way in which the interests of street-level bureaucrats depart from those of managers is their need to process work loads expeditiously, free from real and psychological threats. The fact that street-level bureaucrats must exercise discretion in processing large amounts of work with inadequate resources means that they must develop shortcuts and simplifications to cope with the press of responsibilities. The coping mechanisms street-level bureaucrats develop (see part III) often are unsanctioned by managers of their agencies.

Managers are interested in achieving results consistent with agency objectives. Street-level bureaucrats are interested in processing work consistent with their own preferences and only those agency policies so salient as to be backed up by significant sanctions. These sanctions must be limited. If everything receives priority, nothing does. Work-processing devices are part of the informal agency structure that may be necessary to maintain the organization, even though the procedures may be contrary to agency policy.[21]

This is a neat paradox. Lower-level participants develop coping mechanisms contrary to an agency's policy but actually basic to its survival. For example, brutality is contrary to police policy, but a certain degree of looking-the-other-way on the part of supervisors may be considered necessary to persuade officers to risk assault. Street-level bureaucrats have a role interest in securing the requirements of completing the job. Managers, on the other hand, are properly result-oriented. They are concerned with performance, the cost of securing performance, and only those aspects of process that expose them to critical scrutiny.

Another aspect of street-level bureaucrats' role interests is their desire to maintain and expand their autonomy. Managers try to restrict workers' discretion in order to secure certain results, but street-level bureaucrats often regard such efforts as illegitimate and to some degree resist them successfully. Indeed, to the extent that street-level bureaucrats (and this would include police, teachers, social workers, and nurses, as well as doctors and lawyers) expect themselves to make critical discretionary decisions, many of managers' efforts to dictate service norms are regarded as illegitimate. To the extent that this is the case we have uncovered a condition for non-compliance of lower-level workers. This does not mean that efforts to constrain street-level bureaucrats are in fact illegitimate. Street-level bureaucrats have some claims to professional status, but they also have a bureaucratic status that requires compliance with superiors' directives. It does mean, however, that street-level bureaucrats will perceive their interests as separate from managers' interests, and they will seek to secure these interests.[22]

Street-level bureaucrats conspicuously create capacities to act with discretion and hang on to discretionary capacities they have enjoyed in the past. The maintenance and enhancement of discretion is so important that some detailed illustrations may be useful.

Lower-court judges have recently encouraged the development of a great many alternatives to incarceration, in essence turning the courts into social work referral services. In Massachusetts and elsewhere lower-court judges can refer presumptive offenders to many social programs, the successful completion of which will result in obviating their sentences. These include programs to provide first offenders with counseling, job training, and placement assistance, and alcoholics, reckless drivers, and drug offenders with appropriate counseling. In addition, judges have the services of psychiatrists, social workers, probation officers, and others who might be able to provide treatment as an alternative to imprisonment. These developments have been conceived by humanitarian reformers who believe, along with many judges, that prisons create more criminals than they deter by exposing people to experienced crooks, and by pragmatists, who recognize that the courts have become revolving doors of repeat appearances without deterrent effect.

It is conspicuous to court observers that these programs take a heavy burden off the judge. The judge is now able to make what appears to be a constructive decision rather than simply to choose between the unattractive alternatives of sending a person to jail or releasing the putative offender without penalty. Indirect evidence that these programs fill critical institutional needs is suggested by the Boston pretrial diversion programs. These programs were utilized beyond their capacity by judges, sometimes without regard for the extremely important initial interview or the relatively stringent eligibility requirements the programs sought to impose in order to maximize effectiveness. Dependent upon judges for referrals and, indeed, for their programs' existence, administrators found it difficult to refuse judges who referred too many clients, or inappropriate clients, to them.[23]

The Veterans Administration hospital system is a fascinating bureaucracy because it employs doctors, the preeminent professionals, in highly rule-bound organizations. The country's system of socialized medicine for the indigent veteran has developed an extremely complex series of rules because of simultaneous congressional concern to provide veterans with hospital services, maintain strict cost accounting, and (particularly in the past) not compete with private medical practice. In large part because the VA system was to provide hospital care, leaving to private physicians the business of office consultations, the VA hospitals were prohibited from treating patients on an outpatient basis. This conflicted with the doctors' prerogative to prescribe a level of treatment appropriate to the problem presented. There are many patients who need treatment, but not hospitalization, and to hospitalize such people would be to deny others the hospital space.

However, there was an allowable exception to the rule limiting services to hospitalized veterans. Under the "Pre-Bedcare" category (PBC) veterans who required health services prior to their anticipated admission (for example, blood tests prior to surgery) could be treated. Despite various requirements intended to limit PBC treatment to those whose admission was clearly expected, actual admission to the hospitals from PBC lists was traditionally very low. It seems that doctors, chafing under the restriction that they could not treat patients according to their best estimate of need, were treating patients as outpatients under the fiction that they were expected to be admitted. This supposition is supported by observing what happened when the VA introduced an Ambulatory Health Care (AHC) policy, permitting outpatient treatment for the first time. PBC admissions plummeted, while AHC admissions rose steadily. In one hospital AHC received 148 patients in the first five months of the program, while PBC dropped from 122 to 73 patients during that period. Fifty-one of these patients transferred directly to the AHC program.[24] In retrospect it seems that doctors were able to utilize existing bureaucratic structures to impose their views of proper treatment on the organization, despite organizational efforts to circumscribe their discretion.

Street-level bureaucrats will also use existing regulations and administrative provision to circumvent reforms which limit their discretion. In December 1968, in response to pressure from the Department of Housing and Urban Development, the Boston Housing Authority (BHA) adopted new tenant-selection guidelines designed to insure housing project racial integration. The plan utilized what was known as the "1-2-3 rule." To eliminate personnel discretion in assignments the 1-2-3 rule provided that prospective tenants would be offered places only in the housing projects with the three highest vacancy ratios. If these offers were refused, the application would be returned to the bottom of the waiting list.

The BHA integration plan did not work. Many housing authority employees objected to assigning people to projects in which they did not want to live. They were particularly concerned for their traditionally favored clientele, the elderly, poor whites who populated the "better" BHA projects. Among the reasons the reform did not work were that housing authority personnel were so inundated with work that proper adminstrative controls were not feasible, and in the chaos of processing applications, those who wished to favor some prospective tenants over others were able to do so. Housing officials took advantage of provisions for exceptions to the 1-2-3 rule, interpreting reasonable provisions for flexibility in extremely liberal ways when they wanted to. They volunteered information to favored prospective tenants concerning how to have their applications treated as emergencies or other high-priority categories, while routinely processing the applications of others. Applications were frequently lost or misplaced so that workers could favor tenants simply by locating their files and acting on them, while other files remained unavailable for processing. Meanwhile, public housing managers contributed to the sustained biases of the agency by failing to report vacancies to the central office when they occurred, not informing prospective tenants when units were available, or showing tenants they wished to discourage only unattractive or unsafe units, although others in the project were available. Thus the press of work combined with workers' desires to continue to serve particular clients restored the discretionary powers the new rules were designed to eliminate.[25]

The power of street-level bureaucrats to thwart reforms by manipulating legal loopholes is suggested in a strategy paper prepared by New York City officials to reduce welfare rolls. It indicates managerial awareness of the limits of agency reform without worker cooperation. The paper rejects the possibility of shortening intake hours too drastically, in part because of the chance that "welfare workers would go out of the centers and take applications from people at home, on the street, etc., since application may be made [under existing Federal law] at agency office, in own home, by telephone, by mail, or in any suitable place."[26]

A dramatic example of the instinct to retain discretionary options is provided by the response to the New York State laws sponsored by then Governor Nelson Rockefeller to impose mandatory, severe jail sentences for drug dealers, while providing relatively minor penalties for those caught with small amounts of drugs. The rationale for the law was to provide a strong deterrent to the drug trafficker. Predictably, some people arrested were not the rapacious drug dealers whom the law was designed to deter. This was the case, for example, with drug addicts on methadone who occasionally sold a dosage. The law presented a dilemma for court personnel, who believed that the mandatory, minimum sentence (life imprisonment for the methadone hustlers) was too severe for the offense. In these cases New York District Attorney Richard Kuh began to charge the alleged offenders not with the crimes which they had committed, but rather with crimes for which the punishments were compatible with what he conceived to be the severity of the offense. In this way, the district attorney attempted to provide the discretion demanded by a just court system in the face of legislation designed precisely to eliminate this discretion.[27]

Still another source of sustained differences in the interests of street-level bureaucrats and managers is their continuous interaction with clients and the varying degrees of complexity in this interaction. Modern bureaucracies gain legitimacy by (often rhetorical) commitments to standards of fairness and equity. But street-level bureaucrats are constantly confronted with the apparent unfairness of treating people alike (just as they recognize the obvious inequities of unequal treatment). Since individuals are so much more than their bureaucratically relevant characteristics—age, sex, place of residence, income level, etc.—a failure to recognize these differences sometimes seems unfair in itself. The public housing manager believes that there are degrees of need for public housing not circumscribed by the categories of eligibility. The teacher recognizes that all children deserve her or his attention but thinks some require more attention than others.

Not only are the standards of fairness insufficient to dictate levels of concern, but also street-level bureaucrats, like everyone else, have personal standards of whether or not someone is deserving. The public housing manager may be more sympathetic to the elderly than to other eligibles. Housing inspectors may be sympathetic to the plight of the landlord although nothing in the formal structure of the agency encourages such a bias.[28]

Under some circumstances it may be appropriate to apply standards of service with respect to personal characteristics. Street-level bureaucrats enjoy considerable discretion in part because society does not want computerized public service and rigid application of standards at the expense of responsiveness to the individual situation. The New York district attorney was praised editorially for contriving to circumvent the mandatory sentencing requirement. The VA doctors were acting on behalf of patients and in opposition to limitations on practice when they assigned pre-bedcare status to patients who did not require hospitalization. Clearly discretion provides opportunity to intervene on behalf of clients as well as to discriminate among them. Yet at best bureaucracies are highly ambivalent about personalistic service delivery. At the least it is an enduring source of conflict between the objectives of managers and workers.

Resources for Resistance

In general, lower-level workers always possess minimal resources with which they can resist managers' orientations or achieve a modicum of response from managers in exchange for compliance. If nothing else, since the costs of recruiting and training a worker are rarely trivial, there is always a degree of noncompliance that can be threatened or realized by workers. If it were otherwise, there would be no problem of management.

Public service workers currently enjoy the benefits of collective resources that strengthen their position considerably. Civil service provisions greatly reduce managers' capacity to manipulate benefits and sanctions to induce performance. Civil service provisions for advancement, introduced originally to eliminate biases in promotion, tend to be irrelevant for the skills they purport to test, thus eliminating incentives for meritorious performance. The costs of firing or demoting workers tend to be so great under civil service regulations that managers often prefer to retain workers than to endure a prolonged period of arbitration while the post in dispute remains unfilled, or worse, remains filled by the accused incompetent. This practice results in a mediocre standard of public service performance. Public employee unions in some cases have increased worker protection by building additional safeguards to capricious management decisions into the collective bargaining process.

This does not mean that managers have no control over workers. Formal sanctions, although costly for managers to invoke, are also costly to workers, who thus try to avoid receiving them. Managers also can manipulate discretionary perquisites they control, such as recommendations for advancement or transfer, or shift and work assignments. They also can facilitate or retard individual workers' efforts, granting a day off here, speeding the processing of work there, and generally making a job more or less desirable.

Lower-level workers under some conditions enjoy additional resources stemming from their critical positions in the organization. Sociologist David Mechanic has suggested that under the right circumstances several factors affect the power of lower-level workers. These factors include qualities and characteristics such as expertise, willingness to become interested and to expend effort, and personal attractiveness. They also include structural considerations such as location within the organization, which affects command of information and access and command over organizational tools.[29] These resources enhance the power of lower-status workers to the extent that higher-ranked organizational participants become more dependent on them.[30] It is the situational characteristics which are of greatest interest to us, since the effectiveness of the personal characteristics depend in large part on the worker's organizational location.

Street-level bureaucrats command a degree of expertise, and indeed, of deference, in some policy areas. (And they more or less display the personal characteristics that enhance their influence.) But it is the discretionary role of street-level bureaucrats and their position as de facto policy makers that critically affect managers' dependence upon their subordinates. The sanctioned discretion they exercise means that to demonstrate their own ability and competence, managers are highly dependent upon subordinates without being able to intervene extensively in the way work is performed.

Workers can punish supervisors who do not behave properly toward them, either by refusing to perform work of certain kinds, by doing only minimal work, or by doing work rigidly so as to discredit supervisors. Police officers, for example, can refuse to make vice arrests for a captain they dislike, can refuse to take shortcuts through department regulations in order to achieve results, or can rigidly and comprehensively enforce traffic or parking regulations to the fury of an outraged public and the eventual embarrassment of police officials.[31] Lower-level participants may also refuse to make decisions that their superiors are formally obliged to make, at some costs to superiors. Doctors who informally delegate dosage decisions to ward attendants,[32] or judges who informally allocate sentencing decisions to probation officers, are dependent on their hierarchical subordinates for the smooth functioning of their jobs.

The relationship I have described between street-level bureaucrats and managers has two primary characteristics. First, it is a relationship best conceived in large part as intrinsically conflictual. The role of the street-level bureaucrat is associated with client-processing goals and orientations directed toward maximizing autonomy. Managers' roles in this context are associated with worker-management goals directed toward aggregate achievement of the work unit and orientations directed toward minimizing autonomy. Second, it is a relationship of mutual dependence. Thus managers typically attempt to honor workers' preferences if they are rewarded by reciprocity in job performance. To a degree reciprocity will characterize all working relations; in street-level bureaucracies, however, the resources of lower-level workers are greater than those often possessed by subordinates in other work contexts. Hence, the potential for reciprocity is greater.

This picture of workers and managers in street-level bureaucracies is substantially different from the one usually used to analyze problems of policy making and implementation. Compliance with agency objectives may still be the managerial problem, but it is complicated by the capacity of street-level bureaucrats to resist organizational pressures with their own resources. Some of these resources are common to public service workers generally and some are inherent in their position as policy deliverers with broad discretion.

When relationships between policy deliverers and managers are conflictual and reciprocal, policy implementation analysis must question assumptions that influence flows with authority from higher to lower levels, and that there is an intrinsic shared interest in achieving agency objectives. This situation requires analysis that starts from an understanding of the working conditions and priorities of those who deliver policy and the limits on circumscribing those jobs by recombining conventional sanctions and incentives.

PART II

CONDITIONS OF

WORK

Introduction

STREET-LEVEL BUREAUCRACIES are consistently criticized for their inability to provide responsive and appropriate service. The experience of seeking service through people-processing bureaucracies is perceived by enough people as dehumanizing that the phrase "human services" is often understood as ironic by all but those who work under that label.[1]

The persistence of rigid and unresponsive patterns of behavior results from street-level bureaucrats' substantial discretion, exercised in a particular work context. Like other policy makers, they operate in an environment that conditions the way they perceive problems and frame solutions to them. The work environment of street-level bureaucrats is structured by common conditions that give rise to common patterns of practice and affect the direction these patterns take. At base it is the shared situational context of street-level work that permits generalization about these critical generic political and social roles and the operational policies to which they give rise.[2]

By definition, street-level bureaucrats work at jobs characterized by relatively high degrees of discretion and regular interaction with citizens. Ordinarily, they also experience the following conditions in their work.

1. Resources are chronically inadequate relative to the tasks workers are asked to perform.
2. The demand for services tends to increase to meet the supply.
3. Goal expectations for the agencies in which they work tend to be ambiguous, vague, or conflicting.

4. Performance oriented toward goal achievement tends to be difficult if not impossible to measure.
5. Clients are typically nonvoluntary; partly as a result, clients for the most part do not serve as primary bureaucratic reference groups.[3]

With the possible exception of the last item, to some degree these characteristics follow from the definition of street-level bureaucrats. However, they are worth elaborating because they call into play various behaviors in which we are interested.

Note that these conditions of work may not always prevail. For example, it may be that the welfare department in a small city with a stable, homogeneous, white population is large enough to provide a relatively full range of social services to recipients and perform with relatively clear objectives derived from the relatively homogeneous political culture of the city. Employment and family patterns may be such that there is not a great deal of movement on or off the welfare roles. In such a situation one might expect social workers in that office to behave quite differently from the social workers in a large, more heterogeneous central city.

The analysis presented here depends upon the presence of the aforementioned working conditions. If for some reason these characteristics are not present, the analysis is less likely to be appropriate, although it is instructive to understand why this is the case. If a legal services office encouraged its staff to take only four or five cases at a time in order to maximize the quality of preparation in each case, the lawyers would behave differently than if they worked in an office with much higher demands.

Part II provides a detailed discussion of these work conditions and analyzes their contribution to the problem of providing discretionary social services. Part III builds on this analysis to explore the mechanisms street-level bureaucrats develop to cope with the difficulties and ambiguities inherent in their work.

CHAPTER 3

The Problem of Resources

Bureaucratic decision making takes place under conditions of limited time and information. Decision makers typically are constrained by the costs of obtaining information relative to their resources, by their capacity to absorb information, and by the unavailability of information.[1] However, street-level bureaucrats work with a relatively high degree of uncertainty because of the complexity of the subject matter (people) and the frequency or rapidity with which decisions have to be made. Not only is reliable information costly and difficult to obtain but for street-level bureaucrats high case loads, episodic encounters, and the constant press of decisions force them to act without even being able to consider whether an investment in searching for more information would be profitable. In contrast, other bureaucrats at least sometimes may be able to calculate whether an additional effort should be made to obtain a marginal increase in information. Indeed some organizations may not be afflicted with resource scarcities at all.[2]

Resource inadequacy is not only a theoretical consideration but a highly practical one as well. This is because it appears to the public that resources are manipulable and hence subject to calculated change. However, as we shall see, this is not necessarily the case.

There are several ways in which street-level bureaucracies characteristically provide fewer resources than necessary for workers to do their jobs adequately. The two most important ways are the ratio of workers to clients or cases, and time.

Street-level bureaucrats characteristically have very large case loads relative to their responsibilities. The actual numbers are less important than the fact that they typically cannot fulfill their mandated responsibilities with such case loads. Public defenders sometimes come to trial without having interviewed their clients, or having interviewed them only briefly. Legal services lawyers, while responsible for perhaps 80 to 100 clients whose cases they currently represent, may typically be working actively on only a dozen or so cases.[3] Social workers are unable to make required home visits in public welfare work and are so inundated with paperwork that they are never without a backlog.[4]

Lower-court judges are typically inundated with cases, often causing delays of several months in providing defendants their day in court. Somehow judges must accommodate pressures for speedier trials within the constraints of fairness and equity.[5] In lower courts that hear misdemeanors the volume is likely to be even greater than in felony courts, although the standards of justice are presumably the same.

For teachers, overcrowded classrooms (with meager supplies) mean that they are unable to give the kind of personal attention good teaching requires. High student-teacher ratios also mean that teachers must attend to maintaining order and have less attention for learning activities.

For police officers, the obvious resource constraint is one of time—time to collect information, time to act. A policeman breaking up a fight in a bar does not have time to determine the initiating party and so must make a double arrest.[6] Time to develop even a minimum degree of certainty appears to be unavailable to officers who shoot innocent people because they feared the consequences of what they say was the civilian's intention to reach for a weapon. The problem of having to make a quick decision in life-threatening circumstances is a major foundation of occupational conservatism in police practice. Police reformers are unable to deal adequately with the heartfelt claims of policemen that they require maximum discretion in order to protect themselves. This is the case even though their quick reactions may evoke the very behavior they seek to defend themselves against, as in the case of the citizen whose outrage results from the officer's apparent overreaction to a situation.

Clearly, high case loads affect time for decision making. One observer of a court that heard both felonies and misdemeanors observed that 72 percent of the cases were handled in one minute or less.[7] Even when physical threat is not particularly present, street-level bureaucrats must make quick decisions because of the social reality that they are in the presence of clients who will interpret indecision as incompetence or lack of authority, with consequences for subsequent client interactions.

There are other organizational factors that affect the work of street-level bureaucrats. An emphasis on housekeeping chores, such as filling out forms or drawing up lesson plans, affects the amount of time available to clients. A social worker who spends 60 percent of his or her time doing paperwork has correspondingly less time for client interaction.[8] Support services (secretaries, clerks, investigators, receptionists) can affect the extent to which street-level bureaucrats have time for clients. However, efforts to free street-level bureaucrats of routine tasks so that they may attend to more important aspects of their work do not necessarily reduce the tensions associated with that work or improve the quality of interactions between workers and clients.[9] The reasons for this are elaborated in the next section.

Street-level bureaucrats may also lack personal resources in conducting their work. They may be undertrained or inexperienced. Police rookies, for example, must undergo a long period of informal apprenticeship before they are fully accepted and trusted by more experienced veterans.[10] The recent law school graduate who enters the world of legal services is normally untrained both in interaction with clients and aspects of procedure that bear on the kinds of problems clients are likely to face.

Street-level bureaucrats often experience their jobs in terms of inadequate personal resources, even when part of that inadequacy is attributable to the nature of the job rather than rooted in some personal failure. Some jobs just cannot be done properly, given the ambiguity of goals and the technology of particular social services. Determining whether or not a job is "proper" is subject to uncertainties and implicit negotiation with others. (See chapter 10.) For example, there is no consensus on what techniques or approaches substantially reduce rates of criminal recidivism, although social workers, psychiatrists, and prison officials are supposed to be responsible for rehabilitating offenders.[11]

From management's perspective street-level bureaucrats are resource units to be applied to a task. But because of the nature of their tasks, workers experience their work situations as individuals. One important respect in which street-level bureaucrats respond as individuals is to the stress under which they often work.

This is most obvious in the critical case of policemen, whose behavior often can be explained only by their felt need to avoid danger. They constantly work under the threat of violence that may come from any direction at any time. Because the threat is unpredictable it exists constantly, although the actual likelihood of threats materializing is quite low.[12] Police not only guard against threat but they also characteristically conduct themselves so as to determine whether threatening situations are likely to exist. They tend to be lenient with offenders whose attitude and demeanor denote penitence but harsh and punitive to those offenders who show signs of disrespect.[13] Indeed policemen often appear to test the extent to which an offender respects police authority in order to determine whether he or she is likely to have an improper attitude and therefore be more likely to resist authority.[14] Corrections personnel confront similar situations and develop their own mechanisms to establish control.[15]

Psychological strain results from physical threat. In 1976, 1,500 of New York City's 25,240 member police force were officially examined for psychological reasons, including alcoholism.[16] Law enforcement personnel are not the only lower-level public employees for whom physical danger is a condition of work with which to reckon. According to a U.S. Senate subcommittee report, between 1974 and 1975, 70,000 classroom teachers in the United States reported serious injuries from physical assaults by students. This figure probably understates the situation considerably, since teachers are often discouraged from reporting incidents of violence. Dr. Alfred Bloch, who evaluated and treated more than 200 inner-city Los Angeles teachers who had been assaulted while on the job, likens the psychological impact of these experiences to battlefield trauma.[17]

The threat of physical harm is the most dramatic aspect of the threat under which street-level bureaucrats sometimes work. But virtually all interactions between street-level bureaucrats and clients in some way focus on the workers' needs to assert authority and gain client deference. This is most obvious in the case of teachers who are instructed to first establish discipline as a precondition to successful teaching.[18] However, it is generally characteristic of street-level bureaucrats as well (see chapter 9 for further discussion).

Even without the threat of violence, street-level bureaucrats work in situations which tend to maximize the likelihood of debilitating job stress. One recent study discovered significant correlations between relatively poor mental health and three indicators characteristic of street-level work: resource inadequacy, overload (e.g. high case loads, overcrowded classrooms), and role ambiguity.[19]

There is also a degree of stress in the limited extent to which street-level bureaucrats feel themselves under scrutiny by authorities or others whose negative evaluations might be harmful. This is illustrated well in the testimony of George Kirkham, a law school professor who undertook to prepare for and experience the police role. Kirkham draws attention here to the interaction between feelings of pressure and the haste with which decisions have to be made.

As a police officer, . . . I found myself forced to make the most critical choices in a time frame of seconds rather than days: to shoot or not to shoot, to arrest or not to arrest, to give chase or to let go—always with a nagging certainty that others, those with great amounts of time in which to analyze and think, stood ready to judge and condemn me for whatever action I might take or fail to take. . . .[20]

These points suggest that the salience of solutions to problems of resource inadequacy varies not only with the demands on service and the resources available, but also with the importance to an individual of deriving a satisfactory solution to these problems.

Demand and Supply, or Why Resources Are Usually Inadequate in Street-Level Bureaucracies

Most executives profess that their organizations do not have sufficient resources or at least are hampered by resource constraints. Local governments that turn back federal revenue-sharing funds are the exception to the general rule that organizations perceive themselves as requiring and able to utilize additional resources. Yet street-level bureaucracies, with certain other government agencies, *chronically* experience resource constraints. These agencies are virtually never adequately provided for, and perhaps cannot be adequately provided for. Why is this so?

A distinct characteristic of the work setting of street-level bureaucrats is that the demand for services tends to increase to meet the supply. If additional services are made available, demand will increase to consume them. If more resources are made available, pressures for additional services utilizing those resources will be forthcoming.

The analogy to the development of traffic patterns on the Long Island Expressway is compelling. In the name of relieving congestion during rush hours on this infamous highway, traffic engineers added additional lanes. But every additional lane, while marginally decreasing driving time to New York City, induced more people to use the road. This additional traffic restored the traffic jam that the new lanes had been designed to correct. Utilization increased to meet the supply of road space until commuting time reached the previous level. A new equilibrium was restored with the same degree of congestion during rush hours, although with a higher volume of traffic.

It has often been observed that utilization increases when public services are expanded. Hospital emergency rooms become inundated because they provide free medical care or easy access to care at a time when other health resources, such as family physicians, are less and less available.[21] Mental health centers discover that they may succeed only too well and evoke such a large response from citizens that they have to cut back service.[22] Additional judges do not necessarily decrease court delays because with more judges courts may be more tolerant of lawyers' delaying tactics, thus restoring the lengthy time it takes to bring cases to trial.[23] Neighborhood multiservice-center workers discover they have to abandon plans for systematic client recruitment because the services of the new program are in such demand that new cases prove overwhelming and case finding proves superfluous.[24]

One dimension of service demand is quantitative. Public expectations of and demands for certain public services increase over time. In the case of the police, for example, society expects them to intervene in many more social conflicts—interracial violence, black assaults on blacks, family disputes, juvenile justice—than was the case perhaps forty years ago.[25] Public expectations of personal health care services have become much greater over time, spurred, to be sure, by developments in medical technology and health insurance.

There is a great reservoir of demand for public services generally. In the area of health, as in virtually every other area in which street-level bureaucrats operate, there is no imaginable limit to the amount of health care the population would seek and absorb if it were truly a "free good," available without significant explicit or implicit costs. For some time the greater use of physicians by middle-class people was thought by some to be simply a function of their greater willingness to use doctors, despite the fact that poor health is inversely related to income. Studies have shown, however, that when health care is made available at low cost there is little difference between people of different incomes in their search for medical attention.[26] It is beyond the present capacity of health training institutions to train the number of health professionals it would take to equalize the proportion of health professionals throughout the nation.

More precise and narrowly focused examples of the latent demand for street-level bureaucrats' services are available. At the end of the 1960s for example, it was reasonably estimated that to provide adequately for the legal needs of the poor, 49,000 legal services lawyers and public defenders would have to be employed. At the time there were perhaps 4,000 attorneys, both volunteers and quasi-governmental employees, who were serving in those capacities.[27]

To comprehend the relationship between resources and practice, one must understand the meaning of demand in public services. Demand is not only part of a transaction between citizens and government but is also a transactional concept. It not only requires a demander but also a more or less encouraging supplier. It is meaningless to specify a level of demand unless this is accompanied by a positive (if implicit) degree of receptivity.[28] In more concrete terms, demand for services can be estimated but it cannot finally be *known* in the abstract. It is a function not only of expressions of client preferences but also of government efforts to offer services and to record or acknowledge client responses. Demand as an expression of desire for services is a meaningful concept only if it is accompanied by explication of the extent to which demand was sought out.

Overt expressions of demand for services tend to be more responsive to changes in the perceived availability of services than in changes in the underlying conditions that are commonly supposed to affect demand. In other words, perceived availability of service "pulls" demand, not the other way around. To illustrate: when cities introduce "911" programs providing for central reception of public safety telephone calls, an easily memorized telephone number and publicity to instruct the public in its use, they discover an untapped reserve of requests for public safety assistance. Indeed, New York City at one point undertook a public campaign to urge people to use the 911 system *less* because the increased demand outstripped the city's ability to respond. When Boston introduced its Little City Halls program, providing a municipal presence in the neighborhoods, requests for city services through complaints increased by a third.[29]

Service programs generally can increase the recorded demand on themselves by changing the nature of outreach, the location of offices, or public information about the program.[30] Putative demand for services cannot even take shape until the structures for receiving demands are in place. For example, in Boston 4,000 students were assigned to classes for the retarded in a recent year, whereas only 70 were classified as emotionally disturbed. These figures might suggest that there was enormous demand for special services for the retarded in comparison to the needs of emotionally disturbed pupils. This situation would surprise most specialists in learning disabilities because, to the extent that these labels have some objective referents, these conditions tend to occur in about equal proportions in the population (about 2 percent). It would seem a reasonable inference that the disproportionate demand for services for the retarded was not intrinsic among Boston youth but rather was entirely a function of the availability of special classes for one group and not the other and of the preferences of Boston school personnel for assigning pupils to this category of disability.[31]

The proposition that demand will increase to meet the supply applies qualitatively as well as quantitatively. If there were a fixed clientele (we have just argued there is not) clients would still demand more and improved services, as the population has done historically. This might seem like the ideal toward which to strive, since conditions would be better for street-level workers and clients. However, three possibilities need to be examined.

First, as mentioned earlier street-level bureaucracies usually must choose additional services rather than improvement in services if they have slack resources. Second, claims of qualitative improvements in the form of spending more time on each case are often spurious. Case loads are often informally divided into active and inactive categories. The inactive cases are often not truly inactive but represent cases to which the street-level bureaucrat is unable to attend in the ordinary course of the day. They are regarded as low priority for reasons having little to do with the client but a lot to do with the pressures on the workers. A social worker required to make more home visits than he or she can possibly arrange and still take care of more pressing responsibilities, or a legal services lawyer with a large case load, only a portion of which he or she can act on in the course of a week, have divided their cases in such ways by necessity.[32] When additional workers enter these agencies, they may reduce the formal case load by taking on a portion of each worker's load. But presumably they will only be able to work with the same number of clients as the other workers. Thus they will have the same active case load, and everyone in the agency will have smaller inactive case loads. More clients will be seen or served, but the amount of actual time spent with the average client will not have improved.[33]

Third, even when qualitative changes can be accomplished through caseload reduction, the results are likely to be marginal. An additional teacher in an elementary school of 300 pupils and an average class size of thirty would theoretically reduce the average size of classes to twenty-seven. If this development were reproduced system-wide it would mean a 10 percent increase in teaching personnel. Yet its impact on the classroom work situation would be welcome but marginal for teachers who still have to manage the learning experiences of twenty-seven children.

With limited resources it might be desirable to add specialists rather than relieve all classes equally. Yet the problem remains that the burden on general classroom teachers would not be ameliorated. This is not to condemn such developments, but only to raise the question whether even substantial increases in public personnel budgets can reduce the work-load pressures enough to make a difference in the way clients are processed if other conditions of work remain the same.

When street-level bureaucracies do experience declining demand because of population shifts and uneven age distributions, they encounter different but equal difficulties in relieving case-load pressures. Consolidation or force reductions tend to be administered so as to retain high individual case loads.[34] Relieving case-load pressure may not directly translate into acceptable bureaucratic behavior.[35] In particular, marginal reductions in case load cannot be expected to result in visible improvements in practice. For example, one would not expect teachers to differ substantially in the way they handle disciplinary problems simply because their class sizes are reduced from thirty to twenty-five. Pressures of inadequate resources may still be responsible for questionable practice because: (1) variations in case loads do not cross the threshold below which practice substantially improves; (2) case-load pressures contribute to a milieu that remains even if conditions improve slightly; and (3) the work context of street-level bureaucracies has several components that interact with each other. Case-load pressure may interact with other factors to determine behavior without necessarily varying directly with the behavior in question.[36]

A complication in providing service through street-level bureaucracies comes about because the demand for service is sometimes unpredictable. People who use or claim services cannot be counted upon to time their needs to the exigencies of bureaucratic allocations. This is obviously the case in emergency services, where the essence of adequacy is the capacity to deal with the unexpected. An emergency room staff clearly cannot expect patients to appear at ten-minute intervals. Nor can they be expected to be predictable in their service demands, like patrons of a commuter railroad. It is possible that an exceptionally affluent street-level bureaucracy might be able to handle unpredictable demands for service and provide superior service during off-peak periods. But it is more likely that unpredictability combines with pressing demand to impose considerable costs on the provision of service. Workers may despair of ever catching up or otherwise getting out from under the pressing burden of work. They may become insensitive to the human dimensions of the job.[37] Certainly clients will bear many of the costs of agencies not having the capacity to meet unpredictable demands. Long and unexpected waiting times, broken appointments, short and hurried treatment, are all costs that clients bear from the unpredictable (yet certain to arise) system overload.[38]

Street-level bureaucrats work in situations where the resource problem in most cases is not resolvable. This is either because the number of people treated by street-level bureaucracy is only a fraction of the number that could be treated, or because their theoretical obligations call for higher quality treatment than is possible to provide to individual clients, so that slack resources are devoted to marginal improvements in quality. Conceivably, teachers could have classrooms of ten, legal services lawyers could have case loads of fifteen, and so forth. But the cost of providing service in such ways are so high as to be politically out of the question except in the case of tantalizing, carefully managed pilot or demonstration programs that provide hints of what social welfare delivery might be like if service quality were given primacy. Typically, if such programs succeed, their cost-benefit ratios are regarded as unacceptable and pressures develop to provide service in less costly ways.

This analysis of the demand-supply dilemma should not be taken as counsel of despair. Public policy always requires consideration of the trade-offs involved in providing additional resources for added benefits and incurring additional costs. With added resources more people can be served, just as more people can get to New York City from Long Island, although under stressful conditions, by using an expanded Long Island Expressway. But appreciation of the demand-supply dilemma in street-level bureaucracies does suggest that the problem of the *quality* of service delivery is not likely to yield easily to any imaginable resource increments. Other things being equal, increased capacity results in reproducing the level of service quality at a higher volume for any imaginable increase in resource availability. This proposition is critical because it explains why the steady increase in resources available to street-level bureaucracies in recent years has not resulted in improvements in the perceived quality of client treatment. (Other reasons include the fact that salary raises, which consume increases in agency resource allocations, do not increase resources available to clients, although they may help to maintain staff quality.) Further, it contradicts many often self-serving perspectives on reform, which hold that additional personnel are the most important ingredients in responding adequately to citizen complaints.

Thus street-level bureaucracies are often trapped in a cycle of mediocrity. The better the program and the more responsive it is to the needs of the citizens, the greater will be the demand for the service. This larger demand forces the agency to limit service artificially or impose costs on clients in the absence of a pricing mechanism that would otherwise ration service. The imposed cost of inferior quality or difficulty in receiving services continues until, in the extreme, the agency is returned to the previous equilibrium of indifference to client needs. The more successful the organization, the more likely it is to encounter this dilemma.

It is generally characteristic of free government programs that demand will increase to the point that goods or services can be provided. And in response to this demand agencies providing the goods or services will impose monetary or nonmonetary costs in order to limit demand effectively.[39] Street-level bureaucracies also develop rationing mechanisms to impose costs for services but in doing so they face certain constraints. If indeed they provide vital services—income to the indigent, public safety, education, health care—then there are severe constraints on the sorts of rationing mechanisms they can impose.

Street-level bureaucracies must not appear to be rationing services or depriving social groups of their rights or entitlements. They must give evidence of strenuous efforts to avoid reducing services. They may be asked to "trim the fat," but never to reduce the quality of services or the quantity of vital services. It is one of the best-kept secrets in government how agencies can forever find fat to trim and nonessential services to eliminate, while never affecting "vital programs" and "necessary services."

Agencies forced to reduce expenditures significantly, or otherwise limit service provision, typically publicize the dire consequences of failure to specific groups or sectors to provide budgetary support for what they are doing. (For example, the public university that announces it will be unable to admit a freshman class.) But when it comes to making cuts they will typically attempt to reduce services "across the board" rather than severely injure specific sectors of the population.

The demand-supply dynamics of street-level bureaucracies provide additional understanding of why they seem to be chronically understaffed. The insatiable demand for services in basic social programs results in agencies characteristically responding, and being forced to respond, by adding services or clients, or extending existing resources under pressures of budget stringency. The ethics of public service requires that they provide more of what they do or give rather than utilize additional resources to improve the resource-demand balance.

Sometimes agencies enjoy freedom from close scrutiny on spending. Then they can add qualitative improvements or reduce case-load pressures, as educators have been able to do from time to time. Or, like the police, their services may be in high demand, and they can ride public concerns to new levels of spending for men and machines.

But for the most part street-level bureaucracies, as major components of local public spending, cannot long escape close budgetary scrutiny and thus become the targets of the taxpayers' revolt. In an inflationary era the budgetary convention of asking agencies to maintain effort on the basis of last year's allocation, while costs for goods, services, and salaries are rising, insures that street-level bureaucracies will experience their resource position as chronically inadequate.

CHAPTER 4

Goals and Performance Measures

Supervision and control provide guidance toward bureaucratic goals. Performance measures offer feedback to adjust the system. The clearer the goals and the better developed the performance measures, the more finely tuned guidance can be. The less clear the goals and the less accurate the feedback, the more will individuals in a bureaucracy be on their own. The ambiguity and unclarity of goals and the unavailability of appropriate performance measures in street-level bureaucracies is of fundamental importance not only to workers' job experience, but also to managers' ability to exercise control over policy.

Goals

Street-level bureaucrats characteristically work in jobs with conflicting and ambiguous goals. Is the role of the police to maintain order or to enforce the law? Is the role of public education to communicate social values, teach basic skills, or meet the needs of employers for a trained work force? Are the goals of public welfare to provide income support or decrease dependency?[1] Willis Hawley's comment on public education might well apply to virtually every area of public service work: "[a]lmost every writer on educational administration notes . . . the problem of . . . the multiplicity, ambiguity, and diffuseness of goals."[2]

Public service goals also tend to have an idealized dimension that make them difficult to achieve and confusing and complicated to approach. Goals such as good health, equal justice, and public education, are indeed, as Martin Landau has observed, "more like receding horizons than fixed targets."[3]

Agency goals may be ambiguous because the conflicts that existed when programs were orginally developed were submerged. A typical mechanism of legislative conflict resolution is to pass on intractable conflicts for resolution (or continued irresolution) at the administrative level. The much-studied origins of the poverty program, for example, suggest that different framers of this legislation had different ideas about the objectives of the Economic Opportunity Act of 1964, but could not resolve the inherent conflict at the time the legislation was written.[4]

Agency goals also may be ambiguous because they have accumulated by accretion and have never been rationalized, and it remains functional for the agency not to confront its goal conflicts. Goal conflict in welfare policy persists not because analysts are unaware of ambiguity, but because there is such fundamental disagreement among constituents of welfare policy that Congress has never been willing to address and resolve the conflict directly.[5] Conflicting interests are deeply rooted and each side has marked out territory where it is influential. Each must be content with this arrangement since neither side can prevail.

Another major source of ambiguity may be found in the uncertainty of social service technologies.[6] When there are uncertainties over what will or will not work, there is greater room for admitting and tolerating a variety of approaches and objectives. In such a situation there is often a hunger for discovering successful techniques and an apparent willingness to modify objectives to suit the techniques. The speed with which new ideas in education come and go primarily suggests a search for successful techniques, but also indicates indecisiveness in objectives attributable as much to goal ambiguity as to flexibility.

If goal conflict in street-level bureaucracies is fairly clear-cut (rather than ambiguous), the conflicts characteristically have three sources.

1. Client-centered goals conflict with social engineering goals.
2. Client-centered goals conflict with organization-centered goals.
3. Goals conflict because street-level bureaucrats' role expectations are communicated generally through multiple conflicting reference groups.

CLIENT-CENTERED GOALS VERSUS SOCIAL ENGINEERING GOALS

A worker's concern for the client conflicts at times with the general social role of the agency. This conflict comes to public attention perhaps most noticeably in the case of police complaints that the public demands pursuit of law and order in ways always consistent with norms of fairness and due process. In the corrections area rehabilitation often conflicts with deterrence and isolation of convicted criminals from the rest of society. In public welfare programs fostering the health and well-being of individual recipients conflicts with the goals of eliminating dependency and maintaining the attraction of low-wage work. Conflict between education oriented toward individual achievement and education oriented toward citizenship and discipline also illustrates the tension between primarily focusing on individuals and primarily focusing on social objectives.

Even in areas where one would think that client-centeredness would have unambiguous primacy over other objectives, social engineering objectives often dominate. The politics of legal services, for example, are currently characterized by conflict over whether services should be provided on as broad a basis as possible or whether they should be more concentrated to insure that all poor people who secure legal services can count on having a lawyer's services appropriate to their legal difficulties. In theory there is no question that the professional relationship calls for the provision of services as required. But this professional requirement is usually compromised in organized practice for the poor.[7]

At times client-centered goals primarily support social engineering functions because of the symbolic importance of client-centeredness. Street-level bureaucracies seek to gain client compliance either through the control of resources that the client desires (utilitarian compliance) or, as in the case of police and prisons, through force or the threat of force (coercive compliance).[8] However, it is characteristic of a liberal society to show deference to the norm of respect for the individual. Institutions are given license to organize and manipulate individuals only if they properly defer to this norm. This is simultaneously a normative prescription for behavior and a dominant element in social control.

Although little rehabilitation goes on in prisons the legitimacy of the prison system depends in part on its claims to rehabilitative potential. Although courts process people quickly, often with little time for complete hearings on the merits of cases, rhetoric of guarantees for the "rights of the accused" and the proposition that defendants are "innocent until proven guilty" are powerful supports for a bureaucratized court system regardless whether those injunctions protect defendants from injustice. Claims that actions are in "the best interest of the individual child" energize the rhetoric of school personnel over an extremely wide range of educational policies, despite considerable evidence that the way schools are structured precludes individual attention. Street-level bureaucracies that function through coercive compliance systems such as the police still defer to the norm of respect for individuals. Police legitimacy is strengthened by displays of regularity and due process, although public interest in such symbols varies with the perceived worthiness of the population accorded respect.

The distinction between coercive and utilitarian modes of compliance often breaks down in street-level bureaucracies. Street-level bureaucracies for the most part deal with nonvoluntary clients. This is obvious in the case of the subjects of police arrests; it is less obvious in the case of social services clients who appear to have the option of applying for benefits or refusing them. However, if one takes the view that poor people have no alternatives to seeking essential goods and services through public programs, then analytically the voluntary nature of their involvement in the system becomes suspect. The alternative to volunteering to become a part of the welfare system may be not eating. The alternative to going to a hospital emergency room may be to neglect a serious health problem. If this is the case then to call the client "voluntary" or the mode of client compliance "utilitarian" becomes a bit scholastic.

Thus the norm of due process not only protects the rights of individuals but it also legitimizes the effects the judicial and legal system has on people's lives. Similarly, the norm of fair treatment in public agencies combines with the theoretical right to appeal to legitimize the actions of administrative agencies. (Indeed, the development of standards for client treatment, rights to appeal, and procedures for administrative regularity seem to develop in proportion to client allegations of arbitrariness and unfair treatment. By developing procedural rules agencies may in fact protect the rights of some clients, but they also gain legitimacy in continuing to act with most clients as they did before.) Despite the relatively low status of the clients of many street-level bureaucracies, the importance of deference to the norm of respect for the individual is recognized by the considerable efforts made in recent years to invest clients of these systems with rights, although these rights are often technical and remote rather than practical.

Some street-level bureaucracies such as schools and various rehabilitation programs are both coercive and normative. Schools are coercive in that they require attendance by law, they have strong sanctions against deviant behavior, including expulsion, and they are the only institutions in the society where parents can send children to learn basic skills. They are also normative in that they attempt to motivate children by socializing them to want to participate in the system. A drug rehabilitation program is coercive when it stands as an alternative to jail, but it also is normative because it cannot succeed unless people are motivated to accept the orientation and discipline of the program.

43

In such settings the social engineering objectives may simply be to place people in the hands of skilled professionals. There will be inevitable conflicts between the client focus of professional norms and the dominant framework of the institutions in which the professionals work. A teacher may, as a professional, be oriented to individual evaluation and assistance, but the school as an organization may have as competing orientations discipline, citizenship training, and socialization to norms of general behavior.[9]

In addition, the operating necessities of the organization will likely interfere with providing professional services. The example of the court psychiatrist illustrates this familiar observation. Psychiatrists are trained to render highly personalized and individualized services through interaction with clients in a sustained period of consultation and intervention. Yet the court psychiatrist is often placed in the absurd position of having an extremely brief period to diagnose and label people referred by judges anxious to avoid consigning defendants to the harsh and counter-productive penalties of the prison system. Court psychiatrists are chronically misused because the social function of psychiatric referral by judges outweighs protection of the psychiatric milieu.

CLIENT-CENTERED GOALS VERSUS ORGANIZATIONAL GOALS

Street-level bureaucracies encounter conflict and ambiguity in the tensions between client-centered goals and organizational goals. This distinction echoes some of the considerations presented above and in some ways is continuous with it. The ability of street-level bureaucrats to treat people as individuals is significantly compromised by the needs of the organization to process work quickly using the resources at its disposal.

The fundamental service dilemma of street-level bureaucracies is how to provide individual responses or treatment on a mass basis. Martin Levin calls attention to this conflict in his study of criminal courts. "At the most general level the motives of the judges are primarily two: the defense and maintenance of their traditionally high degree of discretion in criminal court . . . ." permitting them to tailor decisions to the needs, "and successfully coping with their court's case loads." He asserts: "the judges tend to emphasize processing their case loads as an end in itself rather than a means for achieving other goals."[10]

This is a classic example of goal displacement. Effective management of the process preempts the purposes for which the process was developed. The study of street-level bureaucrats may be seen as a study in goal displacement when the norm of individual client orientation becomes subordinate to the needs for mass processing. The typical conflicts here are individual client treatment versus routinization and mass processing, and response to the needs of individual clients versus efficient agency performances.

These dilemmas are related to the public nature of the programs. Just as agencies distributing free goods must develop mechanisms to ration their allocation, political systems must place limits on the demands that organizations can make for additional resources. If, indeed, demand will increase to equal the supply then the inherent impulses organizations display toward growth[11] will lead to increasing organizational scope even though, as suggested above, the quality of service cannot be expected to improve with growth.

Suggestive evidence for this proposition is encountered in the alarm that public officials express when they discover that benefit programs are open-ended. The food stamp program, for example, caused a great deal of official consternation because it entitled many more people to benefits than was originally anticipated, resulting in unexpected costs difficult to control except through categorical cutbacks.[12] Constant harping on the error rate in public welfare or allegations of doctor abuses of medicare claims serve to remind the public and the agencies in charge of these programs that uncontrolled growth in government spending is not officially acceptable. Thus, except in rare instances, such as a new service program in search of a clientele,[13] street-level bureaucracies are under continuous pressure to realize the public objectives of efficiency and cost effectiveness. Pressures will be more or less explicitly articulated depending upon the political climate and a variety of other factors.

Like other organizations, street-level bureaucracies are always constrained by resource limitations. However, it is important to understand that this constraint is experienced as a source of tension within street-level bureaucracies at the operational level. Street-level bureaucrats must find a way to resolve the incompatible orientations toward client-centered practice on the one hand and expedient and efficient practice on the other.

GOAL CONFLICTS AND ROLE EXPECTATIONS

Finally, goal conflicts and ambiguity arise from the contradictory expectations that shape the street-level bureaucracy role. Generally role theorists locate the origin of role expectations in three sources: in peers and others who occupy complementary role positions; in reference groups, in terms of which expectations are defined although they are not literally present; and in public expectations where consensus about role expectations can sometimes be found.[14] To the extent that these sources of role expectations differ significantly one would expect street-level bureaucrats to encounter role conflict and ambiguity (note that goals are one dimension of role construct). There are at least three ways in which the complicated structure of street level bureaucrats' role expectations contributes to goal ambiguity and conflict.

First, to the extent that public expectations affect street-level bureaucrats there is often considerable disagreement about what street-level bureaucracies should primarily do. Street-level bureaucrats within limits may define the ways in which they will pursue their objectives. But often community opinion is diffusely apprehended, creating role conflict. In different cities and within the same city some communities may expect police to enforce the law vigorously and impartially and to have a strong legalistic orientation, while others are content to have the police primarily focus on maintaining order. Some parents want schools oriented toward achievement in basic skills, while others want schools oriented toward developing community values and vocational training. The punitiveness of welfare administration in some cities and the liberal orientation of other welfare offices demonstrate clearly how the same statutes can spawn agencies with vastly different bureaucratic cultures.[15]

These differing perspectives on the purposes of service contribute to goal uncertainty and lead to the following hypotheses. To the extent that communities are indifferent to the nature of bureaucratic policy or fail to express their views in politically salient ways, street-level bureaucracies will perform with internally generated objectives. Conversely, the stronger community sentiment is concerning proper bureaucratic behavior, the more street-level bureaucracies will respond to community orientations. The more heterogeneous community sentiments are, however, the more street-level bureaucracies will experience goal conflict.

Major urban conflicts have resulted in recent times over such diverse perspectives on public services. Should schools promote appreciation of ethnic and racial heritage or should they be devoted to the traditional role of homogenizing and Americanizing urban newcomers? Should public housing managers attempt to integrate their projects racially or should they try to maximize the security and comfort of long-term project residents? Is discipline and punishment more effective for inducing studious attitudes among pupils or is a liberal and flexible approach more appropriate? These are questions that would be answered quite differently by different subpopulations of the country's largest cities.[16]

Racial conflict brings issues of divided community sentiment into sharp focus. Black community residents differ from whites in their law enforcement priorities, the desirability of police intervention in certain areas, appropriate role models for their children in schools, and so on. Moreover, residents of black communities themselves differ in priorities; for example, whether they would prefer high-intensity police protection in order to reduce crime or whether they regard saturation patrolling as community harrassment.

A second dimension of role conflict or ambiguity stems from the significant role of peer groups in establishing role expectations. For street-level bureaucrats, peers are fellow workers (although generally peers can be otherwise, e.g., social peers, family peers, etc.). Only work peers fully appreciate the pressures of work and the extent to which street-level bureaucrats experience the need to have goal orientations that are consistent with resolving work pressures. The greater the strain between various goal expectations, and the smaller the zone of indifference in which street-level bureaucrats operate, the more peer support is critical for sustaining workers' morale.[17]

The subject of peer support is discussed extensively in analyses of the police, the street-level bureaucracy that is perhaps the most controversial and the most subject to conflicting goal expectations. Police must perform their duties somewhere within the demand for strict law enforcement, the necessity for discretion in enforcement actions, and various community interpretations of proper police practice. They must accommodate the constraints of constitutional protection and demands for efficiency in maintenance of order and crime control. They must enforce laws they did not make in communities where demands for law enforcement vary with the laws and with the various strata of the population.[18] Police may perceive the public in these communities as hostile yet dependent. Police role behavior may conflict significantly with individual value preferences and the behavior and outlook of others with whom police must work, particularly judges. Police are expected to be scrupulously objective, impartial, and upstanding, protective of all segments of society even while society does not protect all segments of itself.[19]

A third dimension of the construction of street-level bureaucrats' role expectations concerns the role of clients. Clients are *not* a primary reference group of street-level bureaucrats. They do not count among the groups that primarily define street-level bureaucrats' roles.[20]

This is not to say that children are unimportant to teachers or that litigants and defendants are unimportant to judges. But these people do not primarily or even secondarily determine bureaucratic role expectations. Work-related peer groups, work-related or professionally related standards, and public expectations generally are much more significant in determining role behavior. Recognizing their weak influence in defining workers' roles, some client organizations have demanded inclusion in the constellation of bureaucratic reference groups.[21] Street-level bureaucrats' resistance to client demands may be understood by recognizing that clients are not part of their reference group constellation. The fact that many street-level bureaucrats provide client services or are required to interact with clients in a helpful manner in no way implies that they think that clients should have a say in the nature of street-level practice. Indeed, the organizations that collectively articulate the perspective of street-level bureaucrats, such as teachers' and patrolmen's associations, have fought vigorously to keep their arenas free from citizen involvement.

Yet the matter is hardly simple, as community disputes over greater client participation indicate. Since street-level bureaucrats generally pay lip service to clients' opinions, and as individuals they no doubt often do respect client views, there are internal and professional pressures that incline them toward accepting clients' judgments and soliciting their respect and consent. The cauldron into which clients' demands for a voice in policy have been placed has brewed some of the most vigorous community conflicts of the last fifteen years.

Overt conflict is not the only result of role ambiguity. Lack of clarity in role expectations has been found to impair personal action and reduce workers' effectiveness.[22] Thus role ambiguity affects individual performance as well as organizational direction.

Performance Measures

Job performance in street-level bureaucracies is extremely difficult to measure. The many implications of this statement include the facts that these agencies are not self-corrective, and the definition of adequate performance is highly politicized.

For some purposes bureaucracy itself may be defined in part as a large organization whose output cannot be evaluated through market transactions. Such a definition distinguishes bureaucracies from business organizations, whose behavior is in a sense assessed through profitability.[23] To say that output cannot be evaluated through market transactions draws attention to the fact that bureaucracies characteristically cannot have their work evaluated through an organic social process such as that which is symbolized by the summary on a balance sheet. While in theory a market-oriented organization can learn when it is succeeding or failing through the inexorable realities of profit and loss, bureaucracies receive no similar messages. Hence the measurement and evaluation of performance—the governance of performance—is critical.

Difficulty in evaluating performance may be characteristic of bureaucracies generally but it is particularly endemic in street-level bureaucrats' work. When the output consists of services provided or the validity of discretionary decisions made, it is extremely difficult to oversee or scrutinize these decisions if standards of quality are at issue. The following observations contribute to understanding the problem of performance measurement.[24]

Goal ambiguity, intrinsic to street-level bureaucracies, affects performance measurement. Such goals as developing a well-educated citizenry or securing public safety are ephemeral. But putting these general goals into operation is a practical matter, since we evaluate achievement in terms of goals. As we have seen, there is no agreement in society about objectives of public education and public safety forces. How then to operationalize ambiguous objectives? The extraordinary attention practitioners and theorists in public administration recently have placed on clarifying organizational objectives testifies as well as anything to the general importance of goal clarity for organizational evaluation.

Still another reason that street-level bureaucrats' performance often eludes effective evaluation is that there are too many variables to take into account to make evaluation realistic. It is not only that human beings are complex and that a metric of correct responses is inappropriate. Equally important, there is rarely any way to determine on a regular basis what would have happened to clients in the absence of intervention. A job training program may have a 40 percent placement rate, but to assess its effectiveness one would want to know the employment potential in the trainee group, and what the employment rate of participants would have been without the program. If the program drew its participants from the most work-resistant part of the population, then a 40 percent rate might be extremely good. However, if participants were drawn from a work-oriented part of the population—that is, if the population were "creamed"—then its placement rate might be judged inadequate. Placement rates can only be evaluated if one knows the quality of the material with which programs started.

For example, in the Upward Bound program in the 1960s evaluation of individual projects ultimately proved impossible because there was no way to determine whether programs that got a high proportion of their students into college started with high-risk or low-risk students. The program directors were encouraged to admit high-risk students but no one could tell from testing or background information available on students who was or was not a high risk. Being poor, black, and a student at an inferior high school was regarded as high risk enough. Programs often admitted students with reasonable grades, neglecting students who might have been even higher risks. If those programs succeeded did they succeed because they selected students prudently, or because they ran effective programs? Moreover, evaluation would have to consider changes in the social or economic environment. Changes in national employment trends or civil rights orientations might affect program success in ways not attributable to the program.

To some degree public deference to street-level bureaucrats' autonomy in decision making is also characteristic. This deference is a defining aspect of professionalism and has some applicability in all the areas in which street-level bureaucrats work. While public deference is related to the needs for discretionary judgment, goal ambiguity (leaving goals to be defined by professionals), and decision complexity, it has a meaning of its own, particularly as public bureaucracies attempt to develop performance measures as a precondition to increasing bureaucratic control.

Street-level bureaucrats tend to perform in jobs that are freer from supervisory scrutiny than most organizational jobs, and work norms prevailing in these jobs minimize such scrutiny. This may be because of supervisors' willingness to respect professional claims (for example, teachers in most schools are rarely visited in classrooms by principals, and then only with enough notice so that performances can be staged). Or it may be because workers expected to exercise discretion require some freedom from supervisory control (for example, policemen whose supervisors leave them alone as long as they seem to be performing adequately).[25] Whatever the sources of this freedom, it contributes in itself to the problems of measuring performance, particularly since peer evaluation is one of the ways to achieve accountability in work quality.

Notwithstanding these difficulties, however, bureaucracies *do* establish standards and measure workers' performances against these standards. For example, policemen typically are asked to make a certain number of arrests per month. Social workers are asked to maintain a certain monthly intake and case-closing rate. But these measures are only problematically related to public safety, or to clients' ability to cope with problems that are in part the objectives of these interactions. And they have nothing to do with the appropriateness of workers' actions, or the fairness with which they were made, the net results of which determine the rates on which workers are judged.

Not only are such standards problematically related to goals, but it is not even apparent whether measured increases or decreases signal better or worse performance. The best illustration of this consideration is the problem of inference from crime statistics. Do increases in arrest rates signal improved police performance? Or do they signal deteriorating police performance, indicating an increase in criminal activity and thus in the number of criminals available to catch? Actually, changes in arrest rates may indicate neither, reflecting rather changes in the focus of police patrol. Do decreases in the welfare rolls signal improved bureaucratic performance? They do only if improvement is defined as having fewer people on welfare, the economy that creates the need for welfare remains stable, and welfare agencies do not change their practices affecting clients' willingness to apply. These are but specific illustrations of the observation that agency-generated statistics are likely to tell us little about the phenomena they purport to reflect, but a great deal about the agency behavior that produced the statistics.[26]

Despite the difficulties of performance measurement, street-level bureaucracies do seize on some aspects of performance to measure. They tend to seek reports on what can be measured as a means of exercising control. In turn, the behavior of workers comes to reflect the incentives and sanctions implicit in those measurements.

The relationship between performance measures and behavior was perhaps first highlighted by sociologist Peter Blau when he observed that when the employment agency he was studying began to be evaluated in terms of its placement rate, employment counselors shifted the focus of their work to the more easily employed at the expense of those more difficult to place.[27] This illustrates the general rule that behavior in organizations tends to drift toward compatibility with the ways the organization is evaluated.

Street-level bureaucracies also measure the training and experience of employees as a way of assessing quality. These surrogates represent qualities that are hypothetically associated with good performance. Thus a teaching faculty is assessed in terms of its educational background although the graduate training in question is only problematically related to effective teaching. Street-level bureaucracies often depend on the experience or training of their workers as signs of quality service, although it is not clear that more training or experience is associated with doing a better job. Low-income parents often express concern that experienced teachers exercise seniority rights and migrate to schools in affluent neighborhoods. But experience is problematically related to effective teaching. The less-experienced teacher may be more interested, energetic, ambitious, more recently educated and familiar with new techniques, and more sympathetic toward a low-income clientele. (Of course, lacking good performance measures we rarely have an opportunity to test the relationship between the surrogate measures and their implications for performance.)

The organization itself develops surrogate measures of performance on which it evaluates and is evaluated. Case loads, arrest rates, home visits, and worker/client ratios are all measures of work activity that serve public agencies in the absence of performance measures. These surrogate measures then become reified and guide future performance.[28]

Organizations tend to measure what they can readily quantify without intruding on workers' interaction with clients. Organizational attention focuses on two major considerations. First, a great deal of attention is paid to the way the worker spends his or her time. Classroom control and other demonstrations of discipline are important criteria in teacher evaluations largely because these are aspects of the teacher's classroom that can be observed without intrusion.[29]

Since the determining factor in accomplishment of the goals of the school is the contact between students and teachers in the institutional framework of the school, the main control that the organization has over the action of teachers in the accomplishment of the school's goals is the enforcement of rules concerning teacher behavior. Thus, the administrator can measure teacher compliance with these norms rather than teacher effectiveness since, unfortunately, for many administrators the two are synonymous.[30]

Organizations may develop surrogate indicators of performance and quality, but workers accommodate themselves to these measures and remain independent of organizational control. Since the quality of their accommodations remains unscrutinized, police can meet traffic ticket quotas in a single day or reduce serious crime by recording burglaries as larcenies.[31] Housing inspectors can appear to increase their productivity by inspecting more premises, but this at the expense of lowering their standards and reducing their time spent per inspection.[32] Street-level bureaucracies attempt to promote the validity of surrogate measures to the general public in an effort to appear accountable through performance standards. Although they currently make great efforts to develop information systems to give the impression that they actively seek to increase productivity, there are really few valid statistics where the quality of performance is at issue.

Albert O. Hirschman has usefully pointed out that there are two general ways in which organizations can be self-correcting. Members or consumers may withdraw their organizational support and by so doing signal to managers that something is wrong. Alternatively, they can express their concerns or objections and by so doing help organizations to correct themselves.[33] However, citizens' ability to affect organizations by withdrawing or speaking up depends upon the clarity with which they receive information about the organizations.[34]

An important problem of public bureaucracies generally and street-level bureaucracies particularly is that clients do not receive the kind of information that would permit them to compare or assess their treatment. Nor can they compare the treatment they receive this year with the treatment extended to clients in other years, or compare the performance of their agency with similar agencies elsewhere. Citizens in general and poor people in particular will resign themselves to inferior levels of service if they have nothing with which to compare their experiences and have no basis for thinking that they deserve any better. Their frame of reference, if any, is experiential. But the isolation of most clients from each other makes it difficult to interpret experiences effectively and makes clients highly subject to street-level bureaucrats' definition of their situation.

Recent experiences with educational voucher experiments illuminate the importance of the absence of performance measures in street-level bureaucracies. First, teachers were very resistant to comparison to other teachers and to the staffs of other schools. Second, parents rarely exercised their option to shop around for the best school, tending instead to support the conventional schools. From the standpoint of the present analysis one could hardly expect parents to exercise options when they had no basis for understanding which schools performed better. Whatever problems they may have had with their schools parents may have attributed to difficulties within themselves or their children. In the absence of solid information on alternatives the security of the known quantity was in any case generally chosen over the unknown quantity. Significantly, in the experiments in which school systems were able to differentiate the programs of each school, parents did exercise considerable options.[35]

In summary, the inability to measure street-level bureaucrats' performance has widespread implications for controlling the agencies. Supervisors and agency directors can discipline workers, but not to the point of closely guiding workers' activities toward agency preferences unless they can monitor performance and determine who is or is not measuring up. Nonetheless, surrogate performance measures are developed to provide the agencies and the public with control tools, even if the tools are not quite appropriate and may even be counterproductive to the purposes. These measures do affect workers' behavior, although not necessarily in the direction favored by the agency or the public. And street-level bureaucrats, in recognition of the importance performance measures have to limiting their autonomy, actively resist their development and application.

CHAPTER 5

Relations with Clients

Nonvoluntary Clients

Clients in street-level bureaucracies are nonvoluntary. This point is obvious in coercive public agencies such as police departments, but it also applies when the coercive dimensions of the relationship between the agency and the client are less clear. This is because street-level bureaucracies often supply essential services which citizens cannot obtain elsewhere. Government agencies may have a monopoly on the service, clients may not be able to afford private services, or they may not have ready access to them. Potential welfare recipients in a sense "volunteer" to apply for welfare, for example, but their participation in the welfare system is hardly voluntary if they have no income alternatives.

Where government does not monopolize an essential service it often provides the only such service available to the poor. Health care and legal services, for example, can be obtained privately but only at relatively high cost. The cost of obtaining private assistance in these areas is so great, relative to income, that poor people are forced to seek assistance through public agencies or not to seek assistance at all. The poorer the person, the more he or she is likely to be the nonvoluntary client of not one but several street-level bureaucracies. Relatively affluent people can seek out a private doctor instead of a public clinic. Middle-class families dissatisfied with their school systems can change residences. These options are less available to the poor. This relationship between poor people and public agencies provides grounds for concluding that poor people receive a qualitatively different kind of treatment from the state. Indeed, we might predict that public agencies with poor clients provide different treatment in comparison to those serving more affluent people entirely on the basis that poor people are much more dependent on these agencies.[1]

What is the meaning of saying that the clients of street-level bureaucracies are nonvoluntary? What difference does it make and why do we elevate this consideration to the status of a primary working condition?

If street-level bureaucracies have nonvoluntary clients then they cannot be disciplined by those clients. Street-level bureaucracies usually have nothing to lose by failing to satisfy clients. They will try to manage a large volume of complaints and undoubtedly seek to minimize the extent to which they are perceived as difficult to deal with or unresponsive. But managing complaints successfully is a far cry from changing policy in response to consumer dissatisfaction. Yet, as indicated in the previous chapter, receiving complaints and correcting policy in response to them is one of the few ways organizations can learn from clients.[2]

Sometimes street-level bureaucracies are even rewarded for reducing their clientele. Public welfare agencies in the United States come under criticism for their large number of clients, although a public agency that reached less than half the eligible population in other contexts might be regarded as a colossal failure. At other times street-level bureaucracies are indifferent to the loss of clients or client dissatisfaction. Partly this is due to a proposition developed earlier. If demand for services is practically inexhaustible relative to supply, then the fact that some clients are disaffected by the quality or level of service means only that their places are taken by others who need the service and are willing to accept the costs of seeking it.

Even in situations in which one would assume that street-level bureaucracies would suffer from client losses, the bureaucracies often seem relatively indifferent. Consider the case of public schools in central cities that have lost white, middle-class students and failed to retain lower-class students. Although school revenues are based on average, per-pupil attendance these population losses usually have little effect on school practices.

Perhaps there are ways to explain this lack of responsiveness. The tenure of the more experienced teachers, for example, may mean that they do not consider their jobs threatened by declining school enrollment. Or perhaps school officials think that they are not capable of combatting the attractions of suburban and parochial schools or of influencing achievement levels among drop-outs. Whatever the full explanation of schools' unresponsiveness to declining enrollments,[3] they place surprisingly little emphasis on programs to retain pupils and on public relations designed to promote their strengths and enhance their long-run budgetary status. Instead schools fight for their budgets within the arena of local-interest group politics without great emphasis on consumer satisfaction.

That clients are nonvoluntary has significant implications not only for the direction of public services as a whole but also for the quality of interactions between street-level bureaucrats and clients. Primarily, this is because nonvoluntary clients cannot avoid or withdraw from encounters with workers. Where both parties are free to continue the interaction or leave it, participants will set limits to the costs they will accept before ending the relationship. If the encounter is instrumental, that is, if each participant wants something from the other, they will continue to pursue their objectives within the relationship so long as they value the objectives more than the cost of seeking them. This permits a wide range of implicit bargaining tactics, particularly if both parties have a stake in maintaining the relationship.[4]

However, if one of the parties does not enter the relationship voluntarily or must sustain the relationship because a highly desired good for which there is no alternative is controlled by the other person in the encounter, the nature of the interaction changes. The costs that the nonvoluntary person in the interaction will sustain become much higher. Indeed, the less voluntary the interaction, the less useful it is even to understand the interaction in terms of limits to the costs people will accept, because clients cannot easily withdraw.

Street-level bureaucrats can impose costs of personal abuse, neglectful treatment, or inconvenience without necessarily paying the normal penalty of having the other party retaliate. When medical personnel refer to patients as "garbage," "scum," "liars," "deadbeats," and so forth, there is a temptation to say that this is a reaction to the moral superiority they feel over lower-class people.[5] However, neglect and abuse of patients is a function of the nonvoluntary nature of the association of clients with patients, and not strictly of bureaucracy or class discrepancies. This is suggested by the observation that doctors in private practice can also neglect patients if there is a restricted supply of professionals, but they become much more solicitous when patients have medical alternatives on which to draw.[6]

In the elliptical euphemism used by several street-level bureaucracies, they need not worry that clients will "elope." If clients refuse to continue interacting with street-level bureaucracies, the fault may always be attributed to the client. "Escapees," "dropouts," "incorrigibles," and "socially disorganized" are labels that imply that the exit of the client is attributable to a defect of the client.

Conflict, Reciprocity, and Control

The nonvoluntary nature of clients helps explain why they are not among street-level bureaucrats' primary reference groups (see chapter 4). But this does not mean that clients are helpless in the relationship. Street-level bureaucrats in a sense are also dependent upon clients. Clients have a stock of resources and thus can impose a variety of low-level costs. This is because street-level bureaucrats must obtain client compliance with their decisions, particularly when they are evaluated in terms of clients' behavior or performance.

Order in a prison is a function of adjustments made by guards in exchange for prisoners' general compliance with regulation.[7] So it is with most social organization. To do their work smoothly police officers must obtain the consent of suspects they apprehend. Teachers must secure pupils' cooperation before they can begin to teach. Social workers must obtain the compliance of welfare recipients in case determinations or confront time-consuming appeals. The child who refrains from asking a question after a certain point out of fear of making the teacher angry, the traffic law violator who fails to contest what he regards as an officer's unfair decision, the law client who, although vaguely troubled, is too confused to raise questions about her case, are all actively cooperating in the interactions.

For the most part, except in the more coercive bureaucracies, clients give their consent because (sometimes in combination) they accept the legitimacy of the street-level bureaucrats' position and decision, anticipate that dissent would not be productive, or consider themselves favored by the decision or action taken. Most encounters with bureaucracy appear to be characterized by the consent of clients, but the structure of choices available to clients limits the range of alternative behaviors that they consider realistically available. In short, clients' consent is continuously being managed by public agencies.

Street-level bureaucrats are not required to command. Clients control themselves in response to the superior power of the workers. This is not to suggest that clients are docile because swift retaliation would result from noncompliant behavior. Rather, compliance in most street-level bureaucracies may be said to result from the superior position of the workers, their control over desired benefits, and their potential capacity to deny benefits or make their pursuit more costly.

Compliance also results from the milieu, which comprehensively cues clients concerning behavioral expectations. Readers lower their voices in libraries, defendants talk respectfully to judges, patients wait quietly for doctors, children obey teachers, not directly because of the imminence of retaliation but because they have a diffuse appreciation of "proper" modes of behavior and a diffuse awareness that deviance from these norms may be punished.[8]

Nonetheless, street-level bureaucrats sometimes do display behavior that strongly suggests this inference is warranted. Street-level bureaucrats indeed reprimand or otherwise sanction deviance from acceptable standards of client behavior. They dominate their interactions with clients. They cue and otherwise teach clients to behave "properly." They structure work patterns to maximize control over clients independent of any policy objectives.

The need to control clients is a requirement evident in many work areas, not just street-level bureaucracies. Relationships are always reciprocal to some degree. If one party seeks to control the other, the second party may increase the costs of the first party gaining or exercising control, even if the first is unquestionably more powerful. This observation, which has universal applicability from guerrilla warfare to concentration camps, takes particular shape in street-level bureaucracies in several respects.

First, street-level bureaucrats characteristically are pressed with heavy case loads and demands for quick decisions, so that clients can impose salient costs merely by taking workers' time. Since time may be fairly cheap for clients, or their needs high relative to the value they place on their time, clients potentially have a store of resources with which to affect their relationships with street-level bureaucrats.

Second, street-level bureaucrats are characteristically constrained in the resources they can employ in obtaining client compliance. These constraints consist of professional and bureaucratic standards of fairness and due process that to some degree place limits on what can or cannot be done to or with clients (notwithstanding the most outrageous tales of exceptions to the contrary). They are also constrained by social norms of proper behavior toward other people and by recognition that power should be accompanied by responsibility, particularly when clients are identifiably (indeed defined as) socially or economically needy. This point is emphasized not because street-level bureaucrats are absolutely constrained from abusing their positions, but because what needs to be explained is the mobilization of control in combination with constraints against excessive manifestations of power. Modern bureaucracies which are too heavy-handed lose their legitimacy if their offenses are publicized. Moreover, they are ultimately inefficient if they require significant force to assure adequate client control.

Third, there is an extent to which clients' satisfaction or performance is important to street-level bureaucrats. Successful intervention, expressions of gratitude, and changes in behavior in the desired direction are valued by street-level workers whether or not these developments are reasonably attributable to their work.

Clients sometimes manipulate the gratification received by street-level bureaucrats in order to affect future interactions. Client strategies include passivity and acquiescence, expressions of empathy with workers' problems, and humble acceptance of their own responsibility for their situation. The disadvantaged position of clients forces them to conspire in their own management in order to avoid offending the workers or providing negative evidence about their character. In some circumstances clients can effectively express anger or demand their rights, but these strategies appear useful only in certain circumstances and usually not for long.[9]

While a client has some resources with which to affect a relationship with street-level bureaucrats, the relationship is by no means a balanced one. It is a relationship of "unidirectional" power in which "the capacity to make and carry out decisions is the exclusive, or near exclusive, property of one of the . . . groups."[10] The relationship is primarily determined by the priorities and preferences of street-level bureaucrats, but the character and terms of the relationship are substantially affected by the limits of the job.

The Social Construction of a Client[11]

People come to street-level bureaucracies as unique individuals with different life experiences, personalities, and current circumstances. In their encounters with bureaucracies they are transformed into clients, identifiably located in a very small number of categories, treated as if, and treating themselves as if, they fit standardized definitions of units consigned to specific bureaucratic slots. The processing of *people* into *clients*, assigning them to categories for treatment by bureaucrats, and treating them in terms of those categories, is a social process. Client characteristics do not exist outside of the process that gives rise to them. An important part of this process is the way people learn to treat themselves as if they were categorical entities.

If "reality" is a social construction, general agreement about its characteristics can still be approached if the people who comprise the interaction about the reality are not in conflict, or if they are relative equals. Spectators at a boxing match may approach agreement on what is going on in the ring although they come from different class backgrounds (even here we need to be cautious, since fighting may mean something quite different to people of different classes). Likewise, the boxers may have a similar view of reality because they share the common goal of putting on a show, or because, while in conflict, they are relatively evenly matched.

There is little agreement, however, on the picture of reality where clients and street-level bureaucrats are concerned. This is at least because the two are intrinsically in conflict over objectives and the relationship is drastically unequal. What street-level bureaucrats think they do may have little connection with what clients think is going on. Clients tend to experience their needs as individual problems and their demands as individual expressions of expectations and grievances. They often expect treatment appropriate to them as individuals, and are in large measure encouraged in this expectation by public institutions and society in general. On the other hand, street-level bureaucrats experience client problems as calls for categories of action. Individual client demands are perceived as components of aggregates. Expectations of proper treatment are framed in terms of satisfactory solutions for the optimal processing of the totality of the work rather than in terms of the best solution for individual cases. Clients seek services and benefits; street-level bureaucrats seek control over the process of providing them.

There are four basic dimensions to the control exercised by street-level bureaucrats over clients. Each significantly affects some dimension of client "construction." Briefly, street-level bureaucrats exercise control in: (1) distributing the benefits and sanctions that are supposed to be provided by the agencies; (2) structuring the context of clients' interactions with them and their agencies; (3) teaching clients how to behave as clients; and (4) allocating psychological rewards and sanctions associated with clients entering into relationships with them.

DISTRIBUTING BENEFITS AND SANCTIONS

In allocating benefits and sanctions street-level bureaucrats obviously affect the relative well-being of their clients. They contribute to change and development, to the resources clients control, and to the status clients suffer or enjoy.

While eligibility for public service benefits often may seem cut-and-dried, a considerable part of eligibility is in fact problematic. Rules and regulations provide only a measure of guidance in determining eligibility. This may be because discretion must be used in determining eligibility for the presenting situation, as in the case of a legal services lawyer who must decide whether a prospective client is faced with an emergency and therefore eligible for services under agency policies. It may be because classifying the behavior or background of the client is a matter of discretion, as in assessing whether the behavior of a pupil or prisoner constitutes insolence. Or it may be because the categories into which clients fit are actually problematic and not fixed, as in judicial determination that a juvenile defendant is "a basically good kid in trouble" rather than "a rotten apple."[12] To the extent that the assignment of benefits or sanctions is negotiated between street-level bureaucrats and clients through interpersonal strategies and implicit maneuvering, the allocation of benefits and sanctions are clearly part of a process of constructing the client profile.

STRUCTURING THE CONTEXT

This leads to the second dimension of street-level bureaucrats' control over clients. The most important aspects of interactions with clients are those affecting the structure of the interactions: when they will take place, with what frequency, under what circumstances, with what resources commanded by the parties. The structure of interactions limits and determines the range of behavioral actions from which clients may choose their responses.[13] Street-level bureaucrats organize the context of decision making so that they are able to process clients under circumstances most favorable to controlling their behavior. In this they are not constrained by fear of client retaliation and for the most part can impose on the clients whatever costs are involved. Thus street-level bureaucrats develop routines that prepare people for client status, and their agencies impose standardized ways of processing people to maximize utilization of agency resources (see chapters 7 to 9). In this way disruptive, antagonistic, or uncooperative client behavior is discouraged before it surfaces.

TEACHING THE CLIENT ROLE

A third dimension of control over clients by street-level bureaucrats consists of teaching the client role. We observe the teaching of the client role in schools, where children are socialized to the procedures of orderly classrooms (and to the requirements of modern industrial and administrative work). Children are taught to raise their hands if they wish to speak, walk in twos holding a partner's hand, and organize their work to begin and finish within set periods.

While many such lessons are appropriately treated in terms of the routines established to process work (see chapter 9), there are several aspects of client role instruction that may be taken up here.

Imagine a situation in which a relatively modern bureaucracy has to routinely process clients who have no concept of bureaucratic expectations. Heavy costs may be laid on helpless clients. The dehumanizing mass processing of immigrants at Ellis Island during the mass immigrations from southern and eastern Europe is an example. But where the clients' cooperation is necessary for the bureaucrats to function smoothly—that is, where failure to cooperate, out of anger or ignorance, is likely to impede bureaucratic functioning, the bureaucracy has a stake in teaching clients what is expected of them. This phenomenon has been observed in the case of new immigrants to Israel, who, coming from traditional societies, often lack simple understanding of the functioning of modern social institutions.

Consider, for example, the bus driver who gets out of the bus to teach the idea of a queue—"first come, first served"—an idea which is new to many of his new immigrant passengers. Similarly, the nurse at the well-baby clinic may be seen teaching women, informally, which of their needs are appropriate to the health services and which should be taken to other organizations.[14]

Teaching the client role is not confined to children or immigrants new to modern institutions. While novices may have to be instructed from the start, it is more commonly the case that people are attuned to the requirements of their dependency and only incidentally reminded of proper client behavior. Most of the time people act appropriately, serving as models for others. But they will be spurred to proper behavior if they stray. The uniform, nightstick, and gun of the police officer is sufficient to cue most citizens to respect police authority if they become inclined not to. Teachers have a variety of small rewards (stars) and punishments (minutes after school) to help keep children in line.

Sustained deviance from expected patterns can often have severe consequences for offenders. Legal services lawyers have been observed to walk out of interviews with clients (a very unprofessional thing to do) when clients do not permit them to dictate the terms of the interview.[15] Educators can virtually revoke children's right to education if they persist in disrupting classes. Police expect citizens to obey orders. The occasional incidents in which deaf or mentally handicapped persons are shot by police who think they are normal but defiant citizens provide tragic testimony to the sanctions delivered to people who fail to behave as expected.

There are at least four dimensions of the client role that street-level bureaucrats convey. First, as this discussion has already suggested, they convey cues as to the degree of deference expected. Proper deference will vary from service area to service area. School psychologists may encourage students to demonstrate independence; judges may demand absolute respect for symbols of the judicial process. Police expectations of gang members have been acutely observed.

The police expect law-abiding citizens to express their respect for the law by addressing its representatives with various gestures of deference. It is desired that the suspect's physical presence communicate civility, politeness, penitence, and perhaps fear. In addition, the use of such terms as "Sir" and "Officer" are expected as indications that the humble status of juvenile is properly understood.[16]

Similar observations could be made for each bureaucracy concerning the degree and forms of respect expected by workers.

Second, street-level bureaucrats communicate the penalties for failing to display proper deference. Teachers and policemen manifestly teach lessons in deference by example ("I'm going to make an example of you"). They will not easily let an affront to their authority remain unchallenged, since to do so would be to teach the contrary lesson, that lack of deference will not be punished. Again, lessons of this sort are usually taught subtly. Menace, threat, or punishment will more often be hinted at than carried out.

Third, street-level bureaucrats convey to clients what their proper level of expectations of the bureaucracy should be. This is complicated because at one level the society generally teaches that citizens have a right to equal treatment and responsive services. The ideology of public service urges people to seek safety, health care, education, and other objectives from public agencies. Diffuse public awareness that bureaucracies are characterized by red tape, inefficiency, corruption, and bungling helps to deflate expectations, but it does not do so entirely, since individuals can still hope for and seek out responsive treatment.

At the individual level street-level bureaucrats often convey to clients that they should expect few services. Teachers' tracking of students, even when done informally, precisely conveys to students that they are not expected to learn a great deal. Police directly inform citizens that they cannot expect much action on recovering stolen property. Welfare clients are told by social workers that there is nothing that can be done to increase their benefits.

If nothing truly can be done, it is proper to convey this to clients. The problem is that "nothing can be done" is only another way of saying that the bureaucracy or individual worker does not intend to change priorities. Yet it is often obvious to clients that more could be done if priorities were shifted. The Welfare Rights Organization for a time successfully campaigned to win benefits to which members were already entitled, but which had not been forthcoming because local welfare offices had not sought to maximize client benefits. Similarly, during the rent-strike movement in New York City in

1964–1965, tenants were able to gain priority with local housing agencies because of their association with rent strike organizations.[17] "Nothing more can be done" often really means: "Priorities will not be changed in your case, although they could be." Since priorities could be and often are changed frequently, bureaucracies have a stake in concealing the mutability of policy. (It may be that bureaucratic managers often do not themselves believe or understand that priorities could be changed.)

At the agency level, bureaucracies also attempt to convey proper levels of expectations. Long lines not only discourage prospective clients but also convey that many people have to be processed; hence individual clients should appreciate that workers have little time to spend with them or on their problems. Conducting welfare intake interviews in a single intake office so that workers and clients can overhear all the interviews being conducted conveys to clients that they may not expect privacy. Lower-court arraignment sessions clearly convey to waiting defendants that the judge is very busy, that the court has developed procedures to speed the process, that the court appreciates cooperation with the process, and that most people accept their inability to understand what is going on.

Street-level bureaucrats often attempt to involve clients in the difficulties of their jobs in order to gain understanding or sympathy for their position. Assertions that "I'm just doing my job," or "I'm following orders" help bring the client to an agency point of view. The client is implicitly asked to abandon his or her own interest in the interaction in a friendly, not overtly conflictual tone. But there is little choice involved, since the structure of the institution requires the client to comply or else risk alienating the more powerful street-level bureaucrat. No doubt many workers genuinely assert such claims, and they are often genuinely appreciated by clients. Still, in potentially conflictual stuations these claims function to gain client compliance in a persuasive rather than coercive way.

Fourth, under some circumstances street-level bureaucrats convey information about how to work the system. In so doing, they alert clients to the alternatives available to them under the current structure. Most clients would like to know more about how to negotiate the system, but this information is rarely provided to all clients. Rather, street-level bureaucrats exercise discretion by providing this information on a selective basis. This becomes one of the few ways they are able to favor clients without directly abridging bureaucratic norms of fairness. They make no decisions in favor of one client over another. They simply inform clients selectively how to utilize the system to best advantage. Thus they respect fairness in decision making; it is only information that is selectively distributed. Clients who are so favored, however, receive a tremendous benefit when norms of universalistic decision making operate. Knowing how to position oneself so as to increase the probability of a favorable decision is a substantial advantage.[18]

Sometimes teaching clients how to work the system consists of favoring some clients by providing them with special information. Public housing officials in Boston did this in coaching elderly applicants on how to apply for emergency housing status.[19] Boston housing inspectors did this by reminding landlords that they could petition for certain hearings.[20] Sometimes teaching the system takes the form of discriminating against some clients by denying them information given to others. Welfare officials in North Carolina apparently did this in informing most but not all clients of their right to apply for assistance.[21]

At other times street-level bureaucrats teach clients how to get best results from other bureaucracies. This practice is common among those workers who prepare clients for other agencies. Thus a social worker will instruct a client how to obtain favorable treatment in a referral. A lawyer will instruct a client how best to impress a judge.[22]

Coaching selected clients at times seems innocuous, but it almost always has redistributive effects. The defendant instructed to appear penitent makes others who fail to receive coaching appear defiant in contrast. The public housing officials who coached elderly applicants on how to fit into emergency categories helped these applicants to receive better units more quickly, to the disadvantage of other, equally deserving applicants. Prospective welfare recipients were harmed by the failure of welfare officials to explain their right to apply for services.[23]

To the extent that biased coaching remains secret, one would hypothesize that public legitimacy and regard for the agency would increase. No one would perceive himself or herself to be worse off, while some would feel favored. But to the extent that these biases become known or are exposed, they would tend to undermine the agency's legitimacy.

PSYCHOLOGICAL BENEFITS AND SANCTIONS

A fourth dimension of control over clients consists of producing the psychological benefits and sanctions that result from client involvement with the bureaucracy or accompany client status. There are two aspects to this psychological dimension. The first concerns the rewards and penalties acquired within the process of submitting to interaction with the bureaucracy. The second concerns the implications for the larger society, which responds to client status assigned by the bureaucracy.

In any interaction people see and exchange signals concerning their regard for each other.[24] When one person in an interaction has status and power relative to the other, the signals emanating from that person are particularly potent. Since a person's self-concept is substantially a function of the response of others who are important to the person, interactions with street-level bureaucrats have psychological as well as material implications.

The psychological implications of interactions with street-level bureaucrats may be fleeting where the interaction is not sustained. Police tend to treat people they apprehend scornfully or respectfully depending upon their apparent moral worthiness and the respect they display for the police. To be treated with respect, or with utter disrespect, by these symbols of authority have implications for citizens' views of themselves. People stopped by the police in a sense discover whether they are or are not the kind of person to whom respect is normally granted.

Frequently, citizens do not understand why police have stopped them or singled them out. They attribute an officer's brusque and imperious manner to one of their own personal or physical traits. If they are members of minority groups they may conclude that their racial or ethnic identity triggered police intervention, confirming once again the hazards of minority status and their belief that police officers are racist.

Anger at bureaucrats in general may be attributed to the dehumanizing aspects of having to seek service through bureaucracy. However, for most people apprehension by the police, visits to emergency rooms, or court appearances are single events which have limited implications for personality development. But any of these events may lead to further bureaucratic entanglement, may reinforce patterns of interaction previously encountered, or may signal other bureaucracies that the same (damaging or rewarding) orientations toward the client should be forthcoming in the future.

The greater the involvement of the client with the agencies and their employees, the more sustained and critical the psychological implications of the interactions. For this reason the dependence of poor people on government services creates the context in which interactions with street-level bureaucrats may have substantial psychological implications. At the very least poor people who bounce from one agency to another have reinforced feelings of dependency, powerlessness, and, deriving from these, anger. After sustained exposure to the welfare system, for example, recipients have been found to see themselves as "undeserving" and "lucky to get anything at all."[25]

Institutions that fully dominate peoples' lives have extensive influence over personality development. As Erving Goffman has demonstrated, mental hospitals *teach* patients how to be patients by rewarding behavior that conforms to staff expectations of how mentally ill people behave. Thus they not only teach the client role but touch the person playing the role as well, since for mental patients the role is also their salient personal identity.[26]

The closer institutions get to total involvement with clients, the more their self-images may be affected in a sustained way. Therapists and counselors utilize this fact to reinforce positively the self-images of their clients. Through residency in supportive halfway houses, peer support groups, and other environmental influences, some therapists seek not only to help clients develop psychologically, but also to insulate them from contradictory imagery during the period of involvement.[27]

For most people, the street-level bureaucrats whose psychological reactions are most powerful are teachers. Teachers powerfully convey images to children concerning their expectations of achievement. These images affect the child's self-image, self-expectations, and actual achievement. Through formal, and more insidiously, through informal tracking, teachers indicate to students who is expected to achieve and who is not.

In terms of the outcomes of institutional involvement with citizens, the policy problem is not only that students labeled as likely or unlikely to achieve do perform at expected levels, thereby fulfilling the original achievement prophecy.[28] It is also that determinations concerning the likelihood of success are not even made on the basis of achievement potential, measured however crudely, but are made on the basis of inferred social class, or the biased "harder" data accumulated or reported by other street-level bureaucrats.

In a careful study of a group of primary school pupils, Ray C. Rist observed that kindergarten pupils were placed in putative ability groupings solely on the basis of their dress, demeanor, verbal skills, and social background, before any sustained interaction between the teacher and the children and without testing.[29] The fast-track children received most of the teacher's instructional attention and most of the classroom rewards, although performing honorific chores did not require cognitive skills. The group placed in the lower classroom tracks learned from the teacher that they were not expected to achieve and that they were the kinds of children who could be ignored and ridiculed by authoritative adults (the teacher) and their peers with higher alleged learning ability (the children in the fast track). Meanwhile, the fast-track students were instructed in several ways about their proper self-image. They learned not only that they were brighter than the other children, but also that it was legitimate to scorn the others.

Rist noted that in subsequent grades the relatively poor performances of the slow-track children (perceived as such by the teacher, who had insured that it was so) were reified into fact and formed the basis for other teachers' tracking placements. He also found indications that the lower-track children *were learning* the material, despite the fact that the teacher tended to ignore them. The teacher did not know this because she did not encourage the lower-track (and lower-class) children to display their knowledge, and the cumulative effects of the classroom tracking system discouraged them from displaying their knowledge.

Analogous lessons are communicated in interactions in other street-level bureaucracies. Their potency depends on the extent to which clients have similar dependency and sustained interactions. The reification of street-level bureaucrats' prior judgments in subsequent placement decisions is also common. Judges' decisions concerning severity in sentencing juveniles, for example, depends substantially upon the defendant's record rather than on the severity of the offense.[30] Disposition of students with behavioral disabilities also depends on the previous incidents recorded.[31] In both these instances it is easy to see that young people are subject to the hazard that in the past they may have encountered adults who regarded their behavior as requiring official action, while others, perhaps because of differences in class backgrounds or in the political culture of the institution, did not have offenses recorded.

The example of the informal tracking of primary school children directs attention to the second dimension of labeling by street-level bureaucracies—the implications of client status for the larger society. Not only do slow-track children incorporate in their images of themselves the perspectives of the teacher and the fast-track pupils. The label of "slow learners" also has relevance for other people who play significant roles in the childrens' lives. Parents learn that their children have been assigned to the slow track and may begin to treat them as dull or with anxiety that they have been consigned early to failure. Brothers and sisters may tease. As Rist reports, teachers in later years will treat the children as having the capacities assigned originally by the first teacher. There is little escape from the implications of this labeling. Sometimes people can alter stereotypical images of themselves by presenting massive evidence to the contrary,[32] but in this case the process of interaction is structured so that all the evidence seems to confirm the original diagnosis.

Differences attributed to clients may be regarded as significant when people important to the client respond to him or her differently. When differences reach this level, a person's self-image and self-respect are affected.[33] The status of "criminal," "juvenile delinquent," "welfare mother," and "slow learner" is stigmatic because it goes beyond mere distinctions among people. Society takes these terms as signals to treat people differently. As such, they are simultaneously cues to the people so labeled to regard themselves differently.

Some differences assigned by street-level bureaucrats provide more subtle stigma. For example, being a public housing tenant is not necessarily stigmatic, but living in certain projects may be. Health treatment through medicare may not affect a client's relationship with some clinics, but might have substantial implications in others. The label of "troublemaker" may predict official responses in some schools but not in others.

Prisoners are never fully destigmatized by the society after they have served time. They become "ex-cons." Indeed, mere involvement with a bureaucracy may be stigmatizing, even when the clearly stigmatic label is avoided. This may be the fate of a defendant found innocent at trial,[34] or the patient who is held for examination to determine whether he or she requires treatment for mental illness, even if judged perfectly sane. If others begin to treat one differently as a result of these labels, one may begin to incorporate these views as his or her own self-image.

The particular difficulty with labels ascribed by street-level bureaucrats, as we have seen, is that the characteristics on which they are based are problematic. Judgments concerning the status allocated by street-level bureaucrats depend upon the discretion of the bureaucrat, which in turn depends upon many indeterminate factors, such as training, the social context in which the client is presented, and the presence or absence of similar "differences" in the client population. The fast-track students in the above illustration might have been labeled slow learners in white, middle-class schools (the students and teachers were black). A criminal offense in one setting might be overlooked in another. The social construction of the client, involving the client, others relevant to the client, and the public employees with whom they must deal is a significant process of social definition often unrelated to objective factors and therefore open to the influences of prejudice, stereotype, and ignorance as a basis for determinations.

Some bureaucracies so routinize their processing of clients that significant psychological interactions are minimal. Welfare workers and legal service lawyers, for example, may adhere to interview formats that exclude personal elements and reduce the likelihood of decision making on the basis of interpersonal interactions.[35] Of particular interest to those concerned with the policy consequences of street-level bureaucrats' work is the ways in which the tendencies to treat people in terms of their predicted behavioral characteristics can be avoided. Some bureaucratic settings seem to result in stigmatic treatment and some do not. There are a variety of ways to interrupt tracking patterns without abandoning educational objectives. Over time, recognition of the potential of people previously defined as physically and behaviorally deviant—as in the example of exceptional children—can change. These are aspects of the policy-making roles of street-level bureaucrats that can be influenced only through analyzing the interaction between those who assign status and those who are assigned, and affecting the work context in which the social construction of the client takes place.

CHAPTER 6

Advocacy and Alienation in

Street-Level Work

To deliver street-level policy through bureaucracy is to embrace a contradiction. On the one hand, service is delivered by people to people, invoking a model of human interaction, caring, and responsibility. On the other hand, service is delivered through a bureaucracy, invoking a model of detachment and equal treatment under conditions of resource limitations and constraints, making care and responsibility conditional.

The human model of interaction contributes to the motivation of public service workers, who believe they are helping others, and to the motivation of clients, who are encouraged to confide and trust in strangers and permit themselves to be manipulated and ordered about in the expectation of receiving help or fair treatment. The foundation of support for the human model of interaction rests in the belief that this model benefits clients. Yet it may be called a myth of altruism because the assertion that agencies provide benefits and fair treatment is usually unexamined, not subject to falsification among people who believe it, and a means for structuring a range of further assumptions about public policy.[1]

Whatever the precise functions of this myth, the importance of promoting it may be judged by the intensity with which it is perpetuated. It is perpetuated in professional canons of ethics, which instruct professionals to treat the whole person, to respect and encourage client autonomy, and to respond to the individual rather than to alleged patterns of group behavior. It is perpetuated in schools of training, whose curricula teach bodies of knowledge (for example, the law, or educational psychology) or, rarely, how to treat individuals (for example, interviewing techniques), but virtually never how to juggle case loads or handle large numbers of clients at one time, as initiates will have to do. One of the best illustrations of the solidity of the myth of human interaction in public services is provided by the transformation in the health field of the word "care" from a verb to a noun. Politicians and administrators regularly discuss levels and amounts of care that will be provided, but rarely who will care, and how they will express their caring.

Advocacy

Street-level bureaucrats are often expected to be more than benign and passive gatekeepers. They are also expected to be advocates, that is, to use their knowledge, skill, and position to secure for clients the best treatment or position consistent with the constraints of the service. That street-level bureaucrats should be advocates for clients is articulated explicitly in the professional training and canons of lawyers, doctors, social workers, teachers, and others. Those professions and semi-professions that display the altruism critical to most definitions of professionalism require their members to make clients' needs primary. Other street-level bureaucracies whose claims to professional status are more questionable also display degrees of advocacy in their obligations as public servants to be responsive to the citizens who pay their salaries.

One source of the myth of service altruism is social policy reformers who utilize the discrepancy between reality and stated policy intentions to mobilize support for change. Virtually all policy reforms are advocated in the name of achieving service ideals. (The myth of altruism does not assume ideal policy implementation; it assumes only that policy and people who implement it are well intentioned and that their work constitutes a net social benefit.)

Perhaps even more important in sustaining the myth of service altruism are the workers who attempt to implement the service ideal. Like most social myths this one has a partial basis in reality. Each generation of workers brings to its jobs, in addition to interest in material benefits, dedication to helping people. Those who recruit themselves for public service work are attracted to some degree by the prospect that their lives will gain meaning through helping others.

The myth of human relationships in street-level bureaucracies no doubt

Advocacy and Alienation in Street-Level Work

partly accounts for whatever dedication exists to superior service and for the ability of public services to realize their objectives. However, achievement of advocacy is undermined by several critical factors. Some of these concerns were treated earlier in discussing the structure of street-level bureaucrats' work, but it is useful to review briefly how the structure of work and relations with clients compromise altruism and undermine advocacy where advocacy is appropriate.

The helping orientation of street-level bureaucrats is incompatible with their need to judge and control clients for bureaucratic purposes. This is evident in the following role tensions.

First, advocacy can only be done on behalf of single units, whether they be individuals or collectivities such as a tenants' union. Moreover, the advocate must have enough free attention to devote to the client. This does not mean that only one client can be dealt with at a time. But it does mean that advocacy may be compromised by large case loads and mass processing of clients. For the advocate, large case loads mean that every minute devoted to one client means less time for others. Clearly organizations have to choose what resources to provide, and a suboptimal amount is likely to be available for any client. Street-level bureaucracies chronically tend to allocate relatively low amounts of resources to facilitate workers taking clients' perspectives. Clients are asked to understand this and even to incorporate this understanding into their concept of being a client. Those who fail to do so are punished by bureaucracies, which can impose severe costs on clients who contest the allocation of resources devoted to them.

Second, advocacy is incompatible with organizational perspectives. The organization hoards resources; the advocate seeks their dispersal to clients. The organization imposes tight control over resource dispersal if it can; the advocate seeks to utilize loopholes and discretionary provisions to gain client benefits. The organization seeks to treat all clients equally and to avoid having to respond to claims that others received special treatment; the advocate seeks to secure special treatment for individual clients. The organization acts as if available resource categories had fixed limits (which is often not absolutely true); the advocate acts as if resources were limitless (which is also not true).

Street-level bureaucrats frequently encounter this tension. School counselors are criticized for serving the interests of schools rather than individual children.[2] Doctors have come under considerable criticism for failing to give sufficient priority to *not* spending public monies for patients' health care. This is another way of saying that their advocacy perspective (advocacy for their patients and, perhaps, themselves) is not in balance with their corporate responsibilities.[3] Potentially the same situation exists anytime street-level bureaucrats provide services with open entitlement. For example, the 1972 special education law in Massachusetts directed that educational plans for special needs children be developed and implemented irrespective of costs. State funding for this open-ended provision was not forthcoming, however, and local school systems were required to spend an apparently limitless amount of previously unauthorized funds. In practice these boards did take school system resources into account despite specific provisions to the contrary in the law.[4]

Third, advocacy is incompatible with controlling clients. Street-level bureaucrats usually must make judgments about clients on matters unrelated to appropriate service. They must as well make judgments about credibility, eligibility, and performance. Is the welfare recipient truthful? Does the claimant of legal services truly face an emergency? Is the job trainee certifiably competent? The street-level bureaucrat is almost always a judge as well as a server. Yet it is hard to do both at the same time. Since these are human interactions that are the subjects of judgment, street-level bureaucrats are not free to give themselves unreservedly to clients. They feel the need to make sure that they do not lose control, respect, advantage, or face, or otherwise fail to perform as required by their role. Street-level bureaucrats may attempt to do a good job, but it will be a job tempered by the other psychological and role requirements placed upon them.[5]

Fourth, advocacy is incompatible with the responsibility of street-level bureaucrats to prepare clients for presentation to other workers or other bureaucracies. One of the most substantial checks on workers who deal with clients is the social and other pressures that arise from the fact that a client is later seen and processed by still other workers or is presented to outsiders. To be sure there are norms against peer criticism in some areas, such as medicine, but pressures exerted by the anticipation that others will observe the work are nonetheless substantial. Examples include police officers who anticipate presenting cases in court, public defenders who seek to control clients so as not to embarrass themselves before judges,[6] and employment counselors who try to maintain credibility with employers by recommending only the best candidates for jobs.[7]

Several of these dilemmas are presented by the example of the social workers in Washington state assigned to child protective services. Individuals in these jobs are empowered to investigate and provide authoritative advice to judges in hearings concerning the removal of children from their parents' custody. Yet they are also supposed to provide counseling for parents, primarily from the perspective of serving as an advocate for the child. In this four-sided relationship (agency, judge, parents, child) social workers might well yearn for the clarity an entirely adversarial process might provide.[8]

Alienation

There is another perspective that illuminates the relative attractiveness of street-level positions. Street-level bureaucrats' work is alienated work. This alienation not only affects their commitment to jobs and clients, but, as it also affects the quality of their vocational experiences, it is a significant statement about public policy itself, considering the millions of people who are engaged in street-level employment.

The promiscuous word "alienation" has been overused and under-appreciated. I am not interested here in alienation as a psychological orientation, although psychological orientations no doubt arise from alienated work.[9] Rather, alienation as used here is a concept summarizing the relationship of workers to their work, from which, we may infer, attitudes arise.

Worker alienation summarizes several concerns: the extent to which the worker makes decisions about the work, has control over what is made and how it is fashioned, and influences the disposition of the product. Alienation at times also refers to the extent to which workers are able to express, or need to suppress, their creative and human impulses through work activity. Assembly lines, in which mechanical, repetitive processes are performed, are regarded as alienating for these reasons.[10] Jobs that require workers to deny the basic humanity of others may also be considered alienating.

I have already indicated how some of the shared working conditions of street-level bureaucrats appear to be characteristically unalienated. For example, discretion about clients separates street-level bureaucrats from assembly line workers in two respects. Bureaucrats make decisions about the product of their work and they work with (or on) people, so that they are constantly confronted with the variety of humanity. (For police officers the most rewarding aspect of an otherwise often unrewarding job is the variety of situations and people they encounter.) To the extent that the pressures of the job do not entirely narrow these opportunities, aspects of street-level bureaucrats' work contribute to their fealty toward the diffuse objectives of their agencies.

Street-level bureaucrats often have relatively good relations with other workers. The peer structure in street-level bureaucracies often is quite strong. Street-level bureaucrats work in isolation, but they seek and receive support from other workers. Street-level bureaucrats are no less peer-related than other workers and find gratification in the squad room, teachers lounge, and other places where they congregate.

However, there are several areas in which the alienation of street-level work is fairly extensive. I have already said that the compromises required of advocates reduce the extent to which street-level bureaucrats are able to respond to clients in a fully human way. Moreover, street-level work is inauthentic, in the particular sense of alienation delineated by sociologist Amitai Etzioni. In its emphasis on providing services, mandating workers to act as helpers, and giving them responsibility it "provides the appearance of responsiveness while the underlying conditions . . . subject a person to forces beyond his understanding and control." [11] In defense of the myth of altruism, street-level bureaucracies devote a relatively high proportion of energies to concealing lack of service and generating appearances of responsiveness.

In addition, street-level bureaucrats are alienated from clients—the product of their work—in at least four particular respects: (1) they tend to work only on segments of the product of their work; (2) they do not control the outcome of their work; (3) they do not control the raw materials of their work; and (4) they do not control the pace of their work. [12] These considerations are discussed below.

1. *Working on segments of the product.* One difference between shoe-makers and shoe-factory workers is that the former crafts the entire shoe and thus can draw satisfaction from seeing the fruits of his or her labor. The latter may only cut the heel, punch holes for laces, glue parts together, or perform some other aspect of the shoemaking process. But he or she cannot take pride in having made the article. This analysis of the implications of factory work is as old as the factorization of production and as young as recent industrial efforts to permit workers greater flexibility and variety in work assignments. [13]

Street-level bureaucrats do not work on the entire product, but only on segments. This is the case in two respects. In response to the need to categorize clients they tend to treat them only as bundles of bureaucratically relevant attributes rather than as whole persons. They deal with symptoms, qualifications, and capacities, but not with feelings or superficially tangential facts. The imperatives of processing people into the correct categories tend to overwhelm both professional obligations to treat the whole person and the recognition that responding to clients in narrowly defined areas is likely to miss important dimensions of the presenting problem.

Advocacy and Alienation in Street-Level Work

Understanding that treating parts of people leads to inferior or inappropriate services has generally been the guiding idea behind many critiques of social policy. For example, social workers and psychologists have been employed in hospitals, schools, and courts in efforts to respond holistically to the citizen-client. Reformers recognize that a health problem such as lead poisoning may be a problem of income and law. A problem of poverty may in reality be a legal problem (e.g., being granted a divorce). Education problems may have emotional, physical, or economic origins. The more the society recognizes the interconnectedness of service policy problems, and the more the problems are or remain interconnected, the more the alienation of categorization will impinge on street-level work.

Street-level bureaucrats also tend to work only on segments of the process. In the name of efficiency, convenience, or optimal utilization of resources the world of social services has become more and more specialized. Educators are math teachers, reading teachers, art specialists, dance therapists. The world of special education now includes therapists on various forms of reading disability, various degrees of mental retardation, and various kinds of physical handicaps.

It would be one thing if these specialists had relatively intensive interactions with children so that they could fully plan for them and have the time to realize measurable results. But school programs tend to be filled with specialists who cannot take full responsibility for the product even if they wanted to. This is not an argument against mainstreaming, for no doubt children with special educational needs ought not to be segregated. But mainstreaming in the modern school means going into a system that substantially segments the child's school day. Schools not only specialize by function, but they also are organized so that different workers take responsibilities for different stages through which pupils pass. Different teachers receive students each year as teaching is cross-specialized by grade. The example of specialization in teaching is particularly apt because schools have the most extensive opportunities to interact substantially with service recipients.

There are often considerable costs to specialization in addition to the benefits of expertise and efficiency. Divisions between intake and casework mean that interviews and fact gathering sometimes have to be repeated, which is inefficient. When resource allocation does not permit extensive reinterviewing of clients the result may be inappropriate decisions resulting from the distortion of information between intake and case-work levels. Recent proposals for multi-specialization in special education appear to provide support for the view that clients of special education services have many dimensions, and that treating the whole person is required ultimately for optimal results.

2. *Controlling the outcome of the work.* For reasons closely related to the above, street-level bureaucrats often do not control the outcome of their work. Specialization may mean that they do not see the work through or only participate in a fraction of the work with clients. They do not control all of the resources of the agency they work for. Sometimes they process people for other bureaucracies, which ultimately disposes of cases. Police often complain, for example, that their actions are not supported by judges and prosecutors; they feel uncertain whether their performance of a good job as they define it will result in a desired outcome.

Another reason they do not control the outcome of their work is that clients' problems are not subject to closure. Although street-level bureaucrats are regarded, and regard themselves, as able to solve problems, the problems do not end or are not resolvable. Many public service agencies are called revolving doors for this reason. Street-level bureaucracies that are oriented toward transforming clients, such as judicial institutions and social welfare agencies, are revolving doors because the solutions they offer people are not adequate. People do not stay "fixed." To the extent that this presents street-level bureaucrats with severe dissonance between objectives and capabilities, they develop coping mechanisms to shield them from the implications of the gap between expectations and accomplishment. They are alienated to the extent they experience this discrepancy as loss of control over situations they are supposed to control.

3. *Controlling the input.* Street-level bureaucrats cannot control the nature of the material with which they work. They cannot deploy to greatest effectiveness the skills they possess partly because the conditions of work prohibit effective interaction with clients, and because they do not have control over clients' circumstances even when conditions are favorable for intervention. Even in institutions such as prisons and mental hospitals workers do not control the underlife of the institutions and cannot affect those realities of clients' lives that contribute to their deviant behavior. How frustrating to be a good teacher who has to greet every morning children who are hungry and exhausted from lack of sleep. How frustrating to be a skilled professional attempting to help a welfare recipient whose circumstances conspire to confound every constructive move. It takes a great deal of commitment or cynicism to accept the futility of one's own efforts in such circumstances.[14]

4. *Controlling the work pace.* Street-level bureaucrats do not control the pace of work. I have said that their discretion provides a measure of reward

on the job, but they often do not control the timing of their decision making. This is the case in obviously reactive public service areas such as policing, and in other areas where the amount of time spent on individual clients, or the number of clients requiring attention, cannot be anticipated. Street-level bureaucracies go to great lengths to produce predictability of client demands, either by rationing services in some way or planning for peak period workloads. To some extent they are able to develop devices to minimize the costs of unpredictability. (This is treated in chapter 7.) But to some extent they are not. Then they confront the problem that their work is their master. They get behind in paperwork, are unable to respond to any but the most minimal requests, and believe themselves to be ineffective because they feel they have no slack time to respond fully to any individual situation.

Alienated work leads to dissatisfaction with the job. Job dissatisfaction affects commitment to clients and to the agencies for which they work. The proposition that street-level bureaucrats perform in alienated labor roles contributes to understanding the dynamics of some recent developments in public service organization.

Implications of Alienation

Public service work, particularly in street-level bureaucracies, has become more bureaucratic over time. Civil service and other developments have made worker recruitment more universalistic. This development may also have affected the extent to which workers are able to help clients and see the results of their efforts because treatment of clients has also become more universalistic. Congruity between the social background of workers and clients does not have the same place in public service interactions as it used to. The fabled paternalism of social workers and school teachers in the past may have functioned to give street-level bureaucrats a sense of responsibility and reward for outcomes, even if these gratifications were founded on inequalities and favoritism. Thus the bureaucratization of public service may have been accompanied by increased worker alienation.[15]

To the extent that street-level bureaucrats are alienated in their work, they will be more willing to accept organizational restructuring and less concerned with protecting clients' interests and their own connection with clients. The more tenuous the relationship with clients, the less salient that relationship becomes, and the easier it is to transform the relationship fur-

79

ther. Thus the working conditions that give rise to alienation in work may cumulatively contribute to separating the client from the public service worker. This is significant since in earlier periods public service workers have often championed client rights and benefits. There have been times in American labor history when fledgling public service unions and worker associations bargained for clients as well as for themselves (social workers and teachers, for example). This struggle has become less important as the connection between workers and clients has dissipated.

In general, employers confronted by alienated workers can choose among the following responses in some combination. They can ignore the situation and accept the absenteeism, low morale, poor performance, and other manifestations of worker dissatisfaction. They can restructure the work to make it less alienating. Or they can concentrate on changing the mix of benefits and sanctions that they offer workers outside of working conditions. They can increase pay for work that is less rewarding or improve conditions tangential to the work. Or they can raise the costs of nonproductive behavior.

The trends in public employment since, say, 1960 reflect these alternatives. Public service workers have increased their share of national wealth through higher pay and benefit levels, increased their collective bargaining power, and acquiesced in and often encouraged developments such as specialization, computerization, and fragmentation of responsibilities for clients. Street-level bureaucrats have enhanced their position in the political system to the neglect of aspects of service consistent with more humanistic models of client involvement, or at the expense of taking positions on clients' behalf. These statements no doubt require qualification for particular service areas, but at a general level they suggest linkages between the quality of client services, the structure of street-level bureaucrats' work, and the priorities of a society oriented toward cost effectiveness and the dispensary model of providing for human needs.

PART III

PATTERNS OF

PRACTICE

Introduction

THE "PROBLEM" OF STREET-LEVEL BUREAUCRACY[1]

Street-level bureaucrats work with inadequate resources in circumstances where the demand will always increase to meet the supply of services. Thus they can never be free from the implications of significant constraints. Within these constraints they have broad discretion with respect to the utilization of resources (by definition). In the application of resources to the job they confront the uncertainty that stems from the conflicting or ambiguous goals that unevenly guide their work. They also confront the additional uncertainties that arise from difficulties in measuring and evaluating work performances. A final salient condition of work is that the people with whom street-level bureaucrats regularly interact are not among their primary reference groups, affecting the degree to which client satisfaction has priority. While many aspects of their work promote a client orientation, still others lead to reducing commitment to the work. Thus the portrait of the street-level bureaucrat is one of considerable responsibility in allocating social values but little effective external determination as to how to define and achieve objectives.

To this portrait of work conditions an additional consideration must be added. Street-level bureaucrats manifestly attempt to do a good job *in some way*, given the resources at hand and the general guidance provided by the system as outlined above.[2] Street-level bureaucrats share with others the need to think of themselves in a reasonably favorable light. Most street-level bureaucrats can be taken at face value when they assert that they are doing what they think is the best they can do. Typically, they do not claim that

81

they are doing a perfect job or performing the way the job should be performed; only that they are functioning effectively and properly under the constraints they encounter. The typical teacher, policeman, welfare worker—indeed anyone who regularly meets the public—seems to have an image of himself or herself as working under great strain and with considerable sacrifice to provide clients protection or service no one else would be willing to provide. They see themselves as fighting on the front line of local conflict with little support and less appreciation by a general public whose dirty work they do.[3]

If they have any recognition that their performance is less than adequate under the circumstances they confront, they are likely to seek and find the explanation someplace other than in their own inadequacy. Street-level bureaucrats who are unable to retain a concept of their own adequacy in the job are more likely to leave it or seek other work than to sustain the personal ambivalence that results. This orientation applies even though the civil service system may deaden motivation, and some public employees may be motivated by primarily selfish considerations.

The point that they try to do a good job in some way fulfills the requirements for asserting that the problem of street-level bureaucrats is one of decision making under conditions of considerable uncertainty where satisfactory decisions about resource allocation must be personally as well as organizationally derived. The work context of street-level bureaucrats calls for the development of mechanisms to provide satisfactory services in a context where the quality, quantity, and specific objectives of service remain (within broad limits) to be defined.

There is by now a venerable tradition in organizational studies concerning the search for satisfactory rather than optimal solutions to decision-making problems under conditions of uncertainty.[4] But the analysis of street-level bureaucracy may be somewhat different from other studies because it is not only the *decisions* that become satisfactory rather than optimal, but also the mental and organizational *processes* that must become satisfactory. Thus to understand street-level bureaucracy one must study the routines and subjective responses street-level bureaucrats develop in order to cope with the difficulties and ambiguities of their jobs.[5]

We can now restate the problem of street-level bureaucracy as follows. Street-level bureaucrats attempt to do a good job in some way. The job, however, is in a sense impossible to do in ideal terms. How is the job to be accomplished with inadequate resources, few controls, indeterminate objectives, and discouraging circumstances?

There are three general responses that street-level bureaucrats develop to deal with this indeterminacy. First, they develop patterns of practice that tend to limit demand, maximize the utilization of available resources, and obtain client compliance over and above the procedures developed by their agencies. They organize their work to derive a solution within the resource constraints they encounter. Second, they modify their concept of their jobs, so as to lower or otherwise restrict their objectives and thus reduce the gap between available resources and achieving objectives. Third, they modify their concept of the raw materials with which they work—their clients—so as to make more acceptable the gap between accomplishments and objectives. Much of the patterned behavior of street-level bureaucrats, and many of their characteristic subjective orientations, may be understood as responses to the street-level bureaucracy problem.

ROUTINES AND SIMPLIFICATIONS

In everyday life people seek to simplify their tasks and narrow their range of perceptions in order to process the information they receive and develop responses to it. They create routines to make tasks manageable. They mentally simplify the objects of perception to reduce the complexity of evaluation. They structure their environments to make tasks and perceptions more familiar, less unique. Routines and simplifications aid the management of complexity; environmental structuring limits the complexity to be managed.[6]

Bureaucrats develop routines to deal with the complexity of work tasks. Indeed, for some analysts routinization is virtually equivalent to bureaucratization.[7] For others, routinization inevitably occurs in bureaucracies because of the scarcity of resources relative to the demands made upon them.[8]

The development of simplifications, as mental routinization, predictably characterizes bureaucrats whose work involves processing the objects of bureaucratic attention. At the organizational level bureaucracies officially recognize simplifying cues, such as eligibility requirements, in order to regularize decision processes.[9] However, bureaucrats also develop their own patterns of simplification when the official categories prove inadequate for expeditious work processing, or if they significantly contradict their preferences.

The fact that bureaucracies develop routines and simplifications is hardly cause for comment in itself. However, the structure of these routines and simplifications, and the structuring of the context in which they take place, are worth considerable discussion. Where policy consists of the accretion of many low-level decisions the routines and categories developed for processing those decisions effectively determine policy within the parameters established by authorities.[10] In this sense, as observed earlier, street-level bureaucrats "make" policy.

To put it another way, the routines, simplifications, and low-level decision-making environments of street-level bureaucracies are political. Street-level bureaucrats, as I have been arguing, determine the allocation of particular goods and services in the society, utilizing positions of public authority. To say that their actions are political is to indicate that some people are aided, some are harmed, by the dominant patterns of decision making. If the dominant patterns of decision making are characterized by routinization and simplification, then the structure of these patterns must be analyzed to determine who gets what, when, and how from this sector of government.[11]

The political significance of routines is highlighted by the fact that the policies that result from routine treatment are often biased in ways unintended by the agencies whose policies are being implemented or are antithetical to some of their objectives. For example, the declared policy of the life insurance industry to provide funding for black ghetto enrichment in the late 1960s was undermined by routine processing of loan applications, which tended to follow previously operative procedures. These procedures tended to aid those individuals who were most able to receive credit anyway, to the neglect of the originally targeted population.[12] Draft boards operating under general regulations established by the Selective Service System routinely implemented policies that tended to favor men from relatively affluent families at the expense of those from working-class families.[13] Routines in these instances did not merely facilitate work; they determined outcomes divergent from the stated policy objectives.

At times street-level bureaucrats' routines and simplifications virtually *are* the policies to be delivered. Police routines established to approach motorists who may prove uncooperative are immediately received as an episode in community relations. Similarly, teachers' informal classification of pupils by attributed learning ability effectively determines school stratification policies.

These illustrations have special significance for three reasons. First, they are routines of interaction. Thus citizens may be expected to react—with subsequent implications for worker-client relationships. It is one thing to say that bureaucracies routinize the processing of work, but when the work consists of decisions made about people during the interaction itself, the subjects of routinization will be affected by the processing. This clearly distinguishes analysis of people-processing bureaucracies from analyses of other bureaucratic settings.

Second, while we may generally anticipate routinization and simplification in human affairs, the degrees of organizational routinization and simplification are not predetermined. At least theoretically there is a considerable difference between routinization necessary for minimally efficient functioning and maximum routinization. Moreover, organizations can decide to be less efficient in order also to be less routinized in their client interactions. Indeed, routinization may prove dysfunctional at some point, complicating efficient operations.[14] Similarly, bureaucrats may be expected to categorize clients, but the extent to which they are open to fresh information contradicting facile categorization also is not predetermined.

This is particularly important for street-level bureaucrats who have a public trust to make significant decisions about citizens' welfare. Police, judges, teachers, and mental health workers, for example, are generally obliged to make decisions on the basis of the available evidence rather than presumptions of proper determinations. They are obliged because they have been assigned profound responsibilities concerning the liberty of citizens or the fate of people regarded as incompetent and unable to act in their own best interests.

Third, routines and simplifications are subject to biases from a variety of sources. While they often may be oriented toward fulfilling agency objectives, these measures are also structured to aid workers' job requirements, which may conflict with agency demands. Furthermore, routines and simplifications are subject to workers' occupational and personal biases, including the prejudices that blatantly and subtly permeate the society. The biases expressed in street-level work may be expected to be manifested in proportion to the freedom workers have in defining their work life and the slack in effective controls to suppress those biases. Since street-level bureaucrats have wide discretion about clients, are usually free from direct observation by supervisors or the general public, and are not much affected by client preferences, their routines and simplifications deserve considerable scrutiny. Sociologist Julius Roth, in introducing his study of client treatment in hospital emergency rooms, states this perspective sharply.

There is no evidence that professional training succeeds in creating a universalistic moral neutrality. . . . On the contrary, we are on much safer ground to assume that those engaged in dispensing professional services (or any other services) will apply the evaluations of social worth common to their culture and will modify their services with respect to those evaluations unless discouraged from doing so by the organizational arrangements under which they work.[15]

The analysis of routines developed by street-level bureaucrats must begin with the proposition that they tend to contribute to control over the work environment. This is consistent with perceiving routines as coping behaviors in which the confronting problem is the management of work stresses. The tendency to seek control over the work environment is perhaps evident in most work situations, but again it is worthy of comment because in street-level bureaucracies the search is typically a matter of public policy. Routines could be structured to maximize the achievement of agency objectives. Or they could be structured to maximize responsiveness to clients. No doubt these competing perspectives do account for workers' routines to some degree. However, the extent to which routines are structured to maximize worker control over the work context may measure the extent to which articulated agency policy objectives are difficult to achieve.

The routines of work in street-level bureaucracies appear to be directed toward achieving one or more of four purposes in processing clients.

1. They ration services.
2. They control clients and reduce the consequences of uncertainty.
3. They husband worker resources.
4. They manage the consequences of routine practice.

At times routines and simplifications will be entirely informal and contrary to agency policy. At other times they will be consistent with agency policy and may even be promoted by the agency. It is necessary to overlook this distinction in analyzing street-level bureaucracies because the line between formal and informal routines is often very uncertain. For example, the official policy of one legal services office may be to accept only emergency cases. Another office in the same city may have an open intake policy but the attorneys may informally decide to recruit and work primarily on the most needy cases. In both offices the policy results are the same, but in one office they stem from agency intake policy, in the other from the structure of workers' informal assignment of priorities. Often agencies will adopt as official procedure practices that workers previously adopted informally. When police departments distribute fire hydrant spray caps for recreation, the new policy replaces the previous informal practice of overlooking illegal opening of hydrants by neighborhood residents on hot days.

The following four chapters elaborate some of the routines and simplifications that arise in street-level work in response to job stresses. Although these routines and simplifications originate in the coping needs of individual workers, they nonetheless add up to street-level policy, and they become the patterns of agency behavior with which clients and policy reformers must contend.

CHAPTER 7

Rationing Services: Limitation of Access and Demand

Theoretically there is no limit to the demand for free public goods. Agencies that provide public goods must and will devise ways to ration them. To ration goods or services is to establish the level or proportions of their distribution. This may be done by fixing the amount or level of goods and services in relation to other goods and services. Or it may be done by allocating a fixed level or amount of goods and services among different classes of recipients. In other words, services may be rationed by varying the total amount available, or by varying the distribution of a fixed amount.

This usage is consistent with the familiar application of rationing in wartime. During World War II, for example, automobile tires were rationed by restricting their production for domestic purposes and limiting individual purchases, making them costly, and establishing priorities among users (doctors were privileged in this respect). This chapter considers rationing in street-level bureaucracies that has the effect of fixing (usually to reduce or limit) the level of services. The next chapter takes up rationing that differentiates among clients.

The rationing of the level of services starts when clients present themselves to the worker or agency or an encounter is commanded. Like factory workers confronted with production quotas, street-level bureaucrats attempt to organize their work to facilitate work tasks or liberate as much time as possible for their own purposes. This is evident even in those services areas in which workers have little control over work flow. For example, police often cannot control work flow because most police assignments are in response to citizen initiated calls.[1] Dispatchers, however, make every effort to permit officers to finish one call before beginning another. Officers often take advantage of this practice by postponing reporting the completion of a call until after they have finished accumulated paperwork. In this way police officers regularize the work flow despite substantial irregularity in requests for assistance.

The way in which work comes to the agency significantly affects the efficiency and pleasantness with which it is accommodated. Official efforts to influence the flow of work vary greatly. They range from the mild advisory of the post office providing patrons with information concerning the times when delays are likely to be longest, to the extreme measures taken by a New York City welfare office that closed its doors at noon rather than admit a greater number of Medicaid applicants than could be processed by available personnel in an eight-hour day.[2]

Clearly there are costs to clients in seeking services. In both of the above examples agencies seek to inform clients of the costs and the problems they will encounter—in the first instance, if they seek assistance during days when post office patronage is heavy; in the second, if in ignorance of the situation they attempt to apply for Medicaid and cannot be accommodated because of the high intake demand relative to intake workers. In many instances even the failure to inform clients of likely costs in seeking service constitutes a consumer complaint.

The highest costs are borne by potential clients who are discouraged from or forbidden access to bureaucratic involvement. While exclusion from client status is usually accomplished on the basis of legal grounds, the population of the excluded or discouraged includes many whose exclusion is a matter of discretionary judgment. The ineligibility of tenants evicted from public housing, students expelled from school, or welfare claimants deemed uncooperative depends not on fixed criteria alone, but also on interactions with street-level bureaucrats.

The Costs of Service

To analyze individual influence it has sometimes proved useful to recognize the relationship between citizens' influence and their command of personal resources such as money, status, information, expertise, and capacity for work.[3] People who have these resources tend to be more powerful than those who do not. When people have them they enhance personal influence. When workers for public agencies have them they may be used to direct or subordinate clients or discourage clients from further interactions with the agency.

MONETARY

Street-level bureaucracies can rarely assign monetary costs for services, since by definition public services are free. However, monetary costs *are* imposed in several instructive instances. In income-providing programs citizens' contributions to the income package may be manipulated as policy. Medicare patients may be asked to pay a higher deductible before insurance provisions become operable. Food-stamp recipients may be asked to pay more for their stamps. The effective taxation of earned income in welfare reduces the number of people in contact with this street-level bureaucracy. Clearly differences in monetary costs serve to ration street-level bureaucrats' services.

Programs sometimes force clients to incur monetary costs that discourage them from seeking service. Acquiring records from other agencies to establish eligibility or securing transcripts for appeals can be costly, particularly if travel is involved. Agencies that keep bankers' hours impose monetary costs on working people who cannot appear without losing wages. Appointments sometimes require parents to seek babysitters. Street-level bureaucracies that seek to minimize these penalties introduce evening office hours, or they provide child-care services.

TIME

Just as available time is a resource for people in politics, it is also a unit of value that may be extracted from clients as a cost of service. Clients are typically required to wait for services; it is a sign of their dependence and relative powerlessness that the costs of matching servers with the served are borne almost entirely by clients. It is to maximize the efficiency of workers' time that queues are generally established. A primary reason that clinic-based practice is more efficient than home-based practice is simply that it is patients and not physicians who spend time traveling and waiting. Policemen also allocate time costs by stopping to question young people who, while not guilty of any crime, are judged to require reprimanding.[4]

Some teachers in some school systems make home visits to meet with parents, while others schedule parent-teacher conferences after school on specific days set aside for such purposes. (If there are two parents and one or both work, both are unlikely to be able to meet with the teacher.) These alternative perspectives on parent-teacher conferences measure significant differences in the value placed on time of parents and teachers.

Time costs are often assessed by street-level bureaucrats as delay; they are often experienced by clients as waiting. Bureaucracies can reward clients by expediting service, punish them by delaying service. Court postponements can function in this way, as can an increase in the time between intake interviews and placement on the welfare rolls. Importantly, bureaucracies often have little interest in reducing delay, since more expeditious processing would simply strain available resources.

Assessed time costs may also be experienced as inconvenience, although they are levied as procedure. For example, when an agency refuses to receive complaints over the telephone and requires that they be written, it may cut off complaints lodged frivolously or on impulse, but also discourages complainants who would protest if it were easier.[5] Requirements to complete multiple forms and produce extensive documentation function similarly. It is possible to make an argument that since the real costs of delay and elaborate procedures are the activities foregone while waiting, that is, opportunity costs, it is justifiable that poor people wait longer than the more affluent, since the opportunities foregone are less valued by the society.[6] However, at the very least this elitist view is based on a calculus to the terms of which clients have not consented.

INFORMATION

Giving or withholding information is another way in which services may be rationed. Clients experience the giving or withholding of information in two ways. They experience the favoritism of street-level bureaucrats who provide some clients with privileged information, permitting them to manipulate the system better than others. And they experience it as confusing jargon, elaborate procedures, and arcane practices that act as barriers to understanding how to operate effectively within the system. The emblematic carrier of this characteristic is the court clerk who runs his words together in an undecipherable litany to the dominance of court procedures over citizens' rights.[7] At the bureaucratic level the giving and withholding of information is most obvious in examining how agencies manipulate their case loads by distributing or failing to distribute information about services.

Conventionally, analysts assess the demand for services by studying client rolls and visits. (Demands are statements directed toward public officials that some kind of action ought to be undertaken.)[8] If it is recognized that manifestations of client involvement may not fully reflect client interests, analysts contrive ways to assess underlying needs, for example, through attitudinal and census surveys. From this assessment administrators and politicians make claims about appropriate levels of services.

However, if it is recognized that organizations normally ration services by manipulating the nature and quantity of the information made available about services, then it is easily seen that demand levels are themselves a function of public policy. Client rolls will be seen as a function of *clients' perception* of service availability and the costs of seeking services. Client demand will be expressed only to the extent that clients themselves are aware that they have a social condition that can, should, and will be ministered to by public agencies.

When New York City reduced acceptance rates for new welfare cases at seven centers by 17 percent it accomplished this feat by tightening the application process. This meant not only more careful scrutiny of applicants' claims, but also more documentation and inquisition was required, which contributed a separate measure of rationing.[9]

This perspective is illustrated by indices of need for legal assistance for domestic problems. When a sample of Detroit residents were asked if they required a lawyer for assistance with some domestic-relations matters, scarcely more than 1 percent answered affirmatively. It would have been difficult to predict from this survey that approximately 40 percent of the clients of legal aid and neighborhood law offices originally sought help with domestic problems.[10]

Needs become manifest when the institutions that might provide assistance send out signals that they stand ready to assist. The 40 percent of the clients who originally sought help with domestic matters might have been only a small portion of the population that could have benefitted from such assistance. Some who could have used such services may have been deterred from seeking them. Since legal services are vastly underfunded, even more dramatic demonstrations of need might have materialized if more lawyers had been available.

Information about service is an aspect of service. Withholding information depresses service demands. For example, the campaign to reform welfare by dramatically increasing the welfare rolls was based on the view that a political movement could help overcome the stigma attached by potential recipients to welfare status. It could provide the information necessary to realize a substantial increase in the number of recipients.[11] The failure of public welfare agencies to make sure potential recipients receive the benefits to which they are entitled contrasts dramatically with the success of social security and Veterans' Administration benefits. The difference is that the clients of these two income support programs—the elderly, and veterans—are not socially stigmatized.[12]

Client statistics may not indicate much about the objective needs of the client population but they reflect a great deal about the organizations that formally cater to those needs.[13] Thus growing demand for adult continuing education partly exists in the felt needs of the adult population, but the demand also is responsive to the publicity generated by colleges and universities and their desire to attract students and their tuition. The demand for emergency police services exists to an unknown degree, but the introduction of a 911 central telephone number and dispatch system makes it more likely that citizens believe the police will respond quickly. After the system is introduced the increase in 911 calls will be responsive to organizational factors such as publicity about the service and response time as well as more objective factors such as population growth and changes in the age distribution of the population.

Although the dominant tendency is for street-level bureaucracies to attempt to limit demand by imposing (mostly nonmonetary) costs for services, there are some times when they have a stake in increasing their clientele. They will do this through an analogous rationing process, now directed toward increasing utilization.

Agencies are likely to try to increase their clientele when they are newly established and have to prove their ability to put services into operation. Thus the tripling of service complaints when Boston introduced its Little City Halls program was particularly welcome by its sponsors.[14] Efforts to increase clienteles were generally noticeable when central funding sources launched many subordinate service agencies, which saw themselves competing for funds in the next fiscal cycle. Such agencies would "beat the bushes" for clients in order to demonstrate that they were worthy of future support. Community action agencies and neighborhood mental health centers have been cases in point.[15]

Established street-level bureaucracies may also attempt to increase their clientele if they perceive themselves under attack and calculate that demonstrations of significant service provision, or increases in clientele, might aid their cause. Relatedly, street-level bureaucracies may attempt to increase the number of clients when they are competing against other programs with similar objectives. Such agencies perceive that they are competing for the same client pool, and that only the more successful will survive in the next budget cycle.

This competition also is conducive to quasi-legitimate fraud directed toward making the agencies look better. For example, when drug treatment centers were few they could afford to impose rigorous residential requirements, particularly since clients' commitment to their own rehabilitation was considered critical to therapy. When the number of such institutions increased in the early 1970s in response to available funding, and the population of drug users started to decline, to increase their clientele the centers began to relax their enrollment requirements (for example, by accepting clients who previously would have been judged too difficult to help). They also relaxed attendance requirements, so that a treatment bed might be occupied by someone who was not in fact a full-time resident of the center. Besides drug treatment centers, other organizations that have competed for larger shares of a fixed client pool include mental health centers funded in the same city, and academic departments competing for students within a university.

In theory this bureaucratic competition might provide precisely what bureaucracies importantly lack—a substitute for market place accountability. This, of course, is the idea behind educational vouchers. However, the healing effects of competition are too often mitigated by the residual bureaucratic aspects of the competing organizations. Faculty members in academic departments with declining enrollments are still protected by the tenure system, rewards for research (and bringing in research grants), and other factors that protect them from being assessed solely on criteria of service to students. Similarly, educational voucher experiments have foundered on teachers' tenure, union opposition, and parental inability to express preferences within the system for lack of information on the implications of the available choices.

PSYCHOLOGICAL

Bureaucratic rationing is also achieved by imposing psychological costs on clients. Some of these are implicit in the rationing mechanisms already mentioned. Waiting to receive services, particularly when clients conclude that the wait is inordinate and reflects lack of respect, contributes to diminishing client demands.[16] The administration of public welfare has been notorious for the psychological burdens clients have to bear. These include the degradation implicit in inquiries into sexual behavior, childbearing preferences, childrearing practices, friendship patterns, and persistent assumptions of fraud and dishonesty.[17] Nor have these practices been confined to the "unenlightened" 1950s, although some of the more barbaric features of welfare practice, such as the early dawn raids to catch the elusive "man-in-the-house," are no longer practiced.

93

To take a modest example, women applying for Aid to Families with Dependent Children at times are required to submit to an interview with lawyers, in which they must agree to assist the welfare department in prosecuting the father of their children. Apparently many women are unwilling to agree to this, since it would jeopardize the tenuous but at least partially satisfactory relationship that they may have with the childrens' father. They fear that the support they currently do receive and the positive benefits of good relations with them would be cut off by alienating the fathers, who may not be making substantial incomes anyway. Applicants are thus forced to lie or risk the loss of an important relationship. The interviews are conducted in a legalistic way with little sympathy for the position of the applicant. Many eligible potential clients do not complete the application process, because they prefer not to suffer these pressures and indignities.[18] Like so many monitoring precedures in welfare, it is unclear if monies recovered through these procedures equal the costs of engaging in them.

Psychological sanctions serve to reduce the demands from clients within the system as well as help to limit those who come into it. The defendant in a lower criminal court who asserts that he or she does not understand the charges will be silenced by the hostile response of the judge or clerk who unenthusiastically attempts to redress the complaint. Teachers, by varying their tone of voice, encourage or discourage pupils from asking questions. A lawyer in responding to clients can communicate the opinion that the inquiry is stupid and the client unworthy of a thoughtful response.

The importance of psychological interactions for rationing service is manifest in the extent to which clients will sometimes seek or approve of service simply because they like the way they are treated. Although they later find against them, sympathetic judges sometimes give thoughtful attention to defendants or complainants with weak cases simply in order to make them feel that they had their day in court. The reported gratitude of citizens who are treated in this way may indicate how little people have come to expect from government. It would seem that clients sometimes judge services positively if they are treated with respect regardless of the quality of services. In this connection a study of clients' evaluation of walk-in mental health clinics revealed that "clinic applicants are satisfied with almost any response [from staff] at first so long as the emotional atmosphere of the contact is comfortable."[19] While seekers of mental health services may be particularly sensitive to the quality of initial client-staff interactions there is every reason to think that these interactions form a substantial part of clients' initial evaluations of schools, courts, police, and other street-level services where there are no clearly defined service products to be obtained.

Rationing Services: Limitation of Access and Demand

Queuing

The most modest arrangements for client servicing impose costs on clients. This is evident in the way clients are arranged, or required to present themselves, for bureaucratic processing. Even the most ordinary queuing arrangements—those designed to provide service on a first-come, first-served basis in accordance with universalistic principles of client treatment—impose costs.[20]

Queues that depend upon first-come, first-served as their organizing principle elicit client cooperation because of their apparent fairness, but they may ration service by forcing clients to wait. When clients are forced to wait they are implicitly asked to accept the assumptions of rationing: that the costs they are bearing are necessary because the resources of the agency are fixed. They are also controlled by the social pressures exerted by others who wait. This is one of the functions of the line, waiting room, and other social structures that make it evident that others share the burden of waiting for service.

While resource limitations may be unalterable in the very short run, they are not necessarily immutable. They derive from allocation decisions that consider it acceptable to impose costs on waiting clients. Costs will not be imposed upon clients equally. Long lines processed on a first-come, first-served basis relatively benefit people who can afford to wait, people whose time is not particularly valuable to them, or people who do not have other obligations.

Poor people often suffer in such a system. Not only may clients who appear more affluent get served first because it is thought that the costs of waiting are higher for them,[21] but agencies often paternalistically develop policy as if the costs to the poor were nonexistent. A visit to the waiting room of a welfare office in any inner-city neighborhood is likely to convey the impression that the Welfare Department assumes recipients have nothing else to do with their time. Recipients learn the lesson of people who must seek service from a single source. Like the telephone company, the welfare department is able to pass on to the customer the costs of linking people with service. This system also benefits the average client to the disadvantage of people with extraordinary needs, since initially it has no mechanism for differentiating among clients. However, where the injury to people with extraordinary needs is likely to be severe, as in police work or medical emergencies, the ordering of services is often deliberately structured to search for and respond to this information.

An alternative to the first-come, first-served waiting room or line is the first-come, first-served queue by appointment. This system is also normatively acceptable and theoretically has the advantage of eliminating many of the costs of waiting time. In this queue the costs may appear to be reduced for the average client, but they may still be significant if appointments are crowded together to insure client overlap, as is typically done in health clinics and other medical settings. Crowding appointments may be done for the convenience of bureaucrats whose time is considered more valuable than that of clients, and who thus are guaranteed a flow of clients even if one misses an appointment. The costs of such a queue will also be borne by clients who seek service but cannot afford to wait for it, who are not disciplined enough to make and keep appointments, or who are not sure enough of the likely benefits of service to invest in seeking it. What appears to the street-level bureaucrat as a fair way to allocate time may be seen by the client in the light of past experiences of bureaucratic neglect and taken as a sign that the agency is unlikely to be responsive, or that the problem is unlikely to yield to assistance.

For some clients the costs of waiting may be quite high. In one legal services program approximately 40 percent of eligible clients who received an appointment with a lawyer for the following week did not keep the appointment.[22] This may have been because the problem dissolved during the intervening time, or because merely talking to the intake worker provided a degree of comfort. However, it is equally likely that clients who did not keep their appointments could not keep them but were afraid to say so, were not organized enough to show up at the appointed time, or faced their legal problems without professional advice. Or it may have been that the applicants for assistance interpreted the demand to wait for appointments as a sign that legal services was not likely to be responsive and assumed that, like other public agencies, it would not in the end prove helpful.

In any event, the day a client appears to seek assistance may be the day when he or she is most open to help or the street-level bureaucrat is most likely to be able to intervene successfully. Catherine Kohler Reissman has written about mental health services in an analogous situation.

It is obvious that the disequilibrium created by a crisis is a powerful therapeutic tool that is lost if the situation is allowed to degenerate, through postponement, into a chronic, long-term problem.[23]

Similar to the queue by appointment is the waiting list; clients are asked to wait for what is usually an undetermined amount of time until they can be accommodated. Although it appears to be straightforward on the surface, the waiting-list system has several important latent functions. First, as we have seen in the case of Boston public housing, a waiting list tends to increase the discretion of street-level bureaucrats by providing opportunities to call clients from the waiting list out of turn, or to provide special information that will permit them to take advantage of ways to be treated with higher priority.[24] Waiting lists also permit agencies to give the appearance of service (after all, clients *are* on a waiting list) and to make a case for increased resources because of the backlog of demand.[25] The waiting list appears to record the names of potential clients who are seeking service but cannot be accommodated, although it is obvious to all that many names continue on the list only because the agency has not attempted to discover who is actively waiting and who has long since ceased to be interested.

Some social agencies act as if the waiting list usefully filters potential clients who are truly in need of service and strains out those whose needs are not substantial and who thus drop off. This system of rationing may also provide for a period of time in which spontaneous recuperation may occur, again reserving client spaces only for those who are needy.[26] However, it is uncertain whether continuation on the list is a sign of substantial need or precisely the opposite, a sign that the potential client is successful enough in managing the problem that he or she can wait patiently for services.

A queuing arrangement that maximizes the costs to citizens at the expense of a relatively small number of street-level bureaucrats is employed by lower courts, which typically require defendants to appear on a given day, but notify them only as to the hour they should appear. In a typical situation fifty to one hundred defendants, possibly with a friend or member of their family, must be ready for a hearing or arraignment, with substantial penalties if they do not appear precisely at the beginning of the session (when their names are first called). Here they must wait until the judge arrives, and then wait again while the judge gives priority to defendants in the lockup who may require attorneys, defendants whose attorneys plead that they have to be elsewhere, and defendants whose cases require the testimony of waiting police officers, who themselves are subject to other priorities. Only when these and other priorities are accommodated will the docket be called in alphabetical or some other order.

Defendants may be innocent but by virtue of being arrested are judged guilty enough to pay in time and uncertainty the price that the court exacts for scheduling cases for the primary convenience of the judge. Although practices vary from court to court it is typical that defendants will not be told even approximately when their cases will be called, so that they must wait in the courtroom, possibly for most of the day, until they receive a hearing.[27]

The defendant who has waited through such a day has been instructed in the costs of continued interaction with the court system and must consider whether exercising rights or even pleading innocent in a minor matter, although legally valid, is worth the time and irritation. Some court systems have recently recognized that similar problems, including frequent postponements, inhibit witnesses from appearing and testifying in trials. But the same analysis rarely focuses on defendants and their experiences in court.

This queue by roundup is also typical of jury impaneling, where citizens are called for a week of service and must sit in a jury room awaiting assignment, often for several days, perhaps never to be called. The system officially is justified by the fluctuating and relatively unpredictable demand for jurors, and again is premised on the high value placed on the court's time relative to citizens' time. To insure that there are always people ready to serve, more jurors are called than will be required. If the court could tolerate a postponement now and then for lack of available jurors, and if jurors were called to report serially during the week rather than all at once, less time would be wasted for prospective jurors. But such practices could only be adopted if the time of prospective jurors were accorded more value relative to judges' and lawyers' time than is currently the case.

Clients frequently may be quite willing to pay the costs of waiting. Clients undoubtedly understand that there are times when they will have to wait, unless bureaucracies hire enough staff to meet peak demand. And since demand in most street-level bureaucracies is to some degree unpredictable—even schools often have to hire new teachers or shuffle teacher assignments after school has started—it would be too costly to provide services so that waiting would never occur. Waiting becomes injurious and inappropriately costly only under certain conditions.

Waiting is inappropriate when it exceeds the time generally expected for a service. A person may not resent a two-hour wait in an emergency room to receive a tetanus shot if it is clear that patients with more serious claims are being served first. But the same amount of time spent waiting in line simply to hand in forms to renew a driver's license may be exceedingly irritating. Waiting may also be resented when it involves the violation of an implicit agreement. Waiting is regarded as inappropriate when clients have made an appointment, except when the appointment is considered only an approximation of the time of service (as in the case of office visits to doctors).

Still another situation in which clients resent the costs of waiting arises when they wait unfairly. Thus if a favored client gains access to service more easily than others it will be resented by those who are not favored. Sometimes unfairness in waiting time may be so slight as to go unnoticed by clients. A study of black patients in Chicago hospital emergency rooms revealed that compared to whites waiting time was a little more than three minutes, incurred primarily by claimants with nonemergency conditions who sought help when the emergency room was relatively busy. But this cost is not actually trivial. It is worth noting that a modest three minutes or so, *for the 1,105 blacks in the sample alone*, would add up to a full working day for 2,619 people on a yearly basis,[28] a measure of one of the costs of institutional racism for the blacks of Cook County, Illinois.

Routines and Rationing

The existential problem for street-level bureaucrats is that with any single client they probably could interact flexibly and responsively. But if they did this with too many clients their capacity to respond flexibly would disappear. One might think of each client as, in a sense, seeking to be the one or among the few for whom an exception is made, a favor done, an indiscretion overlooked, a regulation ignored.

This dilemma of street-level bureaucrats is illustrated well by the legal services program. Individually, each attorney is obliged by professional norms to pursue fully the legal recourses available to clients. For impoverished clients this presumably means that attorneys should act on clients' behalf irrespective of cost. Only if this assumption is correct could the provision of legal services begin to redress the balance of power in the legal system, which every observer concedes favors those who command legal resources. But if all clients' legal needs were fully pursued there would be no time for additional clients. The dilemma is exquisite. To limit lawyers' advocacy is to deny poor people equal access to the law. To permit unbounded advocacy is to limit the number of poor people who can have such access. Only a reconstitution of the legal system could overcome the dilemma within the current patterns of inequality: either a radical departure in the amount of subsidies for legal assistance for the poor or a radical simplification of legal procedures.

When confronted with the dilemma of serving more clients or maintaining high quality service, most public managers will experience great pressures to choose in favor of greater numbers at the expense of quality. Their inability to measure and demonstrate the value of a service, when combined with high demand and budgetary concerns, will tend to impose a logic of increasing the quantity of services at the expense of the degree of attention workers can give to individual clients. Street-level bureaucrats, however, may devise ways to sabotage management efforts to reduce interactions with clients. The costs of achieving compliance in the face of workers' resistance may sometimes be more than managers want to pay. An example of such worker resistance is related by Robert Perlman in his study of the Roxbury Multi-Service Center.

Confronted with the complexity and number of demands being made on them, staff members resorted to shielding themselves from the mounting pressures. They extended interviews to postpone or avoid taking the next client. They scheduled home visits in order to avoid intake duty.[29]

Whether street-level bureaucrats oppose efforts to limit their interaction with clients, or whether they accept and encourage such efforts as a way of salvaging an unattractive or deteriorating work situation, is perhaps the critical question on which the quality of public service ultimately depends. Although street-level bureaucrats may sometimes struggle to maintain their ability to treat clients individually, the pressures more often operate in the opposite direction. Street-level practice often reduces the demand for services through rationing. The familiar complaints of encountering "red tape," "being given the run-around," and "talking to a brick wall" are reminders that clients recognize the extent to which bureaucratic unresponsiveness penalizes them.

Routinization rations services in at least two ways. First, set procedures designed to insure regularity, accountability, and fairness also protect workers from client demands for responsiveness. They insulate workers from having to deal with the human dimensions of presenting situations. They do this partly by creating procedures to which workers defer, happily or unhappily. Lawyers and judges, for example, generally accept court procedures that insulate them from erratic client demands. Police officials resist instituting (or more properly, reinstituting) a beat system because they are apprehensive that officers would become too involved with neighborhood residents, and thus perhaps engage in biased behavior. For similar reasons they often oppose assigning officers to the areas in which they reside, and they advocate reasonably frequent changes in assignment.

Social workers may be unhappy with the requirement to process endless paperwork rather than spend time providing client services. But whether happy or unhappy with job routines the fact remains that they serve to limit client demands on the system. The righteous objections of critics that routine procedures detract from primary obligations to serve clients are of little account, since in an important sense it is not useful for the bureaucracies to be more responsive and to secure more clients.

Second, routines provide a legitimate excuse for not dealing flexibly, since fairness in a limited sense demands equal treatment. Unresponsiveness and inflexibility reinforce common beliefs already present that bureaucracy is part of the problem rather than the solution, and they further reduce clients' claims for service or assertions of need.

When routines lead to predictability they may promote a degree of client confidence. As a public defender lecturing his peers on increasing client trust advised: "It's better to tell a client you will see him in two weeks and then show up, than to reassure him by saying, 'I'll stop by tomorrow,' and never show."[30]

But agency practices do not always lead to predictability. When they lead to delay, confusion, and uncertainty they assign considerable costs to clients. At times routines established to protect clients are distorted to minimize contact or services. For example, to insure responsiveness housing inspectors may be required to make more than one effort to contact complainants. However, inspectors may become adept at telephoning complainants when they are unlikely to be home or fail to keep appointments punctually. In Boston this practice "enhanced the prospects of no one being home when the inspector arrived—a practice which when repeated thrice, enabled cases to be dropped."[31]

The significance of practices that subvert predictability, antagonize or neglect clients, or sow confusion and uncertainty is that they are generally *functional* for the agency. They limit client demands and the number of clients in a context where the agency has no dearth of responsibilities and would not in any way be harmed as an agency if clients became disaffected, passive, or refused to articulate demands. Any reduction in client demand is only absorbed by other clients who come forward, or by a marginal and insignificant increase in the capacity of street-level bureaucrats to be responsive to the clients who continue to press.

It is for this reason that we conclude that stated intentions of street-level bureaucracies to become more client-oriented, to receive more citizen input, and to encourage clients to speak out are often questionable, no matter how sincere the administrators who articulate these fine goals. It is dysfunctional to most street-level bureaucracies to become more responsive. Increases in client demands at one point will only lead to mechanisms to ration services further at another point, assuming sources remain unchanged.

The logical but absurd extension of the relationship between demand and services is exemplified by the apocryphal library that reduced costs by closing down. Yet it is a real problem that increased patronage of libraries, museums, zoos, and other agencies providing free goods increases their uncompensated costs when they succeed in becoming more attractive.

Undoubtedly there are dimensions of bureaucratic practice in which increased responsiveness does not add to workers' tasks. Addressing clients politely rather than rudely or indifferently is an area in which greater responsiveness is not necessarily burdensome to the work load. Furthermore, reorganization may result in increasing the responsive capacity of workers. However, most increases in responsiveness—doing more for clients, or even listening to them more—place additional burdens on street-level bureaucrats, who will subvert such developments in the likely absence of any strong rewards or sanctions for going along with them.

There are times when bureaucratic rationing is not simply implicit; limiting clientele or reducing services is the agency's stated policy. In response to reduced budgets or other developments that make client-worker ratios conspicuously high, agencies will reduce the scope of service in several characteristic ways. In reducing services explicitly they will continue to honor the formal norm of universalistic service patterns.

Street-level bureaucracies may reduce services geographically. They may formally narrow the catchment area from which clients are drawn or reduce the number of neighborhoods served by a program. Alternatively, because reductions in service are unpopular, street-level bureaucracies may prefer to reduce the number of centers, effectively cutting services to some areas without formally changing anyone's eligibility. When the borough of Manhattan, for example, consolidated its municipal court system, eliminating district courts in Harlem, it did not formally change access to the court, but informally it substantially increased the costs of using the court system to Upper Manhattan residents.

Services can be limited in terms of clients' personal characteristics. Formally, agencies can change income eligibility levels. Informally, they may limit service by failing to print posters in Spanish or by placing notices in old-age and nursing homes rather than in public housing in order to attract primarily an elderly population.

Street-level bureaucracies also can formally or informally ration services by refusing to take certain kinds of cases. The decriminalization of drunkenness, for example, formally exonerates policemen from dealing with alcoholics (although public disapproval still places pressure on the police to do something about drunks). Informally departments can limit the clientele if officers choose to ignore public drunkenness, or they can reduce its place in departmental priorities.

Even when limiting services is not explicitly the function of rationing practices, service limitation often is not an unintended consequence of bureaucratic organization. Street-level bureaucrats and agency managers are often quite aware of the rationing implications of decisions about shorter office hours, consolidation of services, more or fewer intake workers, or the availability of information. Consider, for example, the efforts of the Budget Bureau of New York City in 1969 to decrease welfare expenditures. In a document remarkable for our purposes the Bureau suggested several ways to save close to $100 million.[32] In addition to reducing allowance levels, which would supply the bulk of the savings, the bureau recommended four administrative changes. Each would explicitly ration services in some way. A new intake procedure was proposed that would require applicants to be actively seeking jobs prior to the intake interview. This would force people to accept low-wage work, and, it was hoped, "more aggressive utilization of existing leverage over the employables would . . . have a deterrent effect on applications for welfare."[33] The authors recognized that for this innovation to be effective a substantially greater capacity of public employment agencies would be required, but there was no discussion of the costs of achieving this increase.

More frequent recertifications would be conducted to induce recipients who were on the rolls but no longer eligible because of changed circumstances to initiate case closings. (More than half of all case closings were then initiated by clients.) This reform would reduce the time between changes in clients' circumstances and the next reporting period.

Closing seven outreach centers would save some of the costs of running the centers, but more importantly, "larger savings are anticipated from secondary effects. . . . The most important of these is the opportunity *to build up and maintain the maximum legal backlog* between intake and eligibility increasing average backlog from two weeks to a full month."[34] Among other secondary benefits of center closings, the authors of the recommendations expected that "the relative inconvenience to the client of self-maintenance on emergency grants (for which application is normally made at the center more than once a week) may have some deterrent effect on [those] marginally eligible for welfare."[35]

Finally, stronger management audits would introduce greater uniformity in the system and provide better checks on welfare employees, who are portrayed in the document as more interested in enrolling clients than in controlling welfare costs.

Of equal interest are the strategies considered but not recommended. These included reducing intake hours, drastically closing intake centers, and requiring clients to provide increased documentation of birth, wages, rent payments, and other details of eligibility. While these provisions were rejected because they might result in unmanageable backlogs and infringe on clients' legal right to a response to their application within a month, the memo clearly recognizes that these measures would deter application rates by increasing the costs of applying to clients.

Provisions of this memo have been described at some length not because they are themselves remarkable but because they illustrate awareness at the agency planning level of the implications of rationing to limit client demand. It is naive to accept the rhetoric of public officials that their actions have the incidental effect of limiting or discouraging client demands. Rather, the opposite assumption is more useful analytically and more accurate empirically; namely, that public employees and higher officials are aware of the implications of actions taken that effectively increase or decrease client demand. They may deny such intentions publicly, of course, since their jobs require obeisance to norms of public service. They may not favor such policies personally, and they may regret that funding limitations preclude being able to serve more clients. Nonetheless, it is appropriate to assume that public agencies are responsible for the rationing implications of their actions.

In 1976 New York City introduced administrative controls that were credited with reducing the acceptance rate for new welfare applicants by half and terminating 18,000 cases a month. But this was accomplished because eligibles were being turned away "by very negative administration of work and parent-support rules," and because half of those terminated failed to show up for recertification, to respond to mailed questionnaires, or to verify school attendance. Their ineligibility was strictly a matter of difficulty or reluctance to pay the costs of remaining on the rolls until forced to do so. Meanwhile, according to an administrator, welfare centers are "overcrowded," "noisy," and "dirty." "Some clients wait four to five hours for service and too often are required to make more than one visit to the center to complete their business. In addition, they don't know the names of people who are serving them."[36] In these and other ways *eligible* clients are asked to pay the costs of seeking relief.

CHAPTER 8

Rationing Services: Inequality in Administration

Free public goods and services may be rationed by imposing costs and fixing their amount. They may also be rationed by allocating them differentially among classes of claimants. In street-level bureaucracies services are distributed differentially for at least four interconnected reasons.

First, as mentioned before, to a degree the society wants bureaucracies to be capable of responding flexibly to unique situations and to be able to treat people in terms of their individual circumstances. This is particularly the case for street-level bureaucracies. Teachers are expected to be interested in the individual child, policemen to be capable of flexible responses, social workers to be attuned to individual needs.

Second, street-level bureaucrats often want to make an improvement in their clients' lives. They derive satisfaction from making a difference for some clients and resist efforts to reduce the discretion that permits them to have this influence.

Third, and most obviously, bureaucracies are simply often required to differentiate among recipients. Everyone is not equally entitled to public services. Eligibility, culpability, and suitability for bureaucratic intervention must all be determined. Indeed, the process of reducing a person to his or her qualifications for bureaucratic intervention essentially *is* the process of becoming a client.[1] In this respect people-processing bureaucracies have two tasks: to develop an appropriate set of categories in terms of which people will be processed, and to map clients in terms of their qualifying or disqualifying characteristics.

An appropriate model for differentiation among clients in people processing is "triage." The term has its origins in a battlefield context. It refers to the decisions of medical personnel to place wounded soldiers in one of three categories: mortally wounded, with little hope of recovery; lightly wounded, not requiring immediate attention; and seriously wounded, but likely salvageable if medical attention is provided promptly. By concentrating on the last category prudent triaging provides a guide to optimizing the use of medical resources in battle. In current usage triaging refers to any medical context (as in emergency rooms) in which potential patients are assigned different treatment priorities.[2]

Triaging provides a useful analogy for bureaucratic differentiation for several reasons. It operates and is mandated in a context of severe resource shortages where the costs of waiting cannot be passed on to clients except with unacceptable consequences. It differentiates among clients, albeit on a sound basis. It requires of field personnel considerable discretion that cannot be reduced to official guidelines. And it clearly operates to the advantage of some and the great disadvantage of others. This is the case because some who are triaged as mortally wounded could be saved if they were given attention. It is not that they are all too far gone; it is only that the *probability* of saving people in this category is lower than considered optimal for expending medical resources.

Triage has its counterparts in many street-level bureaucracies. Building inspections and police patrols are often concentrated not in the most rundown neighborhoods but in those that are considered still redeemable. School children are placed in high tracks to provide resources to those who are considered capable of taking advantage of them. Psychiatrists and psychologists are inclined to accept for treatment people who they think likely to respond to treatment.

In some situations there are powerful reasons to think that differentiating among clients is in itself harmful. Tracking in schools particularly can be criticized as serving no useful purpose so far as the children are concerned, although it is a powerful tool for making teaching and school management easier.[3] However, the problem of triaging in public service is not primarily that it is sometimes destructive. It is that discretionary judgments are subject to *routine abuse.*

This introduces the fourth reason differential distribution of services occurs. Aside from whatever overtly discriminatory practices develop in street-level bureaucracies, differentiating among clients occurs routinely because differentiation often assists street-level bureaucrats in managing their work loads, as in the tracking of school children. Or it may help them cope with the ambiguities and psychological stresses of their jobs. Client differentiation may take place because, confronted with heavy work loads and apparently impossible tasks, street-level bureaucrats seek ways to maximize personal or agency resources, or they attempt to succeed with some clients when they cannot succeed with all. Sanctioned bureaucratic differentiation, for which triage is the paradigm, is open to the potential that street-level bureaucrats will differentiate among clients for reasons having more to do with solving or resolving work-related problems than with providing optimal resource distribution. In this they commonly introduce precisely the sort of particularism that modern bureaucracy theoretically overcomes, however firmly the rules of the agency require universalistic standards of judgment.

I have said that the routines of street-level bureaucracies may well be the policies of the agency, whether or not they are consistent with agency regulations and standards. To lend substance to this observation some of the patterns of practice by which discretionary judgments in these organizations are made should be identified.

CREAMING

Confronted with more clients than can readily be accommodated street-level bureaucrats often choose (or skim off the top) those who seem most likely to succeed in terms of bureaucratic success criteria. This will happen despite formal requirements to provide clients with equal chances for service, and even in the face of policies designed to favor clients with relatively poor probabilities of success. Employment counselors, for example, may send to jobs people who have the greatest chance to gain employment anyway, to the neglect of people who are more difficult to place. The Upward Bound program, dedicated to enriching the educational backgrounds of disadvantaged high school students, constantly had to guard against projects taking students whose chances of getting into college were already fairly high.[4]

Why does creaming take place, particularly in the face of official opposition to the practice? In every case of creaming the agency's incentives reward successes with clients, but they provide no substantial rewards for the risks taken. Since not all potential clients can be served, the reward structure of the agency is adopted as its implicit agenda in the absence of powerful incentives to the contrary. If all clients are equally worthy but all cannot be served, increasing the rate of personal or agency success becomes primary. The situation is complicated by the fact that the criteria for determining who is or is not "high risk" or "likely to succeed" are so problematic that there are few clearcut ways to challenge the worker who may offend selection norms.

From another point of view creaming takes place in circumstances in which there are no controls in assessing success. If teachers were assessed by the rate of progress their students made compared to a predicted rate, then the high achievement students would not necessarily be most highly valued. But in reality teachers are judged implicitly by the status and accomplishments of their students and thus seek to teach high achievement classes or move to middle-class schools. Similarly, employment counselors would value the hard-to-place more if they were given more credit for placing chronically unemployed people than for those temporarily out of work. These considerations return us to a concern for the ways in which street-level bureaucrats' performances are measured.

WORKER BIAS

Differentiation among clients may take place because of workers' preferences for some clients over others. They may prefer some clients over others, despite official norms to the contrary, under at least three circumstances. Ultimately they all reflect the fact that workers find greater gratification in interacting with some clients than with others and have opportunities to act on these preferences.

First, some clients simply evoke workers' sympathy or hostility. Like the Israeli customs officials, workers may be inclined to "give the underdog a break"[5] or may favor clients with similar ethnic backgrounds, as when racial or ethnic favoritism prevails in discriminatory decision making. The Boston Housing Authority workers who tended to favor white elderly applicants probably were responding to both ethnic and sympathy appeals when they selectively provided them with critical information.

It would be as much of a mistake to infer that ethnic or racial appeals always prevail in affecting discretionary judgments as that they never prevail. Bureaucratic norms operate to restrict the range of determinations made in this way. Thus, black police officers may make particular efforts to act in role-prescribed ways when confronting black citizens.[6] Displaying the complementary tendency, white bureaucrats may be more lenient or tolerant with black clients out of fear of being accused of racial biases. The report from San Francisco that black school children tended to receive good grades and were told that they were doing well in school, but in fact were not learning at an acceptable rate, is a vicious example of what can happen when street-level bureaucrats over-react to the potential for biased behavior.

If public officials were simply biased or racist, and if their prejudices were regularly manifested in behavior, the problem of bias in bureaucracy would be more pernicious but easier to root out. At the very least it would be easier to establish policy directives to reduce bias in bureaucracy. But patterns of prejudice are more subtle in the modern bureaucracy dedicated officially to equal treatment. Modern bureaucracy promises to eradicate prejudicial behavior through universalistic treatment; when prejudice does occur, it is more difficult to erase.

A second circumstance of biased behavior is evident when street-level bureaucrats respond to general orientations toward clients' worthiness or unworthiness that permeate the society and to whose proliferation they regularly contribute. This is one of the most well-grounded generalizations that can be made concerning client processing. Juvenile court judges determine sentencing severity on the basis of the apparent worthiness of the defendant.[7] Policemen make decisions concerning citizens on the basis of whether or not they display respect. Trauma-team personnel tend to work harder to save the lives of the young than the old, the high-status citizen rather than the low.[8] Other emergency room personnel make moral evaluations of clients and treat them accordingly.[9]

Where more than one street-level bureaucrat is involved, as in the cases of courtroom processing or multi-disciplinary assessments of handicapped students with special educational needs, it is often the moral worthiness of subjects that is negotiated in these settings.[10]

These observations are consistent with the policies of organizations that tend to focus on morally favored clients instead of those who most require their services. Agencies for the blind tend to be oriented toward children and employable adults although most blind people in the United States are elderly or near retirement.[11] Voluntary hospitals and private social service agencies tend to relocate or reduce their community services when a new group populates the neighborhood for which the services were originally established.

As suggested above, there is every reason to think that the general evaluations of social worth that inform the society will also inform the decisions of street-level bureaucrats in the absence of strong incentives to the contrary. Under what circumstances are these general notions of social worth likely to play a major role? At least three hypotheses seem plausible. First, when street-level bureaucrats have to choose among clients, and biased selection will not incur major costs, general notions of moral worth will prove important. Studies of emergency room bias suggest that blacks tend to receive equal treatment when they have severe injuries, and when the emergency room is not particularly crowded. But when emergency room personnel are under pressure, blacks with nonserious complaints are discriminated against as personnel have recourse to diffuse conceptions of worthiness in decision making.

Second, street-level bureaucrats will fall back on criteria of worthiness when there is no obvious end point to the degree of intervention. The trauma team that struggles particularly hard to save the lives of the young and the more affluent may be applying greater energy because there are no limits to the degree of dedication they could display. Since theoretically they should devote maximum effort in all cases, but in practice cannot (for what is maximum in this instance?), they establish implicit group standards for the circumstances under which maximum dedication will be displayed. Similarly, teachers are in positions in which there is no limit to the amount of dedication they could display to their charges. Choosing among students who are thought to be more worthy of teachers' time is a way of solving the dilemma of discovering limits to a theoretically unlimited, but practically limited, dedication.

This is not to deny that for private reasons doctors and nurses may find saving the life of a child more rewarding than resuscitating an elderly person. Or that teachers may prefer to concentrate on some children rather than others. However, it is to say that these tendencies, however rooted in the workers' personal limitations, also answer deeply felt personal needs associated with the structure of their jobs: to find opportunities for rewards when success is uncertain and unlimited dedication is not possible because assignments are open-ended.

Third, street-level bureaucrats will allow diffuse orientations of moral worthiness to infiltrate decision making when they have explicitly moral judgments to make. Workers in the legal system, and others with quasi-judicial functions such as school disciplinarians and parole officers, are charged with allocating punishments and with the ambiguous tasks of fitting the sanction to the offender as well as the offense. In such circumstances considerations of worthiness play a part. Is the juvenile defendant likely to be deterred from future offenses by lenience or severity? Is the parent fit to entrust with custody of the children? These questions require moral evaluations.

The problem is not that moral judgments are made but that the diffuse moral assumptions of dominant social orientations are likely to influence the decision. Or that dominant values may shape decisions despite competing normative standards that would provide alternative solutions. These are the issues for police officers who must determine when loud and boisterous talking in ethnic neighborhoods or street-gatherings on hot summer nights constitute breaches of the peace requiring intervention. Or consider the police shorthand that permits officers to draw conclusions concerning the victim's complicity in sexual assaults: "If he had time to take his shoes off, it wasn't rape." [12] Yet we know that coercion is most effective when it is so complete that the victim does not resist. Or consider the issues confronting middle-class judges who must decide whether or not to agree to the petition of a welfare department to remove the children of a low-income parent to foster homes. When a home for children becomes "unfit" under law is hardly a matter for objective determination.

A third circumstance in which street-level bureaucrats regularly display biased behavior arises when they are able to act on the view that some clients are more likely to respond to treatment than others. This category of favoritism is similar to creaming except that the motivation comes not from the reward structure of the agency (although this may play a part) but from the gratification that comes with helping people who are thought likely to respond to help. Psychologists and psychiatrists often favor verbally oriented, middle-class patients because their modes of therapy are most rewardingly practiced with such people. Teachers favor children who assimilate information easily because they receive more frequent and positive feedback. [13]

Closely related is the possibility that biased behavior occurs because a group is regarded as unlikely to respond to intervention. Consider the suit of the National Association for the Advancement of Colored People against the New York City Board of Education that charged that black and hispanic problem children were routinely assigned to special schools, yet white children with similar problems were helped in their own schools. [14] Here the NAACP suggests an instance in which the combined preferences of individual teachers results in institutional racism.

A Comment on the Ubiquity of Bias

The bureaucratic sources of bias discussed here are nurtured in street-level bureaucracies. Here work is characterized by high degrees of discretion and resource constraints and the need to control clients in order to process work efficiently. When work is structured as it is in street-level bureaucracies we come to look for the need to differentiate among clients, so much that it seems as useful to assume bias (however modest) and ask why it sometimes does not occur, than to assume equality of treatment and ask why it is regularly abridged.

However, since there is an obvious conflict between universalistic norms and biased practices we need to understand why this contradiction persists in practice. Among the supports of persistent, unsanctioned client differentiation are the following.

1. The context of client differentiation makes performance of all kinds difficult to assess. In particular it is difficult to assess equity of treatment. In some instances it is against the law to collect the data that would be necessary to demonstrate patterns of bias. In other instances there are no sound indicators of service quality, so it is usually impossible to assess workers in this respect.

2. Norms of equal treatment often function to reduce and minimize tendencies toward bias and otherwise provide powerful myths about the way services are allocated. Street-level bureaucrats often believe firmly that they treat all clients alike.

3. When differentiation of clients is observable, it is attributed to formal or informal policies that are alleged to be in the best interests of the clients or the best interest of the greatest number. Slow learners are tracked to help them avoid frustration. Children with physical, mental, or emotional disabilities are segregated in schools to help them avoid the humiliation alleged to result from exposure to more normal children and to concentrate resources on their behalf. Alcoholics who are arrested are thought to appreciate the comforts of a meal and a warm, dry cell. Clients of mental health services are thought to be able to make good use of these services. Those rejected for treatment have their time spared since they are thought unable to take advantage of assistance. There is an ideology of differentiation that at any given time rationalizes, excuses, and justifies the intervention orientations of street-level bureaucrats. (For a further discussion of ideological supports for client differentiation, see chapter 10.)

4. The rule of normality establishes standards of client behavior from which deviation is measured. This helps to insure that a part of the client population will be regarded as deviant. Sociologist David Sudnow has observed that public defenders and judges collaborate in sentencing on the basis of shared expectations of what constitutes a given offense and how it should be sanctioned.[15] Court personnel attach expectations of moral behavior to particular formal offenses so that if the moral content of an offense is more or less than expected for the charge, the charge may be changed even though it accurately describes the conduct in question. In this connection Maureen Mileski reports that in one lower court in Connecticut, judges sentenced those originally charged with serious misdemeanors as severely as those who were allowed to plead to lesser offenses and those charged with higher offenses. It would seem that judges meted sanctions for the behavior and not the formal charge.[16]

Rationing Services: Inequality in Administration

The rule of normality also helps insure that a part of the client population will be regarded as requiring or able to benefit from intervention, and a part will be thought of as unresponsive or unworthy of help. In general, street-level bureaucrats establish expectations of client behavior, both in terms of performance and in terms of their interaction with the bureaucracy. Deviations from these standards tend to be differentiated. Legal services lawyers may be more responsive to particularly cooperative clients.[17] Defendants who fail to show deference to judicial procedures or the agents of the law may be singled out for particularly harsh treatment.[18] An early set of immigration regulations designed to exclude people with mental disorders permitted erratic or "hotheaded" behavior if exhibited by Italians for whom this was regarded as a cultural characteristic (and therefore normal), but regarded such behavior as grounds for excluding northern Europeans, for whom this was designated an abnormal characteristic.

It is probably fair to say that clients will always be differentiated in terms of their perceived relative normality, regardless of how absolutely receptive to intervention they are. This provides street-level bureaucrats with the insurance that they always perceive a set of clients for whom they are necessary. In a school of exceptionally bright children the teachers would learn quickly who was or was not more gratifying to teach. In a client population that was not particularly verbal or middle class, psychologists would still be able to discover quickly who seemed most amenable to treatment. The client world as perceived by street-level bureaucrats is probably much like the children judged to be able to profit from tonsilectomies when this operation was still popular two generations ago. In an experiment recounted by sociologist Eliot Freidson, 174 children out of 389 were selected by a panel of physicians as being able to benefit from tonsilectomies. However, when another group of doctors examined the remaining 215 children, 99 more were judged in need of the operation. And when still another panel examined the rest (116), nearly one-half were recommended for the procedure.[19] One wonders whether service professionals would ever regard at least a portion of a client population as totally unable to benefit from their intervention.

Like the existence of routines, there is nothing surprising about street-level bureaucrats' expectations of normal distribution. The critical question is, again, how are these expectations related to legitimate objectives? The massive problem of children excluded from school provides a case in point. Although their expressed purposes are educational, public schools differentiate extensively on the basis of behavior, excluding large numbers from the school population through suspensions and other punishments.[20] Similarly courts differentiate among people charged with the same offense on the basis not of their street behavior but of their courtroom behavior. In these cases conceptions of normality operate effectively to deny or restrict client treatment.

5. Self-fulfilling prophecies contribute to the persistence of bias by providing spurious confirmation of the validity of differentiation. Greater surveillance of adolescent blacks by the police results in their being arrested at a greater rate than other portions of the population. This tends to confirm that black young adults are the primary delinquency problem.[21] Sending people to prison, where they are exposed to experienced criminals,'where they are labeled as criminal and are later treated as such by society, helps fulfill the prophecy that they were the kinds of people who required severe punishment in the first place.[22] Hospital staffs through subtle signals induce patients to display the behaviors of sick people, confirming that they were mentally disturbed or physically ill in the beginning.[23] The case of schools is perhaps best known. Teachers who expect achievement from their pupils interact with them in such a way as to bring out their full achievement potential.[24] Those predicted to do poorly, however subtly, are more likely to fail.

It should be no surprise that self-fulfilling prophecies run throughout street-level bureaucracies. If clients are differentiated they will respond to that differentiation by accepting in part the implications of the differentiation for their own identities. They will also respond to the role of client by conforming to bureaucracy's expectations concerning client behavior. From this interactionist perspective it is hardly surprising that differentiation of clienteles and the necessity of involvement with bureaucracy lead to the interpersonal dynamics we call self-fulfilling prophecies.

6. In the absence of adequate performance measures and in the context of making significant judgments affecting clients' well-being, street-level bureaucrats depend heavily on subjective assessments of the validity of their practices. This tendency is strongly supported by the feeling that the work they do is so specialized that no one else is in a position to criticize or even comment on their practices. Police, teachers, welfare workers, and other street-level bureaucrats consider themselves isolated from ordinary citizens who cannot appreciate the difficulties and abuse that they experience or the uncertainty of the rewards.[25]

Street-level bureaucrats are receptive to information that seems to confirm the legitimacy of their differentiation of the client world and thus supports their patterns of practice. In this they reflect the general psychological tendency to receive and incorporate information that is supportive of their world view and to filter out information that appears contradictory. They also reflect the general tendency to seek information among peers, who may be expected to be like-minded.

Street-level bureaucrats are conspicuously prone to scan their environment for empirical validation of their views. Their conceptions of clients tend to be consistent with perspectives that exonerate them from responsibility for clients' fate. They are particularly inclined to believe that experience provides the basis for knowledge in assessing the client world. While validity by illustration is logically indefensible it is a significant social fact that influences street-level behavior. We may hypothesize that validity by illustration ("I know it's true because I once had a client who . . .") will prevail in proportion to the worker's need to cope with the uncertainties of decision making and the potential consequences of those decisions. The policeman who draws a gun hastily because another officer was recently slain with a knife when he failed to draw his gun has a powerful argument with which to defend himself when questioned for abridging department policy.

Undoubtedly there are many street-level bureaucrats who refuse to accept the perspectives of their jobs that arise in the occupational subculture. Still, the strength of mechanisms adopted to cope with the work is great precisely because, if they are successful coping devices, they work (by definition). The need to cope acts as a barrier to anomalous information that might challenge the routines and orientations that have been developed over time. Changes in procedures are not necessarily resisted because workers are against change *per se*, but because change threatens the existence of coping routines and orientations that serve to rationalize the work. Similarly, anomalous information is not heard because it contradicts assumptions that make the job more rewarding or rationalizes its contradictions.

7. Unsanctioned, persistent differentiation is supported by the racism and prejudices that permeate the society and are grounded in the structure of inequality. Differentiation is intrinsic to street-level bureaucracy, but social inequality supports it and helps account for the cleavages in terms of which differentiation takes place. Thus the need to routinize, simplify, and differentiate in the context of inequality leads to the *institutionalization* of the stereotypical tendencies that permeate the society. Whatever prejudices street-level bureaucrats as individuals do or do not have, the structure of their work appears to call for differentiation of the client population, and thus there is structural receptivity to prejudicial attitudes. The need for simplification exists, so to speak, prior to the stereotype. The stereotype is nurtured in a context where it functions to divide up the client population.[26]

This does not mean that all street-level bureaucrats are prejudiced or that

115

efforts to reduce biased behavior ought not to be promoted. It does mean that efforts to eliminate prejudiced behavior will tend to yield best results if they address directly the work problems for which the holding of biases is a psychological solution. Workshops that help workers discover that the assumptions they hold about clients are not necessary to function effectively, and those that provide information about techniques of interaction would likely succeed in eliminating biased behavior far more often than more abstract seminars on race relations.

From this perspective the problem of bias is a profound one, not only for the quality of service but also for the legitimacy of government. There can be little official recognition that bias exists if it is bureaucratically functional. Clients and concerned citizens see biased behavior. Street-level bureaucrats on a daily basis see attitudes forged from experience reinforced in their validity. Clients see unfairness; street-level bureaucrats see rational responses to bureaucratic necessities.

This seems to insure a high degree of conflict over public service delivery. Citizen groups will continue to spend great energy conceiving ways to bring accusations of bias to the attention of street-level bureaucracies and designing ways to overcome it. The paraprofessional movement, decentralization, work force integration, and other reform waves have largely been motivated by a desire to overcome perceived biases in a context where the issue cannot be engaged directly, in part for the reasons mentioned here. The problem is made no simpler by the observation that clients come to expect bias and neglect. That differentiation serves bureaucratic purposes is not acceptable to a clientele ready to read indifference into routine procedures and favoritism rationalized as service-related.

CHAPTER 9

Controlling Clients and the Work Situation

Every social order depends on the general consent of its members. Even the most coercive of institutions, such as prisons, function only so long as those affected by the institution cooperate in its activities (even if the cooperation is secured ultimately by force). Typically, cooperation is neither actively coerced nor freely given, but, rather, it emerges from the structure of alternatives.

In the previous chapters I discussed ways in which patterns of street-level practice function to ration services. A second general function of street-level practice is not so much to limit services or choose among clients, but to obtain client cooperation with client-processing procedures. The work that clients are expected to cooperate with may or may not be consistent with agencies' policy declarations. It will, however, be consistent with street-level bureaucrats' conceptions of how to process work with minimal risk of disruption to routine practice.

Street-level bureaucrats' need to control clients as well as the incomplete nature of that control have been discussed earlier (chapters 5 and 6). Here I consider selected aspects of practice that commonly contribute to routine control of clients.

1. Street-level bureaucrats interact with clients in settings that symbolize, reinforce, and limit their relationship. It is practically a cliché to observe that the severe appointments of a courtroom, dominated by a bench behind which a black-robed judge looks down at other courtroom participants, convey the power of the system of laws over the individual. Separate entrances

for judges, commands to stand whenever the judge arrives or departs, and the unintelligibility of the court clerk further contribute to the mysteries of the courtroom.

Each service setting functions somewhat differently, but in their different ways each contributes to client compliance. Many offices in which people seek service are structured to separate clearly the workers from the clients by means of an imposing information desk.[1] Clients, when interviewed, are led to "offices" that, lacking partitions, violate privacy by permitting everyone to view (and listen in on) everyone else's work. Fixed rows of desks in schools, all facing the teacher, physically represent the demand for order that teachers and schools require. Like uniforms, settings facilitate the functioning of the bureaucracies by drawing attention to the location of power and cuing the expectations of clients.

These messages are not accidental. They are fostered by the agencies and generally consented to by the society. It is interesting to observe in modern courthouses the extent to which the traditional courtroom setting—dark, polished wood, the bench, separate entrances, the flags, epigrams celebrating justice—are retained in otherwise nontraditional architecture.

Consider also the tenacity of setting configurations in other public services, and the extent to which departures from tradition appear to be radical. In the public mind a nontraditional school is simply one without fixed desks. Are clients important and valued as people? Provide them with comfortable chairs and sofas on which to sit while they wait, ask them if they are comfortable, and reassure them if they must wait that they have not been forgotten. Are clients of little account? Neglect these considerations and have a small, cramped waiting room with little attention available. It would be mistaken to think of service settings as accidental. It is often a matter of policy that public services are able, or consider themselves unable, to plan for client comfort.

2. Clients are isolated from one another.[2] Public service bureaucracies are organized so that clients have little knowledge of others in the same position. Most client processing is shielded from the scrutiny of other clients. Isolated clients are more likely to think of themselves as responsible for their situations. They are unlikely to see their condition as a reflection of social structure and their treatment as unacceptable.

When client processing is done in public, the impression is accurately conveyed that clients are competing with one another for the attention or favor of street-level bureaucrats. As suggested earlier, in the brutal realities of triage, clients perceive that they gain special treatment or the attention of workers only at the expense of other clients. The bureaucratic defense against special treatment is also germane here: "If I give it to you I would have to give it to everyone." In street-level settings in which clients do know each other—in schools, mental hospitals, prisons—client control is fostered by the competitive systems of rewards, fostering among clients individual orientations rather than collective solutions to problem solving.

Street-level bureaucracies tend to resist organization by clients when it occurs. They tend to regard client organizations as unnecessary, frivolous, likely to be irresponsible, or not representative of clients' true interests. There are no objective measures of the validity of such assertions. From some perspectives any or all might be true. However, these assertions are most usefully regarded as defenses against client organization, intended to diminish their influence among potential recruits or third parties whose support is sought, or to lay the groundwork for an intransigent official response. In the past decade prison inmates, black high-school students, and welfare recipients all have been regularly subject to such official responses when they have attempted to organize.

Public officials often prefer to suppress or disorient client organizations because they can never be sure at what point they will peak or major concessions will be required. However, one lesson learned well by public officials during the past ten years is that it is often possible and desirable to encourage client organizations in order to provide a buffer between individual clients and the agency. Lacking substantive powers or the resources to act effectively, client organizations often provide the appearance of access while actually influencing only those areas in which policy decisions do not materially affect agency behavior.

3. The services and procedures of street-level bureaucrats are presented as benign.[3] Actions affecting clients are always taken in their best interest. Clients are expected to be grateful for benefits they receive. Where street-level bureaucracies constrain clients who are not regarded as guilty—as in schools, hospitals, and noncriminal arrests by the police (e.g., apprehension of alcoholics)—the ideology of benign intervention is particularly necessary to justify practices of questionable value to both client and worker groups. When combined with clients' deference to the more extensive education, training, and expertise of street-level bureaucrats, the ideology that street-level bureaucrats' intervention is in the interest of clients appears to be a particularly important instrument of control.[4]

4. Clients must come in for service. With a few important exceptions street-level bureaucracies require clients to appear for service, rather than have workers go to clients. In part this is a matter of efficiency. As suggested earlier, the monetary costs of providing service would increase dramatically if the costs of having to wait were borne by workers rather than clients. How-

ever, there is more to requiring clients to appear on the bureaucracy's turf than mere economy. Workers face physical and psychological threats when they leave the safety of the office or service headquarters. As the social gap between workers and clients widens, as workers come to regard themselves as more professional, they increasingly resist the home visits that, in many cases, were the keystones of good practice a generation ago. Doctors and other medical personnel are now unavailable for home visits. Teachers ask parents to consult with them at school rather than visit the home. In many social agencies home visits are on the decline.

When home visits cannot be avoided the society one way or another pays for asking workers to undertake them. Social workers who must make site visits to determine the suitability of a home in reports of battered children, and building inspectors who must visit premises to record violations, often insist on working in teams to avoid a feared assault in "bad" neighborhoods. They also arrange to be unable to schedule appointments or find people at home, and they seek special relief for being willing to undertake hazardous assignments.[5]

The most important exception is the police, whose work, by its nature, requires interaction with citizens on neutral or hostile turf. The extraordinary routines in which police engage in order to minimize threat in these circumstances (see below) tend to confirm this view of the importance of the setting for managing clients.

5. Interactions with clients are ordinarily structured so that street-level bureaucrats control their content, timing, and pace. Some of this may be explained by workers' apparent need to collect information and the press of business that forces them to expedite interactions so as to be able to process still other clients. Clearly the multiple forms that clients must fill out, as irritating as they are ubiquitous, function to direct clients' energies to the immediate tasks of client processing.

However, the firm direction exercised by street-level bureaucrats over interactions with clients cannot be explained by these factors alone, for client control is observable in situations in which the next client is not knocking at the door, and in which the norms of service precisely dictate nondirective approaches. Carl Hosticka's study of legal services lawyers' interactions with clients suggests how much control of clients can characterize client-worker interactions presumably oriented toward relatively open relations.[6]

In general the norms of the legal profession call upon lawyers to advance and be loyal to clients' interests; to respect and encourage client autonomy; to insure that clients are involved in and help determine important decisions about their cases; and to treat each case individually, so that lawyers respond to the case at hand rather than to a prior conception of the case. Legal services lawyers might be expected to be particularly responsive to these standards because they work for agencies founded in part to counteract the neglect of poor people by other public agencies and private lawyers, and because they tend to regard themselves as the legal champions of the underdog.

However, in actual interactions with clients legal services lawyers tend to control their clients in ways that undermine these fine standards. In a study of two legal services offices the following were observed.

Interviews are structured by routines developed to expedite the collection of information. Lawyers first ask clients questions to complete a general intake form, then ask questions designed to complete another, more detailed form, which the office secretary identified as most likely to be relevant to the client's case. The dominance of the forms restricts the search process to those categories anticipated by the format, which must necessarily be generally applicable to a wide range of clients.

Clients are observed to make repeated efforts to tell their stories in their own ways, consistent with a nondirective information search process. However, lawyers continually talk them down by insisting on conducting the interview according to the established format. Lawyers profess interest in clients' views, but then shut off discussion or questions by asking leading questions or clarifying small points rather than listening to clients' views.

Data on the structure of the interviews tend to confirm that lawyers dominate. On a measure of dominating the conversation, primarily charting interruptions of one party by the other, clients interrupted 3.8 times during an average 35-minute interview. In contrast, lawyers interrupted clients 10.4 times per interview. On a measure focusing on controlling the topic of conversation, 94 percent of the utterances of lawyers were directed toward controlling the topic; of these, 80 percent of the utterances were questions, 20 percent of them leading questions. Yet asking leading questions is a poor way to obtain information in a free and uncontrolled way.

These data reinforce the impressions gained from directly observing lawyers' interviews with clients. They confirm that interviews are dominated by routinized procedures in which the prior existence of case types is presumed and new clients are fitted to the contours of the previously existing types. Clients are shaped to existing expectations of clients; cases are fitted to existing views of the kinds of cases typical clients present. All this is justified in the names of efficiency, thoroughness, and service.

Significantly, the high degree of routinization may dampen the tendency to differentiate among clients as people. Legal services lawyers do not tend to perceive that clients are significantly different from each other, except in extreme cases. Only clients who are particularly uncooperative, and those who are particularly able to assist in managing their own cases, tend to receive differential responses. Welfare workers also fail to differentiate among clients. Like legal services lawyers, their interaction with clients is so highly structured that variations in treatment are not apparent.[7]

This is not to say that legal services clients or welfare recipients always present unique situations. On the whole there is probably a good deal of similarity in the situations street-level bureaucrats confront. However, the routinization of inquiry minimizes the extent to which street-level bureaucrats can discover unique circumstances requiring flexible responses. Thus we have the ingredients for another self-fulfilling prophecy. In the expectation that most clients will fall into previously defined categories, bureaucracies follow search procedures based on that expectation. Having constricted the kinds of information they receive, street-level bureaucracies find confirmation that, indeed, clients tend to fall into certain well-defined categories.

6. When control of clients is problematic yet critical to task performance or personal safety, interactions between citizens and street-level bureaucrats are dominated by control routines. Some street-level bureaucrats cannot depend on the setting, or on a set interview process, to control clients. These workers will develop routines to make client control a precondition of the interaction.

In teachers' interactions with children and police interactions with suspected offenders, symbols of authority and prior socialization help to insure client compliance with street-level bureaucracy. However, these social control mechanisms are often insufficient. Teachers and police officers both must act immediately to secure the cooperation of the people with whom they are engaged. Inner-city school teachers, for example, consider maintaining discipline one of their primary problems. It is a particularly critical issue in providing educational services when "keeping them in line" and avoiding physical confrontations consume a major portion of teachers' time.[8] Even under less threatening circumstances elementary school teachers are urged to "routinize as much as possible"[9] in order to succeed.

Police rookies are informally socialized by veterans to be tough as a primary requisite of their training[10] and are regarded as dependable partners in large measure by their willingness to use force when necessary. Police officers have most call for mechanisms that will secure compliance with their authority. They depend on such routines for protection from what might evolve into a life-and-death conflict without resorting to a show of arms or other unacceptable deterrents. One way in which they routinize their approach to interactions is to maximize their safety in the event of an attack. Thus, for example, police officers physically position themselves to be in the most advantageous situation if an attack materializes, even if the probability of an assault is low.[11]

Another primary orientation of police routines is to manipulate their public image as ready to use violence if necessary. As one observer describes it:

In most threatening situations, the officer attempts to maintain his edge by managing his appearance such that others will believe he is ready, if not anxious, for action. The policeman's famous swagger, the loud barking tone of his voice, the unsnapped holster or the hand clasped to his nightstick are all attitudes assumed to convey this impression. Decisiveness is readily apparent in such a posture, although the officer himself may have little, if any, idea of what he is about to do.[12]

Still another orientation of police routines is to develop capacities for suspicion and to conduct patrols to identify people who might be guilty of some offense or who might pose danger. Police may find clues to the identity of a potential assailant in a person's walk, dress, style of car, or composure.[13] These routines may be preconditions to effective policing but they also function to provide an early-warning system for the police officer's control requirements.

These procedures may work effectively to help street-level bureaucrats gain control over clients in settings that are not otherwise secure. Certainly they believe that such procedures are necessary for effective performance and would be most reluctant to abandon them. Yet there are some good reasons to think that these control routines help to create a client population that in unknown ways is different from the one that would exist in the absence of these protective devices. Again, street-level bureaucrats may be designing self-fulfilling prophecies in their client-control procedures. By approaching people in a hostile, abrasive, and suspicious manner they may evoke the behaviors they predict. The invoking of authority may lead to rebellion against authority. Thus school personnel may help provoke the behavior problems that interfere with their work, particularly if the authority is not regarded as legitimate.

A person stopped on suspicion may act with hostility toward the police not because of guilt or intrinsic hostility toward the police, but out of a sense of injustice at being stopped. When minority or ethnic communities generally regard the police as hostile to their interests this sense of injustice might easily be triggered. The defense of the police (that such approaches are necessary to do their jobs effectively), requires a degree of sympathy for the police position and a sensitivity to the requirements of the role, which may not be shared by the client population. Thoughtful police officers apparently make valiant efforts to strike a reasonable balance between an approach that induces compliance and one that accounts for the reactions of those who might unfairly be stopped. They are aided in many communities by a considerable degree of familiarity with police procedures, so that the procedures for stopping suspects on suspicion are regarded as routine and not taken personally. Still, the need for control routines represents an ongoing source of tension between the police and the public.

7. Street-level bureaucrats develop sanctions to punish disrespect to routines of order. These sanctions are often particularly significant because they are invoked to affect compliance with bureaucratic order rather than to affect behavior relevant to service. For example, teachers, like policemen, have mechanisms that function to provide clues to potential troublemakers and to exclude from society (in the case of teachers, the society of the school) those whose offenses threaten the working fabric of the institution. Children who are suspended for not having a pass, arriving late to class, being absent excessively, or smoking in the bathrooms are guilty not of educational sins[14] but may find interviews terminated in the rare cases when they are not willing to conform to the (reasonable) procedures demanded of them by attorneys.[15] At another point in the legal process judges tend to sanction defendants on the basis of the seriousness of rule violations, and also on the basis of their lack of respect for agents of the law.[16]

Some insight into the significance for street-level bureaucrats of procedures fostering control over clients can be gained by examining the implications of threatening to deny workers these procedural coping devices. The intensity of the resistance of police officers to citizen review boards can be associated with the fear that people who do not appreciate the pressures and risks of police work will sit in judgment on officers who do what they have to do in order to protect themselves. Teachers in traditional schools similarly fear the removal of the sanctions that, rightly or wrongly, they believe to be effective deterrents to student misconduct.

At times street-level bureaucrats for some reason cannot call on routine processing procedures. This results in great consternation or exaggerated efforts to appear to be in control. For example, welfare workers in the state of Washington experience great frustration in processing gypsies because they have no papers or other means of formal identification to prove birth, death, marriage, or social security status. Gypsies claim to be illiterate and have the habit of lapsing into Romany (their own language) when interrogation gets intense. These welfare recipients are able to evade the normal bureaucratic processing requirements because they are a relatively small sect whose characteristics are not likely to spread to the general welfare population. However, they cause great consternation among welfare workers who fear that their actions might create a precedent for evading the control procedures of the department. Like parents who can allow exceptions to family rules only with a warning to their children that negates any implication of generosity or flexibility, welfare workers typically make such exceptions only with a warning to their clients that they would be well-advised to learn to read and write. [17]

An analogous process of chastising clients toward whom they are otherwise being generous is observed among judges who deal out probationary sentences instead of incarceration. Judges sentencing offenders to probation tend to chastise and moralize more than when they sentence offenders to jail. [18] It is as if the judge, guarding against the possibility that the decision will be called into question by the later behavior of the offender, must compensate for leniency by applying a verbal equivalent of punishment.

Husbanding Resources

Confronted with complex tasks and limited resources, organizations develop work patterns to conserve the resources available. Managers strive to deploy resources more effectively or reduce the costs of work processing. They also may overtly or covertly redefine their objectives, so that what they are trying to achieve becomes easier to accomplish. These fundamental orientations toward resource management—efficiency, productivity, and goal clarification—are at the heart of most organizational reforms in public service bureaucracies and are discussed at some length below, as they affect the quality of work.

In street-level bureaucracies, however, practices oriented towards husbanding resources arise that are not related to management objectives. These are the practices developed by workers to conserve their own job resources. At times they are developed explicitly to conserve resources; at other times they may be explained by the need to conserve resources but are not explicitly developed for this reason. Like the other patterns of practice discussed in these chapters they often have significant implications for the content of public policy.

Street-level bureaucracies are often subject to unpredictable surges in demand. This is obviously the case for police departments and emergency rooms. It is also true of welfare offices, schools, and other agencies in which the work pace would seem more predictable. A client may appear who presents a particularly complicated processing problem and a few children may prove particularly disruptive on a given day. When combined with unexpected but regular breakdowns in agency functioning—such as the need to cover for a co-worker, or the intrusion of some new regulations requiring implementation—these unpredictable circumstances require that street-level bureaucrats have some reserve capacity to respond.

Workers faced with unpredictable surges in work load will attempt to secure safe time that they can deploy if necessary, time that usually functions to cushion the work day. "Where workloads or resource supplies fluctuate, the individual is tempted to stockpile. . . ."[19] This is the significance of the police dispatcher's tacit approval of officers who, upon completing an assignment, delay calling in until they have completed leftover paperwork. Cushioning the work day is rationalized in public services in which there is a well-recognized need for reserve capacity. Police departments and emergency rooms may be expected to deploy resources for peak load duty, but only within certain reasonable limits. In these services there must always be a planned excess capacity if they are to function effectively. In contrast, public services without generally recognized emergency functions are, if anything, expected to operate above capacity. When schools operate on double shifts or welfare workers have excessive case loads these institutions are not considered to be malfunctioning except by a small group of concerned and attentive citizens.

In such situations street-level bureaucrats have a strong incentive, when they can, to let the work expand to fill the amount of time available. This Peter Principle is commonly perceived to result from laziness, inertia, and inability to plan. While it may be related to these things, it is also rooted in the bureaucratic need to cope with the unpredictability of demand.

Workers recognize that any sign that they are not working to full capacity will be greeted with additional assignments, as there are always additional assignments to be made. Thus there is no incentive to complete an inspection or an interview quickly, because the time liberated by efficiency will be reassigned to conduct another inspection or interview. This is not the case when workers have quotas to meet or business appointments to conduct. In these cases workers are rewarded by processing assignments more quickly since they will be able to enjoy or utilize for other purposes the time liberated by their efficiency.

The validity of conceiving street-level bureaucrats as acting to conserve work time may be judged in part by the vehemence with which workers seek to protect their current work loads. Case loads are invariably too heavy. Responsibilities are always burdensome. These arguments are difficult to inspect rationally. Efficiency specialists will seek to disclose an untapped horde of resources and appropriate them for the agency. Workers' representatives will demonstrate the good uses street-level bureaucrats make of their slack time, if they have any—doing paperwork, preparing for assignments, or taking a breather so as to remain effective—and will demand compensation if this work must be done while workers are off-duty. For clients slack time remains a target of apparently greater available resources, of which both individual clients and groups of clients might take advantage.

The possibilities that workers are overworked and slothful remain. But it is more helpful to see the problem as structural. Workers have no protection against the accretion of responsibilities because of incessant demands and the irrelevance of performance measures of service quality. Given the need for reserve capacity to meet unpredictable demands, the husbanding of resources follows.

At the organizational level there are some conspicuously typical ways in which problems of the need for reserve time are handled. Organizations relieve their staffs of the need to treat irregular processing problems by developing special units and special procedures to process problem cases. These mechanisms are discussed at some length below (pp. 133–139).

Another way in which street-level bureaucrats conserve resources is to create the conditions for making decisions as free as possible from the implicit pressures of affected parties. For example, when education personnel in Massachusetts were required to design an educational plan for all children with special educational needs in the presence and with the active participation of the parents, these meetings were often preceded by private meetings of the evaluating teams. It is reasonable to infer that the teams met without the parents in order to present the parents with a united front and to avoid having to make a decision on the spur of the moment in the presence of outsiders.[20]

Another illustration is provided by Boston housing inspectors. These workers are required to give complainants a copy of the violations they record following an inspection. This regulation was introduced to make the actions of the inspectors visible to tenants who complained and to leave a record of the visit. However, inspectors are not required to leave with tenants a copy of their "inspector's report," which sets out the actions taken by the inspector after leaving the premises, including the actions taken on the violations found. Thus the tenant may receive the impression that the inspector's visit was fruitful. In reality the inspector may decide not to take legal action on the violations, and this decision is not taken when the tenant can review or have access to the process. Moreover, if the inspector decides that there is no cause for action on the violations, the tenant would only learn about it if she or he inquired later why no action was forthcoming.[21]

Similarly, lower-court judges can be observed to reserve decisions for later announcement when they think one of the parties to a case would be highly reactive, or if a worthy but guilty party to a case would be disappointed by a decision.

The desire to make decisions about people in private, particularly when they are likely to be negative or disappointing, is entirely understandable. Yet public policy often calls for street-level bureaucrats to make decisions in public precisely so that they can be exposed to, if not influenced by, the presence of those affected by the decisions. Such policy incorporates the theory that clients are likely to become more a part of bureaucrats' reference groups if they are present at times when decisions are made. Thus it is a matter of concern that street-level bureaucrats often are able to shift the field of decision making to a place where clients cannot intrude. The associated tendency to obscure the locus of decision making so that no individual need be confronted by disappointed or aggrieved clients similarly threatens client interests.

A final set of practices that function to husband resources have in common the effective transferring of decision-making responsibility about clients to other public workers. Street-level bureaucrats do this by permitting lower-level functionaries to exercise discretion in their place (screening), by accepting the judgment of others so that independent assessments need not be made ("rubber-stamping"), and by referrals.

SCREENING

Most people-processing organizations have a formal role for workers who stand as buffers between street-level bureaucrats and clients. Although street-level bureaucrats formally make the critical decisions about clients' status or provide the services, there remains an important formal role for other workers. This is to provide information to clients, to determine the proper slot for clients when discretionary decisions are minimal, or to protect street-level bureaucrats from inappropriate client pressures (as defined by the agency).

Thus street-level bureaucracies commonly employ receptionists, clerks, secretaries, and other facilitators to provide information in person or over the telephone, to assist clients in locating the proper place in the bureaucracy, and to make informal judgments as to whether they should persist in seeking help. This statement is equally applicable to the receptionist in a legal services office, a health aid in a VA hospital, an operator in a 911 police emergency call system, and a secretary of the local public housing authority.

The role of screener would not be cause for comment if screeners performed their jobs as they are defined in theory—that is, making decisions involving minimal discretion. However, in important respects screeners often come to function as street-level bureaucrats, exercising discretion in important areas of people's lives, although without the authority to do so. Emergency room registration clerks determine the order in which patients are seen by doctors, and even whether patients will be seen at all.[22] Secretaries can be helpful or unresponsive to potential clients, by their manner conveying whether or not the agency is likely to be receptive, and by helping or not helping potential clients characterize their situations in ways that will gain them favor. Like registration clerks in emergency rooms, the way secretaries characterize cases affects the ultimate processing by street-level bureaucrats.[23]

Perhaps an extreme example is provided by the public-housing applications clerk who identified prospective tenants she considered desirable, placed them in projects before vacancies became generally available, and informally rejected acceptable applications by placing them in a special file in the back of the applications file drawer. She did all this while working for an agency whose formal procedures called for fair and nondiscretionary behavior on her part.[24]

Wherever workers encounter the public they are in positions to play the gatekeeping functions of determining eligibility, conveying information, and presenting the face of the agency to clients as benign, indifferent, or hostile. Thus whether the low-level worker's tasks are tightly circumscribed, as in VA hospitals or police emergency telephone systems, or they present considerable opportunity for the exercise of informal discretion, as in public housing, these agency buffers can vitally influence citizen access to public benefits.

RUBBER STAMPING

A different kind of screening is used as the basis for decision making by street-level bureaucrats who routinely adopt the judgments of others as their own. Sometimes the views of others determine the actions street-level workers will take; sometimes they will determine the effort workers will devote. Popularly we call this "rubber stamping," although the process is often more complicated than this pejorative label implies.

For example, judges commonly accept the decisions of police officers or probation officers in lower-court criminal cases and more or less ratify these decisions in their determinations.[25] In some domestic relations courts the recommendations of social workers on the placement of children in contested divorces almost invariably provide the guidelines for judicial action, although their reports are supposed to be only advisory. The same has been observed of adoption agency workers and judicial consent to placement.[26] According to Jerome Carlin, in many specialized judicial settings that deal with the poor "it has become common practice to delegate authority for decision making to administrative personnel: referrees, commissioners, probation officers, medical examiners, marriage counselors, and others."[27]

A particularly significant delegation of authority has taken place in commitments to mental hospitals and in other situations in which mental competence is at issue. Commitments or findings of incompetence often may take place without hearings or, for that matter, any other proceedings in which contradictory evidence might conceivably be presented, simply on the basis of petitions for hospitalization or the reports of physicians.[28] These practices, however modernized or reformed to some degree in recent years, provides insight into the abrogation of discretionary decision-making functions under some circumstances.

Judges are not the only ones who accept the recommendations of others in making their authoritative decisions. Teachers use the judgments of childrens' previous teachers in their informal classroom track assignments, as early as the second grade, according to one study.[29] Public defenders make judgments about the worthiness of offenders on the basis of the charges made by police officers.[30] Emergency room doctors accept a clerk's judgment as to whether an individual requires immediate assistance or is a drunk and therefore should be treated after other patients, although the "drunk" may not smell of alcohol and may have serious medical requirements that would otherwise command the doctors' attention.[31] Perhaps the most mechanical application of previously applied labels is that of emergency room personnel who give immediate attention to all patients who arrive in an official vehicle, such as a police car, regardless of their condition.[32]

It is fairly easy to understand why bureaucrats would consistently accept the judgment of others in making determinations. Street-level bureaucrats confront problems in which they must make significant decisions about people and complex situations without being able to interrogate people fully or investigate the background of their claims. The assertions of other professionals, who are assumed to know their jobs and are charged with responsibility for making appropriate assessment in their own work, provide significant and legitimate cues to decision making in the absence of other sources of information.

It is entirely rational to depend upon the cues of respected others in making decisions. People do this all the time—when asking friends to recommend a mechanic, or a movie, or a mover. Unfortunately, what is rational private decision making may subvert public policy. Judges, rather than policemen, probation officers, or social workers, are charged with judicial determinations because they are theoretically in a better position to seek and hear information from all sides, and procedurally in a better position to protect the participants in a case. From a limited perspective this may be the best they can do. But when judges pass on responsibility they negate the theoretical safeguards their responsibilities represent in favor of the safety of expert or informal opinion.

Public policy is also subverted because street-level bureaucrats are generally obliged to make decisions based upon the case at hand. When clients are presented with or come accompanied by labels that predict the treatment they will receive, they do not obtain a response to the case at hand but rather to the stereotype their label evokes. Thus the "troublemaker" in school, the "drunk" in the emergency room, and the "rotten apple" in juvenile court receive responses to their labels and not to the behavior or circumstances that brought them into association with public agencies in the first place.

Still another difficulty with processing clients through prior identification by others is that the professionals whose decisions are effectively substituted for the decisions of those formally charged with authority in these cases are themselves subject to the decision pressures of street-level bureaucrats. The probation officers or social workers with many investigations to make and little chance of making them thoroughly take shortcuts of characterization and judgment that are similar but not identical to those made by the officials to whom they report. Thus the social worker is horrified to discover that her ambivalent, highly tentative report on placing children in a divorce proceeding, rendered under great pressure, highly qualified to reflect the uncertainty of findings, is taken as authoritative and as an appropriate basis for action, despite the pleas in her report for further, intensive probing. Hers is the only information that the judge has to make a decision. The feelings and actions of both social worker and judge are understandable. But however understandable, the interests of family members in a fair and humane decision may be jeopardized.[33]

REFERRALS

A final set of practices operating to conserve resources is associated with referrals. Referring a client from one agency to another obviously serves the client's interest when there is an identified, specific client need and resources are available from the receiving organization. However, there is a class of referrals which, whatever its contribution to client well-being, appears to function more to process heavy case loads in resource-poor agencies than to fulfill specific client needs. Street-level bureaucrats may make referrals as one of the least costly ways to process clients without providing services. Thus agencies may maintain benign images of helpfulness and service, without explicitly having to turn clients away.

This use of referrals is partly a result of the extraordinary demand for resources relative to the supply. Public agencies, responsibly seeking to meet clients' needs, attempt to link them with other agencies when their own resources become swamped. This works to the satisfaction of all when resources are available in other agencies, but it turns into a referral merry-go-round when other agencies become similarly inundated. When the Roxbury (Boston) Multi-Service Center opened its doors, it expected to provide black community residents with links to other social agencies to which they might not otherwise go. However, the agency shortly experienced as many referrals *from* other agencies as it was making *to* other agencies. It may be inferred that other Boston social agencies, under-staffed relative to the demands on them, saw the new Multi-Service Center as a resource that they might now exploit.[34]

Referrals also may represent a way in which agencies protect themselves by providing symbolic service when actual services are not available. Jeffry Galper puts it audaciously when he suggests the analogy of the parking problem in large cities: "there are never enough spots for all in need, but at any one time some cars are cruising the streets, looking. Referral is a way of dealing with clients in need without really dealing with them.[35]

Referrals also have some of the qualities of court delays and waiting lists. More people can be accommodated into the service structure at one time, although no more service is actually provided. And referrals can result in inducing people to stop seeking services because they consider their need less important now relative to the costs, or they have been encouraged to resolve their problems on their own. Whatever explains the drop-off from the referral net, it functions to some extent to ration the community services available.

Controlling Clients and the Work Situation

Managing the Consequences of Routine Practice

Street-level practices ration service, organize clients' passage through the bureaucracy, and conserve scarce organizational and personal resources. For various reasons these practices sometimes prove inadequate, or they evoke client reactions that cannot be handled through routine procedures. Cases that deviate from routine processing are not exempt from routinization, however. Instead street-level bureaucracies call on additional practices to manage the first-round costs of processing people in routine ways. These practices function to absorb dissatisfaction with common procedures, thereby permitting agencies to continue to process the majority of cases routinely.

Ideally, complex systems ought to have procedures that come into play when extraordinary circumstances occur. Schools, for example, must have fire drill routines. However, organizational practices that manage deviance from routinization often function in ways that, from the perspective of the client, have little to do with providing optimal services.

Street-level bureaucrats regularly refer difficult or problem cases to other people employed in their organization. Often this is uncomplicated, as when novices ask supervisors or more experienced workers to handle clients who present difficulties. The referral of difficult cases to more experienced workers hardly requires comment. From the point of view of service quality, the problem arises when referrals are made not because cases defy workers' abilities, but because they interfere with routine procedures. They must be treated as special by a bureaucracy which cannot afford to hear complaints or vigorous dissent from decisions at the same time that other clients *with similar claims but less inclination to speak out* are also being processed. The problem is kicked upstairs, not to seek expertise but to manage dissent or noncompliance. Thus street-level bureaucracies introduce the "pressure specialist"[36] to hear and decide on clients who pursue their cases vigorously.

The pressure specialist serves in several ways. Dissenting clients are siphoned off, permitting routine procedures to be imposed for the vast majority. Pressure specialists also perform onerous tasks that would otherwise taint the entire staff. For example, severe punishments in schools are usually meted out by an administrator or designated disciplinarian, protecting teachers from having to punish severely students whom they are simultaneously asked to instruct.

The availability of a pressure specialist in some respects protects the worker from the clients' strong negative feelings by providing an alternative to decision making. Rather than listen to clients complain, or worry that a decision may evoke client hostility, the worker can process the case through a pressure referral. Thus the worker's legitimacy is partially protected by the availability of a channel that places responsibility for difficult decisions in the hands of others.

Workers can use the availability of pressure specialists to enhance the prospects of favored clients. For example, welfare workers often take pleasure in artfully presenting cases to supervisors in such a way that they are likely to endorse the worker's judgment. Or street-level bureaucrats can scuttle clients' prospects without clients' knowledge by giving the appearance of bureaucratic neutrality but privately providing damaging information to supervisors.

The possibility that decisions can be appealed also enhances the legitimacy of the bureaucracy to the client. For this to work on a sustained basis, however, two conditions must be met. First, and quite obviously, it must look like channels for appeal are open. Second, and less obviously, these channels must be costly to use, rarely successful, and, if successful, certainly not well publicized. The reason for this is simply that if appeals channels were inexpensive to use or likely to be successful they soon *would be* used by clients seeking increased benefits or a favorable disposition. The channels of appeal would soon be clogged, and the manifest unfairness that some clients receive more than others because they sought more would undermine the system.[37]

Thus appeals ordinarily require long delays, the services of advocates, complicated administrative procedures associated with filing, and general hostility from the challenged agency.[38] Recent innovations responsive to client pressure often require public agencies to publish the requirements for appealing and inform clients of their rights to appeal, provide responses within a specified time period, and offer counsel to clients seeking appeals. These innovations still require considerable determination and energy from individual clients.

Public agencies also seek to insure that appeals cannot be sought collectively. The appeals process can function so long as a single client cannot gain redress for a class of clients. So long as individual clients cannot win benefits for groups, public agencies can ration the claims of large numbers of clients in many ways, and thus gain protection from an inundation of client demands.

These observations are generally supported by examining the volume of appeals in public agencies. For example, through the early 1960s there was almost a total lack of appeals from welfare decisions, although federal law required each state to establish an appeals procedure. In New York City, where a relatively liberal welfare environment prevailed compared to the rest of the country, only 15 appeals were taken in 1964, although half a million people were on welfare at the time.[39]

Appeals can also be discouraged by the high probability that they will not succeed. Allegations of police brutality are rarely made through official channels because of the conviction that they will not receive a sympathetic hearing from the officers who sit on the hearing boards. In Rochester, for example, where 102 complaints alleging "unnecessary force" were registered in the five- to seven-year period after 1965, only two were upheld by the police internal inspection office; of the 368 alleging unnecessary force and other improper behavior, forty-six were sustained.[40]

At times street-level bureaucracies institutionalize the pressure specialist, creating a special unit to deal with cases with which the agency is generally troubled. In many municipalities landlords are not vigorously prosecuted for housing violations, in part because judges do not give high priority to housing cases when cases of apparently greater public urgency—assaults and narcotics, for example—are also brought before them.[41] However, at times the failure of the courts to prosecute landlords vigorously threatens to undermine the legitimacy of the court systems. In such cases local housing courts, like the one established in Boston, can segregate these troublesome matters while reserving court time for the regular case load.

Tactical patrol forces provide police departments with special capacity to allocate officers to high crime neighborhoods and situations with high potential for violence. Special classes for disruptive students and those with learning disabilities absolve teachers from a need to deal with these control problems. This has significant consequences for children assigned to these classes, as well as for mainstream students deprived of their presence. Even if a justification for such segregation can be mustered, the highly subjective nature of classifying students for such classes draws attention to the organizational rather than the educational functions they serve.

A typical response of many public agencies to the claims generated by minority and women's rights movements has been to establish special units to hear citizen complaints and to take responsibility for institutional change in these areas. Police departments have established internal review boards (sometimes with outside citizen participation) and community relations units to present a sympathetic face to the black community. Public school systems have hired community relations specialists and affirmative action officers to take responsibility for the complaints of minorities and women and to articulate agency perspectives consistent with the interests of these groups. These steps have contributed to increased minority and female employment in the bureaucracies, symbolic rewards to these constituencies, perhaps genuine changes in the attitudes of some agency personnel, and possibly greater responsiveness to clients in some circumstances.

However, these innovations also function to protect the bureaucracies from pressures for change, and they insulate street-level bureaucrats from the need to confront certain client populations. Police departments channel what they label minority cases to human relations units when questions about racial attitudes are raised, freeing ordinary officers from having to resolve them. The affirmative action office takes responsibility for recruiting women to the work force, absolving the people who normally do the hiring from having to change their attitudes about female employees. Moreover, the ordinary worker recognizes the essentially symbolic and nonintegral nature of the new unit and may display toward it the same antipathy extended toward the group it is supposed to represent. Thus community relations officers are correctly made to feel that they are not respected by patrol officers.[42] Equal opportunity officers responsible for integrating work forces have to struggle to obtain respect from within the institutions that hire them.

Special units often end up taking responsibility for areas that are properly the general responsibility of other bureaucrats. They provide a symbolic approach to deeply devisive issues, and by providing street-level bureaucrats with a safety valve in their confrontation with clients, they may do as much harm as good with respect to changing the general orientation of agency personnel. Sociologist Albert Reiss Jr. puts it simply: ". . . the development of a special 'human relations' staff, will remove an important function from the domain of the line worker. . . . Without specific provision for implementation in the line, there is little opportunity to apply human relations to the treatment of clients."[43] Of course police officers can hardly avoid human relations in the broadest sense. But it is critical that a human relations *unit* may absolve them from ultimate responsibility for the way they behave in certain situations.

EMERGENCIES

The most common structural device for managing the consequences of routine is the emergency. Emergency practices, whatever their other functions, solve major service dilemmas for street-level bureaucracies.

Most people are generally familiar with some emergency procedures. Hospitals assign emergency status to people with certain medical conditions and accordingly take extraordinary actions on their behalf. Ancillary health protection agencies such as ambulance services and fire departments take extraordinary actions when an emergency is identified. Police dispatch assigns degrees of priority to calls in which intervention would most likely save lives or result in the apprehension of felons.

Emergencies are not confined to the reactive, life-saving public services Americans have become so familiar with through television. New welfare recipients can receive emergency grants upon applying; continuing recipients can receive them if they are burned out or experience other disasters. Housing inspections may be expedited if they are classified as emergencies, and in some cities housing may even be repaired by public agencies if an emergency is judged to exist. Public housing applicants receive priority if their need for housing has emergency status. Mental health clinics are instructed to take only clients with acute problems who present a danger to themselves or others. Legal services offices sometimes accept only clients who have emergency legal needs. It is the rare aid-giving agency that does not provide emergency assistance, the rare service-providing agency that does not admit emergency cases to its rolls.

Yet what is an emergency? There would probably be some consensus that the word denotes a situation that requires prompt attention, threatens the sustained existence of the subject, and calls for extraordinary actions on the part of others.[44]

However, the use of emergency treatment categories or assignment of clients to them may not reflect these circumstances. Police emergencies calling for preemptive responses include situations in which an emergency is designated primarily because it seems likely that offenders could be caught. Yet the potential for apprehending criminals is not necessarily related to life saving. The highest priority is informally assigned to situations in which officers are the ones whose lives are threatened. Here the highest priority depends on the occupation of the subjects.

It is relatively easy to find other examples in which emergencies depart from this definition. As indicated previously, emergency rooms accord special treatment to patients who arrive in police vehicles, regardless of their medical condition. Public housing officers and welfare workers can show favoritism by instructing selected clients how to be categorized as emergencies. New York City developed an emergency response to deteriorated housing conditions that accorded priority to conditions brought to the attention of city agencies by rent strikers and other tenant groups.[45] Here emergency status was affected by who sounded the alarm.

Clearly the category of emergency in public services is organizationally and situationally determined. A condition is emergent in public services only if it is called so by an authoritative agent. Patterns usually emerge to give shape to emergency practice, so that by convention one can often tell when a condition is likely to be regarded as an emergency. However, an emergency does not exist outside of the organizational needs of the agency and the relationship between the bureaucracy and the clients.

Street-level bureaucracies define emergencies in two ways. They create the emergency categories, and they determine when clients or cases fit those categories. In creating the categories they assign priorities but also determine the reach and limits of their own flexibility. By determining which cases are emergencies they allocate bureaucratic resources with respect to formally relevant and nonrelevant attributes of the case.

With the recognition that emergencies are situationally determined, the function of emergency procedures may be summarized as follows.

1. Emergency procedures aid in the rational allocation of resources. They are created to direct resources to the most urgent cases. In this respect emergency measures differ from triage procedures, which seek not the most urgent cases but the most urgent cases likely to respond to treatment. Most discussions of emergency procedures focus entirely on considerations of rationality: how to discriminate among cases most effectively and how to deploy resources most effectively.

2. Emergency procedures facilitate resource mobilization on behalf of cases. Doctors (and patients if they can) evoke emergency procedures in ambiguous situations in order to obtain hospital resources.[46]

3. Emergency procedures permit treating part of the case load comprehensively when resource constraints preclude treating all cases fully. Thus street-level bureaucracies are able to direct a full range of resources to *some* of the case load, thereby preserving a concept of what service could be under ideal conditions, and salvaging some of the bureaucracy's legitimacy and the service ideals of agency personnel.

The difficulty with serving part of the case load is that while some receive special treatment, people with equally severe needs are neglected. Clients with objectively equal claims do not present themselves to the agencies or do not evoke emergency procedures, although their condition or circumstances may be as severe as those who are treated as emergencies.

4. Emergency categories permit agencies and individual street-level bureaucrats to be selective and to make exceptions. Thus they find one way to overcome the requirements of fairness and allocate resources according to private or unofficial conceptions of need.

5. Emergency procedures permit street-level bureaucrats to provide resources to those who threaten the smooth functioning of the agency. For those who complain or object to the way they are treated, emergency procedures serve as safety valves to deal with contentious, potentially trouble-

some situations. Emergency status is sometimes accorded clients whose severe problems would tend to discredit the agency charged with responding to them. In this case emergency treatment is likely to be forthcoming in relation to the embarrassment potential of the client's condition or situation. The client with persistence, higher status, or better access to the media (through representation by an organized group, for example) is more likely to have high embarrassment potential than a client who lacks these characteristics.

Emergency treatment contributes substantially to the routinization of street-level bureaucracies by providing ways to manage some of the negative consequences of routinization. It provides a *routine way* to make exceptions without destroying the legitimacy of the organization. While allocating resources, emergency treatment also permits street-level bureaucrats to exercise a measure of control over their work by selecting some clients for special treatment. In addition, it protects the agency from criticism and public scrutiny by providing a way to deal with cases that present either the greatest objective or political problems.

For those clients who receive special treatment, of which emergency designation is often the prerequisite, the public agency is particularly responsive. Yet all clients would like to be treated with the same degree of responsiveness. Hence the maneuvering of some clients to be labeled as emergencies. Individual clients and client-oriented groups have an interest in expanding the emergency categories so that more and more clients receive emergency designation. But if all clients are treated as emergencies, none can receive emergency help. Organizations with responsive emergency procedures end up designing additional rationing mechanisms to limit the client demand. Facilities and services become swamped as clients attempt to receive the special treatment they have momentarily come to expect. At times the disorder that ensues can result in an enlargement of public service responsibilities. Emergency rooms take on additional personnel and welfare offices become less secretive about emergency grant procedures when clients become educated about their rights.

However, if clients remain nonvoluntary and dependent with respect to street-level bureaucracies, the limits of this creative disorder are likely to be reached shortly. Organizations with responsive emergency procedures end up designing additional rationing mechanisms to limit client demand, or they restructure emergency services in order to absorb the demand without threatening organizational functioning.[47]

CHAPTER 10

The Client-Processing Mentality

The drill sergeant who insists that soldiers stand tall, keep their eyes straight, and march in precision achieves results without knowing the state of mind, predispositions, or previous military experience of the recruits. He is untroubled by the needs of individuals and is at ease with mass processing. Street-level bureaucrats are not so favored. Their work involves the built-in contradiction that, while expected to exercise discretion in response to individuals and individual cases, in practice they must process people in terms of routines, stereotypes, and other mechanisms that facilitate work tasks.

Workers defend these patterns psychologically. They regard their adaptations to the job not only as mechanisms to cope with resource limitations, but also as functional requirements of doing the job in the first place. Thus what to critics seem to be compromise solutions to resource constraints may, from the workers' perspectives, be desirable and necessary components of the work environment. To attack the routine is to appear to attack the structure. Clients who challenge bureaucratic routines are taught this lesson when administrators act to control them or respond defensively to questions about agency procedures.

However, this does not entirely explain how workers cope or exhaust the types of psychological adaptations apparently required by these jobs. For one thing, it does not explain how street-level bureaucrats rationalize the discrepancy between service ideals and service provision. At least two additional perspectives on the psychology of street-level work must be considered in accounting for street-level bureaucrats' persistence and relative job satisfaction.

First, street-level bureaucrats modify their objectives to match better their ability to perform. Second, they mentally discount their clientele so as to reduce the tension resulting from their inability to deal with citizens according to ideal service models. In short, street-level bureaucrats develop conceptions of their jobs, and of clients, that reduce the strain between capabilities and goals, thereby making their jobs psychologically easier to manage.[1]

This is particularly significant because street-level bureaucrats' views of their work, and of clients, are matters of great public concern. Street-level bureaucrats are often accused of being biased against particular racial or ethnic groups or they are thought to be particularly cynical or unreliable in fulfilling obligations toward particular social groups. The proposal that workers' attitudes in large part are formed in response to their work setting contradicts some popular views. Popular wisdom often identifies the source of workers' attitudes toward clients and their jobs in prejudices acquired in upbringing and social background. Such perspectives lead to recommendations to hire better educated personnel or provide further education and training in public and human relations.

All too often such perspectives fail to take account of the influence of street-level bureaucrats' work on their attitudes. It is apparent that street-level bureaucrats change their attitudes from the time they are recruited to the time when they begin to experience work problems. Differences in the class backgrounds of recruits tend to disappear in training and trainee socialization.[2] Furthermore, there is evidence that educational background, which is closely related to class, is not an important predictor of the attitudes of workers who experience extreme job stresses. In this connection, sociologist Eliot Freidson has reviewed studies relating doctors' educational background to performance and concludes: "There is some very persuasive evidence that 'socialization' does not explain some important elements of professional performance half so well as does the organization of the immediate work environment.[3]

This is not to say that biases toward clients do not intrude in street-level work. However, focusing on the social backgrounds or experiences of workers will not yield a persuasive theory of bias in street-level bureaucracy. Such a theory should account for the development and persistence of attitudes as well as their direction.

Taking a different view, the origins of bias in street-level bureaucracies may be sought in the structure of work that requires coping responses to job stress. Attitudinal developments that redefine the nature of the job, or the nature of the clientele to be served, function in this way. Considering the structure of work helps explain the persistence of biases and the difficulties inherent in interrupting them.

However, the content of coping responses may well reflect the prevailing biases of the society. The need for biases may be rooted in the work structure, but the expression of this need may take different forms. Stereotyping thus may be thought of as a *form* of simplification. While simplifications are mental shortcuts (of many different kinds) that summarize and come to stand for more complex phenomena, stereotypes are simplifications in whose validity people strongly believe, and yet they are prejudicial and inaccurate as summary characteristics for groups of people with nominally similar attributes.

This approach to analyzing the client-processing mentality detaches the existence of attitudes toward clients and jobs from the content of those attitudes. It suggests that attitudinal dispositions will be rigid or flexible in large measure according to the degree they help workers cope with job stresses. On the other hand, it suggests that workers' attitudes and resulting behavior may be challenged and helped to change if: incentives and sanctions within the structure of the job encourage change; the structure of the job is altered to reduce workers' needs for psychological coping mechanisms; it can be shown that workers can cope successfully with job stresses without depending upon undesirable simplifications; efforts are made to make simplifications conform to actual job requirements rather than to unrelated biases. These general guidelines are grounded in recognition that the persistence of inappropriate attitudes is related to the work experience, and they can best be helped to change by focusing attention on the requirements of work.

The following sections treat in greater detail the tendency of street-level bureaucrats to cope with job stresses by modifying their conceptions of work and their conceptions of the clientele to be served. At the same time they show the relationship between attitudinal coping responses and the patterns of practice that the attitudes support.

Modifications of Conceptions of Work

TENSIONS BETWEEN CAPABILITIES AND OBJECTIVES

Withdrawal from work is one way that people respond to job stress. They may withdraw in fact, or they may withdraw psychologically. At the extreme, the tension between capabilities and objectives may be resolved by quitting. Or, in anticipation of this tension, people may decline to apply for public employment in the first place. Idealistic young teachers quit because they cannot tolerate the pettiness of their supervisors or their inability to teach as they would like or were trained to teach. Zealous young attorneys leave jobs as public lawyers in despair over making an improvement in the lives of their poor clients. In some ways these idealists are potentially the most dedicated public employees. In other respects they are least suited to do the work. In any event public agencies are left with a work force least bothered by the discrepancies between what they are supposed to do and what they actually do.

They and others who withdraw from the work force mute the extent to which withdrawal behaviors are evident in street-level bureaucracies. Thus, adaptive attitudes developed may be more moderate than would be the case if those least able to cope had remained on the job.

Those who do not actually withdraw from the work force may withdraw psychologically without actually quitting, rejecting personal responsibility for agency performance. The outward manifestation of these withdrawal orientations are familiar to managers and people attentive to labor-management relations: absenteeism, high turnover, goldbricking, slowdowns, and general withdrawal from involvement. These reactions are all outward signs of attitudinal responses to the sometimes overwhelming and insuperable difficulties of gaining gratification in task processes and achievement. At base are psychological developments that function to help workers maintain a distance from their failure or inability to realize the symbiotic goals of personal gratification and task realization.[4]

The problems of actual or psychological withdrawal from work are complicated in street-level bureaucracies by several considerations. There are numerous incentives outside the job context itself that operate to reduce the extent to which workers leave public service. Civil service systems protect against arbitrary management decisions, but they also increase the costs of firing workers or taking actions against them. In addition, workers accrue rights by virtue of their tenure in public employment, providing powerful incentives to remain in jobs despite low or declining job satisfaction. For example, the right to retire after twenty years' service, or pension rights that increase with tenure, encourage street-level bureaucrats to remain in jobs despite the inherent pressures.[5]

Indeed, it is possible to argue that these and other conditions of public employment, when combined with the difficulty of measuring job performance, are powerful enough to reduce workers' contributions to agency objectives to an absolute minimum once a degree of seniority has been achieved. The cynical view is that public workers have very little incentive to perform. However, while some street-level bureaucrats may retire on the job, the vast majority continue to be reasonably dedicated to occupational objectives as they come to define them.[6]

In addition to the usual material and psychological incentives operating on the job, street-level bureaucrats often enter public service with some inter- est in client-oriented work, embrace professional orientations that call for al- truistic behavior toward clients, and continually interact with clients, thus regularly confronting client characteristics and concerns. Moreover, street- level bureaucrats do not abandon agency objectives entirely because the discretionary nature of their jobs and the organizational milieu in which they work encourage them to develop private conceptions of the agency's objec- tives. They strive to realize these modified objectives and measure their day- to-day achievements in terms of them. They rationalize ambiguities and con- tradictions in objectives by developing their own conceptions of the public service (which they may share with other workers). Taking limitations in the work as a fixed reality rather than a problem with which to grapple, street- level bureaucrats forge a way to obtain job satisfaction and consistency be- tween aspirations and perceived capability.

Accepting limitations as fixed rather than as problematic is significant for two reasons. First, it discourages innovation and encourages mediocrity. It is one thing to say that resources are limited, another to say that the practices arising from trying to cope with limited resources are optimal. Yet the ten- dency to equate what exists with what is best is strong when patterns of prac- tice must be defended psychologically to avoid confrontations with work fail- ures.

Second, as I have argued, organizational patterns of practice in street- level bureaucracies *are* the policies of the organization. Thus, workers' pri- vate redefinition of agency ends result directly in accepting the means as ends. Means may become ends in other organizations, but lower-level work- ers rarely have as much influence on the drift in goals as in street-level bu- reaucracies.

PRIVATE GOAL DEFINITIONS

As we have seen, individual workers develop procedures to allocate re- sources efficiently. Some of these practices are approved or indulged by their organizations, others are unsanctioned. Parallel developments occur in conceptions of the work to be done. Just as organizations confronted with dif- ficulties in achieving objectives may retreat on objectives in order to obtain a better fit between their capabilities and goals,[7] so too workers can and do modify their conceptions of the job in order to close the psychological gap between capabilities and objectives. Thus judges may be oriented toward punishment and deterrence or corrections and rehabilitation. Teachers may be oriented toward classroom control or toward cognitive and personality development. Police officers drift toward concerns with order maintenance or law enforcement.[8] Possessing a simpler concept of the job than the one theoretically prevailing in reality, street-level bureaucrats are able to fashion an apparently more consistent approach to their work.

Street-level bureaucrats also impose personal conceptions of their jobs when they make superior efforts for some clients, conceding that they cannot extend themselves for all. At times this perspective results in favoritism toward certain social groups, but it may also apply without group bias. A case in point is the public defender who must select only a few cases to push to trial, settling the others as best he or she can.[9] Teachers similarly rationalize their inability to pay close attention to all children by drawing special satisfaction from the progress of children who do receive particular notice.

In these cases efficiency is still the norm and effective triage is again the ideal. But the benefits gained from modifying goals to make them consistent with serving a few, when not all can be served well, are not public benefits. On the contrary they are enjoyed mostly by the workers (and presumably by the clients who receive special attention). Moreover, they are not open to popular judgment or normally available for policy analysis. The individual street-level bureaucrat is not, in a sense, free to abandon private conceptions of the job without taking on still more of the tensions that go with it. Because these personal conceptions are adaptive responses they tend to be held rigidly and are not open for discussion.

The patterns of practice developed by individual workers often only make sense in the private conception of the job held by the worker, while supervisors and the public still expect allegiance to a more complex set of goals. For example, a police officer who fails to make an arrest upon observing an unlawful incident may strike an observer as negligent. But if the officer privately understands his or her job to be one of maintaining order and community harmony, with law enforcement in the neighborhood a secondary matter, this behavior may be acceptable according to the officer's private definition.

In the same way, a teacher who spends a great deal of time with a few students will not consider fair any criticism of this practice if he or she defines the job as, at best, the provision of sufficient attention to a select group. It is difficult to investigate conceptions of the job and trace their relationship to performance. Yet this may be necessary if one would try to reorient street-level bureaucrats in their work.

Private conceptions of the job have their counterparts in official policy. In some cases agencies themselves solve workers' problems by imposing a particular orientation on the work. At other times, the adaptive defensive attitudes of street-level bureaucrats toward their jobs are incorporated in the service orientation of their agencies although still officially unsanctioned. Thus the staff of some schools develop collective perspectives on their work and some police departments develop a shared view of patrol practices, contrary to the preferences of supervisors. Recruitment of like-minded people to the service contributes to collective adaptation to bureaucratic stresses by excluding staff members who would challenge work-force goal consensus.[10]

SPECIALIZATION

Specialization of function in bureaucracy is usually treated as fostering efficiency, permitting workers to develop skills and expertise and concentrate attention on their work. For some analysts specialization is synonymous with modern bureaucracy.[11] Specialization is frequently and increasingly characteristic of street-level bureaucracies. Welfare departments separate social services from eligibility determinations. Legal services agencies separate individual client servicing from law reform units. Schools breed educational specialties.

Like other contributors to efficiency, specialization solves problems for workers as well as for their organizations. In particular, specialization permits street-level bureaucrats to reduce the strain that would otherwise complicate their work situation. A lawyer in a law reform unit need not balance the demands of incessant case-load pressures, while his or her colleague who has high case-load assignments is relieved from considering the larger issues that clients' cases present. The social worker concerned with eligibility is relieved of concerns for clients' social integration, while the income maintenance worker need not worry whether clients receive undeserved support.

It is undoubtedly appropriate for some workers to be trained in areas that others are not trained in. Not every teacher, for example, need know French or Hebrew or Chinese for schools to provide training in languages other than English. But some specialization relieves other workers from developing skills they should have. As I have suggested, community relations specialists relieve others of responsibility for concern with treatment of minorities. Special community advocates may function to relieve others of responsibility for being advocates themselves. Even the case of language specialization is not so obvious as it might first appear. For should not all teachers in some city schools know Spanish to be able to converse with a large proportion of their students? Why should the Spanish teachers and the teachers of Hispanic background have responsibility for communicating with Spanish-speaking students? Specialization in this case relieves the other teachers of an important complication in their work lives.

Specialization permits street-level bureaucrats to avoid seeing their work as a whole. Once specialized they are expected, and expect themselves, to pursue an agenda that calls for the deployment of a restricted set of (perhaps highly developed) skills toward the achievement of a result defined by those skills. Specialists tend to perceive the client and his or her problems in terms of the methodologies and previously established processing categories that their training dictates.[12] Rare is the specialist who retains a comprehensive conception of the client and the alternatives available for processing. In some fields, such as special education, critics have advocated the training of *general specialists* capable of working with children with any learning disability or physical or psychological behavior. (This confirms the obvious: teachers should be well trained for the job, and the base of practice and theory from which they should operate has expanded significantly.)

Public institutions generally have conflicting or ambiguous goals for good reason. They embrace ambiguity, contradictions, and complexity because the society is unable and unwilling to abandon certain fundamental aspirations and expectations in providing public services. Specialists undoubtedly bring important skills and orientations to organizations that cannot develop them in their staff as a whole. Yet specialization and task specificity should be analyzed to discover those circumstances in which the costs of relieving street-level bureaucrats from contradictions and ambiguities may be higher than the benefits.

IDEOLOGY AND MILIEU

Another dimension of goal consolidation is provided by the occupational or professional ideology that governs street-level bureaucracies. Ideology provides a framework in terms of which disparate bits of information are stored, comprehended, and retrieved.[13] In street-level bureaucracies ideology also can serve as a way of disciplining goal orientations when many goals compete. When a school becomes an open classroom school or reverts to a traditional model the directors are saying something about their goals as well as their methods. The same is true in the case of correctional facilities that assert the primacy of custody over treatment.[14] By stressing some objectives over others, administrators partially solve the problem of what kind of institution they will run. Thus hiring becomes more rational because objectives are clearer, and employees have a clearer sense of what they are expected to achieve.

In recent years considerable attention has been devoted to the trend towards "medicalization" of social problems. Advanced by physicians and supported by a public anxious to think that there are "solutions" to behavioral "problems," the medical model has intruded into the worlds of education and corrections, and other environments in which human development is at issue. This trend has been correctly understood as undermining the political and social status of individuals, who, labeled "diseased" or "sick," are expected by the society to accept others' definitions of their circumstances and means for recovery. The significance for social control is substantial. What in other times might be understood as rebellious behavior may now be processed as mere sickness, implying no indictment and certainly no culpability on the part of social institutions that may have contributed to the genesis of the behavior.

Why has the medical orientation become so prominent? The influence of physicians and the high regard in which most people hold them surely provides part of the answer. But this does not fully explain the attraction of the medical orientation to say, educators, who in some respects have competing professional perspectives.

A substantial addition to understanding the attraction of the medical milieu in education, corrections, and other fields may be gained by recognizing the ways in which the introduction of a therapeutic milieu contributes to simplifying the goal orientations of public service workers. It provides a defense against personal responsibility of the worker by resting responsibility for clients in their physical or psychological development. It provides a theory of client behavior to help explain the complex world of the street-level bureaucrat. And it provides a clear statement of clients' problems in terms of which responses can be formulated. The hegemony of the medical model may be explained not only by the influence of physicians but also by the way it helps street-level bureaucrats solve problems of goal complexity.

This is not to say that goal clarification and reconstruction of work objectives have no value. Schools that assert that reading is primary may be able to achieve results that elude schools with more diffuse goals. There are undoubtedly physiological dimensions to deviant behavior in some instances, although the pharmacological cure is sometimes worse than the disease. The question is whether or not public institutions make their objectives and orientations manifest and the costs of their choices clear, and whether or not it is appropriate to abandon some goals or concentrate more on others.

DEFENSES AGAINST DISCRETION

Street-level bureaucrats sometimes cope with their jobs by privately modifying the scope of their authority. Imposing restrictions on the scope of their powers frees street-level bureaucrats from perceived responsibility for outcomes and reduces the strain between resources and objectives.

Denying discretion is a common way to limit responsibility. Workers seek to deny that they have influence, are free to make decisions, or offer service alternatives. Strict adherence to rules, and refusals to make exceptions when exceptions might be made, provide workers with defenses against the possibility that they might be able to act more as clients would wish. "That's the way things are," "It's the law," and similar rationalizations not only protect workers from client pressures, but also protect them from confronting their own shortcomings as participants in public service work.[15] At times these assertions are best understood as strategies to deflect clients' claims. But at other times they are best understood as rigidly held attitudes that partially have their origins in, and are bolstered by, distress over the gap between expectations and perceived capability.

Agencies often impose rigidities on their workers. For example, in the late 1960s, when the welfare rights movement began to pressure welfare workers to make discretionary grants to large numbers of recipients, welfare departments throughout the country eliminated discretionary special-grant awards for furniture and other items. Thus the departments removed from workers a discretionary option. This circumscribed their power but also eliminated the tension between the workers' desires to help clients and their need to control disbursements.

Another way in which agencies help solve employees' role tensions is by extensively promulgating rules specifying official procedures. From the point of view of reducing role tensions it is less important that rules are not necessarily followed than that they are available as authoritative materials with which street-level bureaucrats can renovate job conceptions to better fit work realities. Thus rules not only order work but also function to order workers' role conceptions.[16]

Earlier chapters have focused attention on street-level bureaucrats' development of work routines to process clients and otherwise treat their responsibilities. These routines often represent more than mere instruments of efficiency. Street-level bureaucrats also develop attachments to modes of practice. They appear to feel that their jobs require the routines. In some street-level bureaucracies, routines of practice become so dominant that workers seek to negotiate the routines rather than to obtain the objective for which routines were presumably developed.

Legal services lawyers, for example, have been observed to discourage clients from raising questions and penalizing those who refuse to follow the preferred procedures. Similarly, welfare workers have been observed to disfavor clients who do not permit them to conduct interviews according to standard formats.[17] These and other examples of rigid adherence to procedure suggest the significance for workers of pursuing means instead of ends.

DEFENSES AGAINST BUREAUCRACY

Earlier chapters have also stressed the tenacity of street-level bureaucrats in resisting efforts to limit their discretion. They may assert discretionary dimensions of their job *to a greater degree than called for in theory* in order to salvage a semblance of proper client treatment as they define it. Typically, they develop conceptions of their job that focus on good treatment of some rather than inadequate treatment of all.

Most of the time escapes from bureaucracy tend to favor some kinds of clients over others. (This tendency is discussed later in the treatment of modifications of conceptions of clients.) Sometimes the escape from bureaucracy appears simply as a refusal to accept the decision-making formulas of the work. The social workers who started making home visits rather than doing intake, because they felt that additional clients could not be well served by the agency, illustrate this inclination.[18]

Another dimension of the escape from bureaucracy is suggested by street-level bureaucrats who in client processing redefine their jobs by taking into account the informal but likely consequences of their actions. Judges and prosecutors, for example, often make charging and sentencing decisions based on their expectations of the consequences of subjecting defendants to the results of sentencing, although formally they are not supposed to consider the quality of correctional institutions in their deliberations. These tendencies have earned some judicial personnel considerable criticism for the resulting leniency of their approaches.[19] Similar reconceptualizations of the job were evident among the public housing personnel who, contrary to official agency policy, took into account the consequences of placing some favored applicants in undesirable housing projects, as previously discussed.

Is escape from bureaucracy desirable? Does it represent a tendency toward responsiveness whose absence is too often deplored? Certainly to the beneficiaries of these orientations it represents responsiveness. However, the dilemmas of street-level bureaucracy remain unresolved. Workers who undermine intake practices by favoring some clients deny minimal services to those who fail to get entered on the agency rolls. Public housing applicants who do not receive treatment are disadvantaged because fewer places are available in the better projects. Judges and prosecutors who develop private conceptions of proper considerations in charging and sentencing contribute to defendants' welfare as best they can, but they also skew the population of the correctional institutions in ways responsive to their private conceptions of appropriate sentencing. And to judge by the proliferation of mandatory sentencing legislation, they force the development of inflexible policy to restore the formal order. However one might sympathize with court personnel who take discretionary actions in clients' interests, one cannot conclude that they substantially resolve the dilemmas of confining the scope of discretion and negating the consequences of rule-bound bureaucracy.

Modifications of Conceptions of Clients

Street-level bureaucrats are expected to treat all people in common circumstances alike. Paradoxically, many factors operate to make favoritism and unequal treatment characteristic of modern bureaucracies. These factors include the inherent subjectivity of required judgments, the difficulty of assessing street-level bureaucrats' work, the inadequacy of feedback as an influence on behavior, and ideological considerations that justify client differentiation. These concerns have been treated in the previous three chapters focusing on patterns of practice developed to make jobs easier to manage.

However, a discussion of the importance of practices resulting in client differentiation would be incomplete without reference to the *psychological* importance of client differentiations as a coping strategy. Client differentiation is a significant aspect of street-level bureaucrats' rationalization of the contradictions in their work. It is not simply that street-level workers prefer some clients over others. These preferences also make it possible to perform flexibly and responsively with a limited segment of the clientele. Thus workers do for some what they are unable to do for all. The street-level bureaucrat salvages *for a portion of the clientele* a conception of his or her performance relatively consistent with ideal conceptions of the job. Thus as the work is experienced there is no dissonance between the job as it should be done and the job as it is done *for a portion of the clientele*. The worker knows in a private sense that he or she is capable of doing the job well and can better defend against the assaults to the ego which the structure of street-level work normally delivers. The teacher's pet is not only an obedient child but also one who confirms to the teacher the teacher's own capability.

There is another important reason to consider street-level bureaucrats' conceptual modifications of the clientele. Just as differentiation of clients supports rationing and other practices of organizing work, it also supports private modifications of conceptions of work. Conceptions of the job imply conceptions of the clientele. One cannot practice without an implicit model of the people on whom one is practicing. An open classroom demands a conception of children as requiring relatively greater freedom and flexibility than are available in a traditional classroom. A psychiatrically oriented drug center is founded on a different model of human motivation than a center organized around peer interaction and self-help.

Street-level bureaucrats who are unable to provide all clients with their best efforts develop conceptual mechanisms to divide up the client population and rationalize the division. The differentiation of clients discussed in previous chapters thus not only provides a rationale for allocating scarce resources, but it also serves to help street-level bureaucrats justify their jobs to themselves. The frequency with which street-level bureaucrats are observed to divide up the client world conceptually suggests the importance of this dimension of work in sustaining street-level practice.

The psychological importance of private reconceptions of the clientele can be traced in the primary divisions of the client world. For example, unsanctioned distinctions between worthy and unworthy clients narrow the range of clients for whom street-level bureaucrats must provide their best efforts. Street-level bureaucrats often respond more favorably to clients who are helpful or cooperative in their own treatment, or who appear to be particularly responsive to help. Orienting services toward cooperative clients, or clients who respond to treatment, allows street-level bureaucrats to believe that they are optimizing their use of resources. At the same time these perceptions help condone service denials (or even routine treatment) by permitting the private judgment that some clients absorb more than their fair share of resources.

Perhaps the most familiar syndrome of private reconceptions of clients concerns locating responsibility for client difficulties. Assumptions about who or what is responsible for clients' situations are significant conceptual instruments by which street-level bureaucrats distance themselves from clients. For example, the tendency of helping professionals to blame the victim, attributing the cause of clients' situations to the individuals themselves without considering the role of social and environmental contexts, locates responsibility in a place that absolves the helper from blame.[20]

There are many examples of blaming the victim. Chronically unemployed men are described as shiftless and unwilling to work when their situations might be attributed to the structure of employment and previous job availability. Students' learning difficulties are explained by focusing on their lack of motivation rather than on the skills of the teachers and the atmosphere of the school. Blaming clients for failing to keep appointments protects street-level bureaucrats from the possibility that prior interviews have discouraged or alienated them. Instances of teachers beating children who clearly display signs of mental disturbance provide particularly brutal illustrations of the apparent need of at least some street-level bureaucrats to attribute self-direction to noncompliant clients.[21] If the client is to blame, street-level bureaucrats are shielded from having to confront their own failures or the failures of the agencies for which they work.

An opposite but functionally equivalent mode of perceiving clients also serves to absolve street-level bureaucrats from responsibility for service failures. This is the tendency to take an entirely environmental point of view and perceive clients exclusively as the products of inadequate background conditioning. Thus if children are perceived as primitive, racially inferior, or culturally deprived, teachers can hardly fault themselves if their charges fail to progress.[22] Similarly, job training counselors who explain failures by clients' low motivation stemming from the discouragement experienced by ghetto youth can avoid dealing with their own failures to make the program meaningful.

Undeniably, there are cultural and social factors that affect client performance, just as there is a sense in which people are responsible for their actions. However, it is important to note that these explanations function as cognitive shields, reducing what responsibility and accountability may exist in the role expectations of street-level bureaucrats. Moreover, because these explanations of responsibility are illegitimate in terms of formal agency policy, they remain beneath the surface, unstated. Thus when they implicitly form the basis for decisions about clients they contribute to misunderstanding and to the resulting hostility of clients toward the agencies acting upon them.

Given the imbalance in power between clients and their agencies, not all clients will respond with hostility to decisions based on these implicit assumptions. Perhaps more commonly, clients accept the implicit assumptions of responsibility; then these conceptual structures contribute to client compliance with agency policy. Clients may accept responsibility for their circumstances without reference to the environmental conditions that they experience. Or they may regard their situation as hopeless because their environment is so antagonistic to improvement. Each attitudinal set works against personal movement and growth.[23]

This is not to say that one can easily strike out for one explanation of responsibility over another. Structural explanations of clients' circumstances are important in order to direct attention to changing the political, economic, and social structures that circumscribe and dictate the possibilities of action. For if environmental factors do not prescribe life changes they certainly structure the range of opportunities.

Similarly, in important respects clients to some degree must be responsible for themselves. Without this assumption there can be no client growth within the current structure of arrangements and no client contribution to changing those arrangements, individually or collectively. Erving Goffman's insight into the relationship of client responsibility to absolving explanations, developed in his study of prisons, mental hospitals, and other "total" institutions, has generally wider applicability.

Although there is a psychiatric view of mental disorder and an environmental view of crime and counterrevolutionary activity, both freeing the offender from moral responsibility for his offense, total institutions can little afford this particular kind of determinism. Inmates must be caused to *self-direct* themselves in a manageable way, and, for this to be promoted, both desired and undesired conduct must be defined as springing from the personal will and character of the individual inmate himself, and defined as something he himself can do something about.[24]

These views of social responsibility do not originate with street-level bureaucrats, of course. But they are adopted and rigidly held by workers faced with the contradiction that they ought to be able to make a difference in clients' lives, but commonly cannot. These views explain failure away, and permit workers to develop more comfortable relations with the contradictions in their work.

Not all street-level bureaucrats develop these attitudinal patterns. Conspicuously, some public services develop different patterns of attribution of client responsibilities from others, and variations can also be found within individual public services.[25] The task of those interested in promoting the quality of street-level bureaucracy is to help sustain the ambiguity in allocating responsibility. It is undoubtedly an important measure of street-level bureaucratic services that some workers find a way to keep in balance their views of client responsibility and environmental causality and their own potential for intervention.

Street-level bureaucrats hold private views that affect the distribution and quality of services, and they hold these views intensely. Their biases, when they exist, are difficult to interrupt. Why should this be so when street-level bureaucrats, more than most people, have regular opportunities to disconfirm stereotypes?

A partial possible explanation has already been suggested. First, segmentation of the client population complements work practices that are themselves compromises, and it also complements the resulting reconceptions of work objectives. In other words, patterns of practice, conceptions of the job, and conceptions of the clients must fit together if street-level bureaucrats are to resolve work contradictions successfully. Private conceptions of the clientele will be developed in proportion to the need to come to a private resolution of the contradictions in the work.

Second, conceptual modifications of the clientele tend to accept and build upon general social attitudes, and thus are reinforced in everyday life. Favoring clients who are underdogs or discriminating against clients considered socially unworthy may partly be explained by the sympathies and antipathies of the general society. Sociologist Howard Becker reports that children may be morally unacceptable to teachers in terms of values centered around health and cleanliness, sex and aggression, ambition and work, and age-group relations. These considerations are particularly likely to be salient when class discrepancies between teachers and pupils are significant.[26] These responses to childrens' characteristics are not likely to be unique to teachers. But when teachers do respond to children in these terms, their responses have implications for public policy.

Other conceptions of clients appear to enhance feelings about job accomplishments even when they seem to run counter to prevailing social norms. Consider the case of social service workers who would rather be assigned to child abuse than to child neglect cases. Although child abuse is a particularly unattractive crime the anomaly appears to be explained by the greater likelihood that child abuse cases will respond to intervention, while the typically passive child neglector is less likely to respond to social workers' assistance.[27] It would appear that clientele segmentation is usually consistent with prevailing social norms, but it is not wholly explained by them.

Third, various aspects of the ways in which street-level bureaucrats receive information about their work contribute to conceptual modifications of the clientele. Illustrative validation, self-fulfilling prophecies, rationalizations that excuse failure, and selective retention of information tend to confirm rather than disconfirm workers' attitudes about clients.

Finally, street-level bureaucrats work in a milieu in which their co-workers have similar needs to segment the client population. Thus attitudes prejudicial or beneficial to certain clients are likely to reverberate among, rather than be contradicted by, other workers.

Street-level bureaucrats have a need to modify their conceptions of clients quite apart from but usually consistent with the prejudices of the general society. And they work in a structure that tends to confirm the validity of their biases. The general argument of this section, based on observations that street-level bureaucrats consistently introduce unsanctioned biases into client processing, suggests that it would be difficult to eliminate client differentiation without changing the structure of work for which these biases are functional.

This is not to say that any particular bias is necessary to cope with the work. No doubt classes of clients may be treated in markedly different ways if administrators pay enough attention to specific behavior of workers. But without changes in the work structure one ought to expect that biases will soon develop in other areas, or that the old biases will soon emerge in new forms in the absence of considerable vigilance.

PART IV

THE FUTURE OF
STREET-LEVEL
BUREAUCRACY

CHAPTER 11

The Assault on Human Services:

Bureaucratic Control,

Accountability,

and the Fiscal Crisis

This chapter examines the current application of administrative measures to secure accountability among street-level bureaucrats. I argue that bureaucratic accountability is virtually impossible to achieve among lower-level workers who exercise high degrees of discretion, at least where qualitative aspects of the work are involved. Nonetheless, public managers are pressured to secure or improve workers' accountability through manipulation of incentives and other aspects of job structure immediately available to them. When considered along with other objectives public managers seek, the results may not simply be ineffective but may also lead to an erosion of service quality.

Current perceptions of fiscal crisis heighten concerns for bureaucratic accountability. State and local politicians seeking to cut or constrain budgets must look to street-level bureaucracies if they want to reduce public payrolls. As schools, welfare offices, and police departments confront demands for personnel cuts, the issue of accountability arises with urgency. If public workers cannot demonstrate accountability, all the more reason to slash their numbers. And if their numbers are reduced, all the more reason that politicians seek ways to hold the remainder accountable so as to assure clients and the public that essential government tasks will continue to be performed responsibly.

Accountability is the link between bureaucracy and democracy. Modern democracy depends on the accountability of bureaucracies to carry out declared policy and otherwise administer the ongoing structures of governmentally determined opportunity and regulation. If this is the case, accountability must mean more than simply having to answer to a superior, or expecting to be called to account for one's actions. This is because these definitions leave open precisely what is at issue: whether there is any reliable relationship between what superiors seek and what subordinates do.

Taking a different tack, I propose that people should be considered accountable when there is a high probability that they will be responsive to legitimate authority or influence. This definition of accountability directs attention to two important aspects of the concept. First, accountability is a relationship between people or groups. One is always accountable to *someone,* accountability is not abstract. Although the term is sometimes used loosely confusion results unless we specify both parties in the accountability relationship.[1]

Second, accountability refers to patterns of behavior. Only if a pattern of behavior exists can predictability, and therefore accountability, exist. In practical terms this means that efforts to change or improve accountability cannot succeed unless patterns of behavior change or improve. For example, medical and police review boards do not increase accountability unless general relationships with citizens or superiors change. This is no more than saying that laws are only effective if they not only punish transgressions but also deter illegal behavior.

From this perspective attempts to increase accountability through administrative controls may be seen as efforts to increase the congruence between worker behavior and the policies of agency executives through the use of sanctions and incentives available to the organization. Manipulation of administrative controls is not the only way to secure accountability. Recent efforts and speculation have also focused on improving accountability to consumers by recreating the conditions of a market (for example, voucher proposals), to the public by changing the structure of government programs (for example, school decentralization), and to the law by seeking judicial relief. Some emphasis has also been placed recently on improving accountability to professional norms by enhancing employees' status and training. Yet of all these efforts to obtain *bureaucratic accountability* represent the range of actions available in the short run to people who manage public agencies. Whatever theoretical advantages exist in other approaches, efforts to obtain bureaucratic accountability will have the greatest immediate impact on workers and clients alike.

To utilize organizational incentives and sanctions, at least the following conditions must prevail. These conditions are the prerequisites of a bureaucratic accountability *policy*.

1. Agencies must know what they want workers to do. Where the objectives are multiple and conflicting, agencies must be able to rank their preferences.
2. Agencies must know how to measure workers performance.
3. Agencies must be able to compare workers to one another to establish a standard for judgment.
4. Agencies must have incentives and sanctions capable of disciplining workers. They must be able to prevail over other incentives and sanctions that may operate.

The preconditions of an accountability policy may exist in many bureaucratic contexts, but they do not apply where street-level bureaucrats are concerned. Efforts to improve bureaucratic accountability policies in these contexts may undermine rather than enhance service quality and may systematically *decrease* service quality when certain conditions of public bureaucracy prevail.

The essence of street-level bureaucracies is that they require people to make decisions about other people. Street-level bureaucrats have discretion because the nature of service provision calls for human judgment that cannot be programmed and for which machines cannot substitute. Street-level bureaucrats have responsibility for making unique and fully appropriate responses to individual clients and their situations. It is the nature of what we call human services that the unique aspects of people and their situations will be apprehended by public service workers and translated into courses of action responsive to each case within (more or less broad) limits imposed by their agencies. They will not, in fact, dispose of every case in unique fashion. The limitations on possible responses are often circumscribed, for example, by the prevailing statutory provisions of the law or the categories of services to which recipients can be assigned. However, street-level bureaucrats still have the responsibility *at least to be open to the possibility* that each client presents special circumstances and opportunities that may require fresh thinking and flexible action.

If this is the case, street-level bureaucrats must irreducibly be accountable to the client and to an appropriate response to the client's situation and circumstances. These considerations cannot sensibly be translated into authoritative agency guidelines, although it is on behalf of their agencies that street-level bureaucrats are accountable to clients. It is a contradiction in terms to say that the worker should be accountable to respond to each client in the unique fashion appropriate to the presenting case. For no accountability can exist if the agency does not know what response it prefers, and it cannot assert a preferred response if each worker should be open to the possibility that unique and fresh responses are appropriate. It is more useful to suggest that street-level bureaucrats are ordinarily expected to be accountable to two sources of influence—agency preferences *and* clients' claims.[2]

There are other sources for the assertion that street-level bureaucrats are ordinarily expected to be accountable to clients in possible conflict with the agencies for which they work. The most important of these is that most street-level bureaucrats are professionals or they work in occupations aspiring to professional status. In either case a fundamental expectation attached to the job is that client needs are primary and that the extension of public trust depends upon accountability to people as individuals when they are encountered in the course of work. Social workers, teachers, and, of course, doctors and lawyers, are expected to respond to the individual and the presenting situation, however strongly their work situations mitigate against flexible responses.

This is a great strength and also a great weakness of the public services. It provides a measure of responsiveness to clients when the organization of bureaucratic service tends toward neglect or rigidity. But by virtue of providing another focus of accountability it also means that street-level bureaucrats are less controllable.

Holding Workers to Agency Objectives

Despite the dual focus of accountability inherent in the street-level bureaucrats' roles, public managers are drawn to making street-level bureaucrats more accountable by reducing their discretion and constraining their alternatives. They write manuals to cover contingencies. They audit the performance of workers to provide retrospective sanctions in anticipation of which it is hoped future behavior will be modified. They insist workers specify objectives in the hopes that accountability can be more effectively monitored.

These management tools at times may be effective in controlling workers. Manuals specifying proper procedures may help standardize responses and provide instruction. Performance audits may create greater awareness that management is observing performance, and may thus lead workers to take greater care. Specifying objectives is always likely to be instructive and it directs workers' attention to the relationship between the available resources and the goals they are trying to achieve.[3]

However, street-level bureaucrats may subvert efforts to control them more effectively in the name of accountability. In these and other examples of attempts to increase control it is relatively easy for workers to tailor their behavior to avoid accountability. For one thing, they are likely to be the source of information management receives concerning their performance. They are fully able to provide information about the presenting situation that makes the action taken appear to be responsive to the original problem when it may not have been. This is less blatant falsification than it is auspicious shading of the truth and sincere rationalization.

It is extremely difficult for management to contradict workers' reports for several reasons. A critical piece of information is the state of mind of the worker and his or her analysis of the presenting situation. Since street-level decisions are made in private it is extremely difficult to second-guess workers, since the second-guessers are not at hand to evaluate the intangible factors that may have contributed to the original judgment. For this reason, the records kept by street-level bureaucrats are almost never complete or adequate to the task of post hoc auditing, and when records are kept, they are written sketchily and defensively to guard against later adverse scrutiny.[4]

Record keeping can help insure that procedures are followed (since falsification is normally not the issue). Health practitioners can be made to run certain tests, social workers to ask certain questions, police officers to follow certain procedures. But the records cannot force accountability on the appropriateness of the actions to the presenting situation.

Another major difficulty with obtaining accountability through management control arises because of the dependence of street-level bureaucracies on their workers. Since the services delivered by schools, police departments, or legal services offices fundamentally consist of the actions of teachers, police officers, and lawyers, these agencies are constrained from controlling workers too much, particularly in challenging their performance, for fear of generating opposition to management policies and diminishing accountability even further. The weakness of management incentives to sanction negative performance contributes to a climate in which vigorous challenges to street-level bureaucrats' autonomy in decision making is presumed to have possible negative net consequences for service delivery, by destroying morale and inhibiting worker initiative.[5]

Are there negative aspects to management control efforts, or are these efforts simply generally ineffective? There are several respects in which control practices can actively subvert service quality.

First, specification of methods of client treatment under the guise of obtaining accountability may actually result in reductions in client services. There is often a thin line between inducing workers to better conform to agency policies and inducing workers to be open to fewer options and opportunities for clients. For example, during the Nixon Administration the Department of Health, Education, and Welfare attempted to increase welfare employees' accountability by auditing their error rate in accepting clients for welfare. This policy reduced services by providing incentives for welfare workers only to reduce errors that favored clients. Federal guidelines did not then call for reducing error rates for the potential welfare population as a whole. If it had done so the applications of all welfare applicants would have been audited, both those accepted and those rejected. Scrutiny of welfare workers' decisions strictly in terms of whether or not they were too lenient amounts to narrowing the role of welfare workers, reducing their accountability to clients and to professional standards of conduct.

Second, supervision of subordinates with broad discretion and responsibilities requires assertions of priorities in attempting to increase accountability. Police departments may scrutinize traffic tickets, vice arrests, or interracial encounters between police and citizens. But they cannot meaningfully hold officers accountable for everything all the time. If everything is scrutinized, nothing is scrutinized. Thus efforts to control street-level bureaucrats not only affect those areas that are management targets, but they also affect those areas that are not the focus of management efforts, since by implication those efforts will not come up for surveillance. Efforts to increase accountability in some areas may come to be regarded as the only areas in which accountability will be sought and behavior scrutinized.

Third, many management control efforts provide a veneer of accountability without in fact constraining behavior very much. Management control systems have symbolic value, providing concerned publics with reassurances that employees are accountable even when they are not. Introduction of management systems at least temporarily permits agencies to deflect criticisms as citizens find it very difficult to challenge the emperor who officials say is fully clothed, appearances and personal experiences to the contrary notwithstanding. [6]

GOAL CLARIFICATION

One of the conspicuous features of many public services is the ambiguity and multiplicity of objectives. How can accountability be achieved, ask the critics, if public officials are unclear about their objectives? The desirability of clarifying (and then putting into operation) agency objectives to increase accountability stems from the force of this observation and recognition that a bureaucratic accountability policy requires specification of objectives (as suggested above).

Surely it is desirable to clarify objectives if they are needlessly and irrelevantly fuzzy or contradictory. Surely it is easier to run an effective agency if you know what you are supposed to be doing. However, while agency goals may be unclear or contradictory for reasons of neglect and historical inertia, they may also be unclear or contradictory because they reflect the contradictory impulses of the society the agency serves. Schools attempt to instruct, but they also inculcate attitudes toward social behavior and citizenship. They do this not because educators are fuzzy but because both these objectives are favored by parents (and because there is no convincing case that they are mutually incompatible). Criminal justice institutions are oriented toward punishment and rehabilitation not because judges and corrections officials are simpleminded but because the society has impulses toward reforming as well as deterring criminals.

The public service areas of education, corrections, and welfare in recent years have all been subject to efforts to increase accountability through goal clarification. Educators have sought to concentrate on reading to the exclusion of other educational objectives; corrections analysts have sought to build up the role of punishment and make it more certain at the expense of emphasis on rehabilitation; welfare reformers have successfully separated decisions on income support from social service provision. The dilemma for accountability is to know when goal clarification is desirable because continued ambivalence and contradiction are unproductive, and when it will result in a reduction in the scope and mission of public services. The problem of goal ambiguity has contributed to the discrediting of institutions providing services in social work, corrections, and mental health, and to the dismantling of many programs to provide assistance in these areas. But it requires the most serious inquiry to determine the long-term implications of requiring the former and potential clients of these institutions to have recourse exclusively to noninstitutional community and personal resources.

PERFORMANCE MEASURES

The development of performance measures is critical to a bureaucratic accountability policy. Administrators make great efforts to develop performance measures in order to control employees' behavior.

There is no question that public services can be enhanced through development of valid performance measures. In such cases public service workers can be held accountable for producing results in the same way that machine operators can be charged with producing a certain volume of output in a given period of time. However, public service workers, like machine operators, must also be assessed for quality control, since producing a volume of items is meaningless without consideration of the standard maintained in production. Here, paradoxically the search for performance measures can interfere with the quality of public service.

In theory quantitative measures of performance should be fairly easy to obtain and consent on their validity reasonably uncontroversial. This is not always the case in street-level bureaucracies, however, for several reasons.

First, street-level bureaucrats will concentrate on the activities measured. If police officers are assessed on traffic ticketing or vice arrests, activity in these areas will increase. This is entirely predictable when we recognize that police have control over their search activities and can choose to concentrate on one dimension of their job or another. By virtue of simply putting attention on some tasks over others street-level bureaucrats can improve their performance on most quantitative measures managers introduce. If welfare workers are assessed on their error rate, the error rate will go down because workers pay more attention to it. If teachers are assessed or even remotely evaluated on the proportion of their charges who pass year-end examinations, more will pass as teachers "teach the test." This is neither surprising nor in itself deplorable, but simply highly probable. Whenever management undertakes to concentrate on measuring a dimension of performance workers correctly accept this as a signal of management priority. A problem is created, however, when the measure induces workers to reduce attention to other aspects of their jobs and when there is no control on the quality of work produced.[7]

Relatedly, street-level bureaucrats will make choices and exercise discretion by directing their activities in ways that will improve their performance scores. This phenomenon did not begin and end with Peter Blau's classic report of the employment counselors who, when assessed in terms of successful placement ratios rather than the case load they carried, made greater efforts for easy-to-place clients at the expense of more difficult cases.[8] The phenomenon of "creaming" in recruiting for social programs has similar dynamics. Workers select for their programs clients likely to do well in them, in order to improve the appearance of success. As James D. Thompson says, "[W]here work loads exceed capacity and the individual has options, he is tempted to select tasks which promise to enhance his scores on assessment criteria."[9] This generalization obtains for individuals and also for the work units of which they are a part.

Fraud and deception can also intrude into performance measurement. The Washington, D.C. police took pride in their record of reducing serious crimes until a study revealed that police officers were reporting that most burglaries involved items valued at less than fifty dollars. Significantly, the definition of a serious (that is, felonious) burglary is defined in part as involving the theft of over fifty dollars in value.[10] The incentives to under-report the value of items in burglaries are the same as those that induced New York City sanitation men to water their garbage so their trucks would weigh the expected amount when they appeared at the landfill site, even though the drivers had not completed their runs.

It may be claimed that these problems—inducing behavior to conform to the measure, neglecting other responsibilities, and inauthentically performing according to the measured standards—are simply difficulties that skilled management experts can overcome. In particular, management often seeks measures of resource deployment, depending on the inference that the provision of resources is a surrogate for (and, to be sure, a prerequisite to) service delivery. This inference is acceptable when the qualitative issue is resource deployment, as in the case of police dispatch, ambulance response time, and neighborhood shift allocations in sanitation services.[11]

The difficulty arises in the inference that resource deployment of a particular sort bears a relationship to the quality of service delivery. For example, case-load activity might be used as a quantitative measure of performance, since it indicates formal relationships between street-level bureaucrats and clients. Class size indicates associations between teachers and children. Court dispositions indicate relationships between defendants and judicial personnel. But in all these instances there may be inverse relationships between the quality of street-level bureaucrats' involvement and the number of clients they process. If simply having people processed or having them attached to public service workers were the issue, these measures would bear a meaningful relationship to desired service. But our expectations of these public services are different. It is not sufficient that people are assigned a social worker, sit in a classroom, or have their cases heard. We also expect that they will be processed with a degree of care, with attention to their circumstances and potential. Thus there may be no relationship, or an inverse relationship, between quantitative indicators of service and service quality.

The more discretion is part of the bureaucratic role, the less one can infer

167

that quantitative indicators bear relationship to service quality. Even in such an apparently straightforward measure as the number of arrests made by police officers or the number of people treated in emergency rooms, we have no idea whether the arrests were made with care or that treatment met appropriate standards. Sophisticated management specialists acknowledge the problems of inferring quality from quantitative indicators.[12] But this does not prevent them from using quantitative measures as surrogates for service quality or ignoring the problems of inference in their utilization.[13]

Of course the reason quantitative measures are used so often is that actual performance is virtually impossible to measure. It is perhaps useful to put this quite bluntly. We cannot measure the quality of street-level bureaucrats' performances, particularly in terms of the most important aspects of their jobs. Aspects of performance can be measured and assessed, and many surrogates for performance measures can be developed with important implications as management tools. But the most important dimensions of service performance defy calibration.

Measures of performance quality are elusive for reasons analogous to the difficulty in circumscribing street-level bureaucrats' discretion. If clients or presenting cases should be treated as if they might present unique situations, then it is impossible to reduce responses to sets of appropriate and previously indicated reactions. To put it another way, the more street-level bureaucrats are supposed to act with discretion, and the broader the areas of discretionary treatment, the more difficult it is to develop performance measures. If we are not agreed as to what comprises good teaching, how can we measure it? If we are not willing to deprive police officers of discretion because on the street they need to be able to make judgments based on an appraisal of the total situation, how can we propose measures of quality arrests and interventions with citizens? If every client should be treated as if he or she may require responses tailored to the individual, how can we specify the requirements of a good interview?

It may be argued that we may still assess service quality by developing outcome indicators. But here similar questions arise. First, service quality measures are meaningless without adequate controls to assess levels of difficulty. The same outcome may have required radically different service because of the difficulties presented. For example, the same student achievement levels might represent excellent work on the part of a teacher of students with learning difficulties and poor work on the part of a teacher with bright and motivated students.

Without controls there can be no comparability of units of analysis, unless the often unwarranted assumption is made that levels of difficulty are equal.

Thus teachers resist being measured by the progress of their pupils unless adequate provision is made to control for their students' previous levels of achievement (and, more important) for their students' capacity to learn. Thus police officers would object to utilizing arrests per capita per available officer as measure of performance unless controls were introduced for the propensity of criminal behavior in the district. Comparing districts by outcome tends to be useless because of the inadequacy of such controls.

Some advocate that measures such as these be deployed in order to discover deviations from normal practice, so that workers who deviate from the norm can be brought into line. These proposals have some merit, but here the problem is that unless one is confident that the best workers or districts are doing a good job, such comparisons may simply institutionalize mediocrity.

Recent attention has also focused on utilizing surveys of client satisfaction to obtain information on workers' performance. Resistance to such surveys arises out of professional skepticism that performance that pleases clients may not be related to high-quality practice. The popular teacher may not be the most effective instructor; a popular judge may not be the fairest judge. Still, in a comprehensive assessment program, client satisfaction surveys have their place if client satisfaction is indeed deemed desirable (as it usually is).

Street-level bureaucrats' interactions with clients tend to take place in private or beyond the scrutiny of supervisors. Interviews are held in private offices and under norms of confidentiality. Teaching is done in classrooms that principals and supervisors do not normally enter; if they do, they provide notice so that the teaching, like a performance, may be changed by the presence of an audience. Police officers, although they do take action in public, normally do so without observation by other officers or supervisors. The exception is the officer's partner, who is compelled by police norms to shield his partner from criticism. Of the street-level bureaucrats we have studied only judges tend to make their important decisions in public.

This fact provides a barrier to an important potential source of performance measurement. It might be possible for street-level bureaucrats to scrutinize each others' work and provide assessments of quality. But given the structure of these agencies such scrutiny would be highly obtrusive in relations between workers and clients and very costly if engaged in on a widespread basis. Thus public service agencies rarely engage in direct observation of their line workers, but depend upon the written record supplied by their workers (the reliability of which was discussed earlier).

Accountability and Productivity

Thus far I have focused discussion on some of the major difficulties in developing an administrative accountability policy. But are there any negative effects of such policies? For example, what is the harm of attempting to develop performance measures? It may be difficult to measure performance, but perhaps we are simply at the beginning of the development of a management tool. Perhaps the current measures of performance are not entirely adequate, but they may have their uses, and they may be increasingly refined.

This is the rhetoric of those who are committed to achieving bureaucratic accountability and recognize the inadequacy of current measures, but who apparently have faith that their approach is ultimately correct.[14] This line of discussion would have us believe that there are some benefits to current efforts to develop accountability through improved performance measurement, that these benefits are likely to increase, and that there are no significant costs. Surely management benefits from operationalizing and attempting to develop measures of worker performance. Even if the preferred behavior cannot be adequately measured, performance measurement and monitoring can signal workers powerfully concerning which aspects of performance are most salient.

However, in the current period bureaucratic accountability policies also have negative consequences because of the competing demands on, and of, administrators. Currently, public agencies are under enormous pressures to minimize costs and increase productivity. They are under pressure to reduce government expenditures or keep them from rising. They are under pressure to increase productivity in order to maintain services, or claim that they are maintaining them, in the face of financial stringency. And they are under pressure to increase productivity in order to justify employee pay increases, which they are under particular pressure to grant because of the impact of inflation on wages. (The only way to stabilize government budgets when services cannot be reduced beyond a certain level and costs are rising is to increase the productivity of the present work force. Organized workers argue that they have no incentive to increase productivity unless they can share in the gains made because they work harder and cooperate with the reorganization of work often entailed by productivity reforms.)[15]

Productivity in the public sector summarizes the relationship between the utilization of resources and the resulting public services product. Productivity may improve in three ways: when costs remain the same while public services increase; when costs decline while services remain the same; or when costs increase but services increase still more. Schematically, there are two dimensions to public services implied here—one qualitative, the other quantitative. If the quantity increases or remains the same, but services have declined qualitatively, productivity increases have not necessarily taken place.[16] If more garbage is picked up on the streets without increasing the crews, but half of it is strewn back on the streets, productivity has not increased. The debasement of service is what infuriated New Yorkers when transit workers were given an increase in pay based upon alleged gains in productivity. It appeared, however, that the Transit Authority had been able to provide services with fewer personnel only by increasing the time between trains and reducing the number of cars in operation.[17] In this view the transit workers had been falsely credited with improved productivity.

These are the essential elements of productivity. In practice, however, debasement of services is rarely taken into account, although the problem is given lip service by productivity theorists. This may be true for several reasons. First, if the quality of service is difficult to measure, so is reduction in service quality difficult to measure. Second, there are many ways to save money by eroding the quality of service without appearing to do so. They include offering services on a group rather than an individual basis, substituting paraprofessionals, often paid from other sources, for regular staff, and, conversely, forcing professionals to handle clerical and other routine chores, reducing the time they have to interact with their clients.[18] Additionally, street-level bureaucrats can narrow the range of situations in which they will act. Examples include legal services offices that decide to take only emergency cases, police departments that decide to neglect selected infractions, and schools that offer reduced programs. Each of these techniques permit managers to give the appearance of maintaining services while reducing costs.

Third, in the current period pressures experienced by public managers to reduce the budget and improve productivity are pressing and general, while the constituency for maintaining service quality is disorganized, weak, or nonexistent. Only clients experience service quality reduction, and they are severely constrained in comparing their experiences with others and organizing collectively to oppose service quality debasement. Ironically, the greatest opponents of service quality debasement are street-level bureaucrats themselves. For them debasement often means harder work, less job satisfaction, and greater individual problems with clients. Yet they are cross-pressured by the interest they have in helping their agencies appear financially responsible and by their collusion with public officials to share financially in productivity increases.

But there is more to the debasement of public services than pressures and interests. A large part of the problem stems from the orientation toward measurement, precision, and scientific management itself. Consider the formula *productivity = service quantity and quality/cost.* Two of the determinants of productivity, service quantity and cost, are easy to measure; the third, service quality, is virtually impossible to measure. Managers under pressure to improve productivity are likely to try to cut personnel or obtain more work from existing personnel because these are the terms of the equation for which measures are available and which managers can manipulate. Thus staffs are reduced to bare bones without reduction in responsibilities. Thus staffs are asked to do more without increases in personnel.[19]

Street-Level Bureaucrats and the Fiscal Crisis

There is always an implicit tension between resource constraints and the inexorable demands for public service. However, this tension is rarely manifest politically. The budgets (and employment rolls) of street-level bureaucracies rise not only with increases in population to be served, but also with higher standards of what citizens are entitled to, a decline in the availability of comparable private services, and the perceived need for more effective and improved agencies of social control, coercive or manipulative. The impulses to increase expenditures in these areas rarely have been challenged in terms of resource constraints. In the period since World War II federal government subsidies to state and local public services have postponed or softened the confrontation between revenues and expenditures in areas such as public health, education, police, and welfare. However, the current period, characterized as a fiscal crisis among state and local governments, forces recognition of the relationship between what people get from government and what jurisdictions are willing to pay.

At best the term "fiscal crisis" is reserved for situations in which financial agreements and long-standing patterns of practice can no longer be honored, as when a political jurisdiction cannot meet its payroll or honor its commitments to lenders. But the term is also used much more loosely to mobilize people to believe that there is something wrong or that there is a problem associated with current and projected expenditures relative to available revenues and other income. If political and economic elites are successful in promulgating a sense of crisis they are able to make manifest and set the terms of confrontation between governmental expenditures and income. If in other times social services, for example, grew in response to perceived societal needs, in a fiscal crisis the imperatives for service development are subordinated to the demands of perceived revenue limitations.[20]

Like other political confrontations, the management of fiscal crises has redistributive consequences. The costs of responding to the needs of expenditure constraints do not fall evenly or randomly on the population as a whole, but rather affect different segments of the population differentially. The fiscal crises of the cities provide a focus and an apparently benign rationale for attacking and injuring the provision of public services. And they demonstrate the vulnerability to attack of high levels of public service quality.

The fiscal crisis of the cities affects the quality of service delivery in two significant ways. First, services are rationed in various ways, maintaining the appearance of service while reducing and debasing it in practice. This is not to say that legitimate savings cannot be realized by eliminating "real" waste and duplication that may exist.[21] However, in city administration these "real" savings tend to be concentrated in areas in which questions of resource deployment are paramount, not in areas in which the provision and nurturing of interactions with street-level bureaucrats is at issue. It is conspicuous, for example, that when administrators take pride in productivity savings it is in the sanitation department that the greatest successes are often realized. In police departments dispatch (deployment), not interactions with citizens, is the area of concentration in productivity campaigns. Most street-level bureaucracies have to contend with impulses to reduce the amount of time workers spend with clients, not the reverse.

For public officials the problem of managing the fiscal crisis consists of reducing expenditures while minimizing the apparent impact of the cuts. This is why cuts will initially be said to eliminate waste and duplication whether or not waste exists or duplication takes place. Rationing typically means increasing the costs to clients of seeking services, while maintaining the service shell, or reducing services to decrease potential benefits. Both prospects are likely to lead to lower client demand. Closing neighborhood branch offices while continuing to offer services from a central (downtown) location is a typical technique for achieving this. Reducing the number of telephones or receptionists reduces the number of inquiries. Increasing the response time in investigating a complaint reduces the efficacy of complaining and hence future volume. City agencies often experience decreasing ability to process citizen needs at the same time that they are experimenting with techniques to improve their performance. The public message regarding agency responsiveness becomes mixed, to say the least.

When public managers decide to fight demands for service reduction they say that all waste, duplication, and nonessential services have been cut, and that any further cuts will be in essential services. Their ability to make this claim depends on general public perception of the importance of the agency and public employees' collective capacity to resist. Thus schools can make the claim more effectively than welfare agencies, police departments more effectively than sanitation departments. Cuts in service provision obviously may affect service quality, but is is impossible to determine from public rhetoric where the politics of distributing urban resources to public employees ends and injury to service delivery begins.

A second dimension of response to the fiscal crisis is personnel reductions. Personnel practices are particularly important because salaries comprise the bulk of urban budgets; thus savings must be sought in the area of public employment.

Personnel practices in the fiscal crisis tend to follow a path of severity. Administrators first make it more difficult for agencies to replace workers who leave. Next administrators suspend hiring, then slow wage increases or freeze wages, then begin to lay off workers. All of these steps have implications for service provision but the most important point is that each of these steps reflects increasing penalties to public employees, regardless of the implications for clients. Priorities are set by imperatives of labor-management relations, not by the needs of clients for service provision.

Increasing the difficulty of replacing workers and freezing employee rolls represent managers' efforts to realize savings through attrition. They attempt to reduce personnel rolls by not replacing those people who retire or otherwise leave their jobs. Since in normal circumstances the rate of exit in almost any line of work is substantial, a significant reduction in employment can be realized over several years without firing anyone. Realizing savings through attrition accomodates public managers' needs to keep peace with organized public employees, but it creates substantial costs for service provision above and beyond the obvious reduction in force. Since workers do not retire or otherwise leave their jobs in response to agency priorities, the incidence of turnover is unevenly distributed in the work force. This means that important gaps in service provision occur. Workers important to the operation of a particular office, or those who possess critical skills, may be the ones to quit rather than the most marginal employees. If the critical positions they vacate are left unfilled, the injury to service provision is obvious. But even if they are filled by employees who remain they are unlikely to be filled well.

In the street-level bureaucracies with a high level of job specialization the vacancies will be filled by employees who lack the required skills or resources. Fifth-grade teachers will be assigned to kindergarten classes, and physical education instructors will become math teachers when there are excesses of the former and need for the latter. But even in street-level bureaucracies with low levels of specialization it will be difficult to fill the vacancies adequately. Police departments, for example, assign desk officers to active patrol in order to maintain the patrol force when additional officers cannot be hired. But those officers assigned to desk jobs may be more suitable for sedentary positions than the officers they replace. Moreover, except for retirees the people who leave public service work in the fiscal crisis will tend to be the more employable, so that the work force at the same time becomes mediocre through attrition.

The squeeze of the fiscal crisis is particularly tight because in many ways it reflects national rather than local conditions. If a city were financially strapped in an otherwise healthy economy, young public employees would be able to find work in other locations. However, all governments more or less experience pressure to hold the line on costs at the same time, since the fiscal crisis is significantly a function of national economic and political trends. Thus no longer are there jobs waiting for young teachers or social workers in the suburbs, or California, or elsewhere, as in the past.

Street-level bureaucrats' performance is not tied directly to wage incentives. Promotions and raises, when they are given out, do not depend so much on job performance as on personal relations, additional outside training, work-load handling, and other factors unrelated to client servicing. Moreover, promotions to positions of greater responsibility are rare, since the job hierarchies in most street-level bureaucracies schematically resemble relatively flat pyramids, with existing jobs undifferentiated at the bottom of the scale. When most teachers can look forward only to being teachers, most police officers only to being police officers, incentives to high-quality service may flag unless specially encouraged.[22]

For these reasons it is probably incorrect to argue that wage freezes directly affect workers' motivation. Their impact is likely to be somewhat different. First, wage freezes and slowdowns affect the likelihood that workers will stay in their jobs, and they force people out of jobs without firing them. Again this affects the distribution of age and skills in street-level bureaucracies. Older workers will stay to protect and build pension benefits. Younger workers will be more likely to leave public employment, somewhat tempered by the availability of jobs elsewhere.

In periods of high inflation wage freezes effectively reduce workers' real income as well as their income relative to workers in other sectors. The feelings of deprivation that may result from diminishing workers' income in these ways are quite different from attitudes toward wages that street-level bureaucrats may have had in other periods. While wages may not play a major role in creating incentives to performance, effectively reducing wages may have a significant impact on street-level bureaucrats' attitudes toward their jobs.

Street-level bureaucrats may be accountable to managers and clients, as mentioned above. But they are accountable to clients *on behalf of their agencies and the public purposes they represent.* To reduce workers' wages is to shred these bonds of accountability by bringing to the surface aspects of the wage relationship that otherwise remain obscured by the claims and ideology of professional status and attitudes. People who accept the relatively fixed civil-service formulas for wage increases will not easily accept receiving less than they did receive, particularly as the motivation for street-level work leads some employees to regard their work as voluntaristic to some degree, that is, undercompensated to begin with. As wages are effectively reduced street-level bureaucrats may be expected to look more to their benefits and remuneration and less to the service dimensions of their job.

Decruitment practices, of which firing workers is the most drastic, have similar implications.[23] When workers are not replaced their responsibilities are distributed among those who remain, usually without reducing the responsibilities they already have. Increasing the responsibilities of other staff without increased compensation or work resources is the white collar equivalent of the onerous assembly line speedup.

In this connection consider the modest complaint of a New York City school teacher over staff reductions, increased responsibilities, and reduced resources.

I have never been quite sure what ["increased productivity"] means exactly. However, if it means what I think it means, they would like to see us work harder than we ever did before. If this is so, then all the proponents of "increased productivity" will be delighted to know that we are doing remarkably well in that department.

For example, we have official classes of 45 or more youngsters and ten minutes in which to take attendance, read circulars, distribute notices, make reports (in duplicate yet), answer questions, etc. In many cases we have classes which have rosters of

49 or more children with 30 chairs in the room or typing classes of 47 with 32 type-writers. Add to this emergency coverages of classes, cafeteria patrol or other building assignments, program problems, shortage of supplies and equipment and much more—all of this with reduced staff—not to mention the mounds of work we take home with us. The pressures under which we work can never be understood by any-one who is not involved in day-to-day school activity. Yes, we have indeed increased productivity, but in so doing we have decreased our effectiveness as human beings to our students, our families and ourselves.[24]

Or consider the impact of the budget freeze on human services in Mas-sachusetts, when staff attrition resulted in greater physical and chemical re-straint of mental patients in state institutions. As "hundreds and hundreds of staff quit their jobs, unable to cope with the conditions and trauma imposed by a freeze which imperiled their physical safety and adequate care for resi-dents for whom they bore responsibility,"[25] programs to make patients more self-sufficient were entirely abandoned and the institutions went from care facilities to "warehouses" for the mentally disabled.

When workers are fired, managers also abridge the implicit contract with employees by bringing to the surface the reality of job insecurity in what previously had seemed secure employment. Again, those who remain carry the work load of those who were fired. While some increased and heroic ef-forts may be forthcoming it is equally likely that work will be processed in ways which reduce the amount and quality of time street-level bureaucrats can spend with clients.[26]

Again, this decruitment does not take place according to calculations of impact on service, but in response to the ethics of seniority. For example, different public agencies are typically asked to reduce their forces by a cer-tain fixed percentage. Politicians do not want to choose between services and so establish a decision rule for work-force reduction. Street-level bureau-cracies that do choose between units or services undermine the strategic implications of their choices by providing those with seniority the chance to "bump" less senior employees from their positions in sectors of the service that are untouched by the budget cuts.

For some enterprises reductions in personnel rolls can be cleansing but public agencies cannot take advantage of opportunities to eliminate ineffec-tive workers. Particularly affected by decruitment are younger workers and those who have been recently hired, often members of minority groups. It is difficult to specify the impact of decruitment precisely but we can see that it falls unevenly on those with more recent training and new ideas and those with fresh perspectives. It falls less heavily on those with more experience, an arguable benefit.[27]

These observations concerning reductions in work force should not lead us to conclude that street-level bureaucracies should be the size they are, or larger, or that they should never be smaller than they presently are. The fact is that we know very little about the proper size of street-level service delivery units. A public school deprived of its specialists might actually serve students better by throwing regular teachers back on their own resources. The important point is that when public bureaucracies are growing, jobs usually are created in response to perceived needs, and workers are hired with reference to credentials and apparent qualifications. But when they are forced to shrink, public bureaucracies rarely remove workers in response to decisions concerning the most effective utilization of reduced available resources.

Who speaks for service quality in the era of performance measurement, productivity campaigns, and fiscal crisis? Public managers, with better control over costs and resource deployment than over the quality of the product, sacrifice service quality in the name of efficiency and productivity. Street-level bureaucrats more and more are reduced to production units whose work is speeded up and whose managers appear content to sacrifice quality in order to maintain volume. In the process the conditions of work are eroded and workers are unable to utilize many of the coping mechanisms and attitudes that helped sustain their jobs under difficult conditions in earlier periods. Thus, the fiscal crisis raises the salience of the wage relationship and diminishes the salience of service. This is ironic since the wage and benefit demands of organized public employees have been widely regarded as one of the primary causes of the fiscal crisis in the first place.

The federal role in this aspect of the fiscal crisis is worth noting. Funds available through counter-cyclical revenue sharing and the Comprehensive Employment and Training Act (CETA) underwrote city payrolls for several years. This helped many cities avoid confronting the enormity of their financial obligations to street-level bureaucrats. However, current policies based on the view that the federal role in managing the urban fiscal crisis is less important than limiting the federal budget threaten all at once to reveal the incapacity of cities to retain public employees. Restricting CETA funds to the chronically unemployed may be sound manpower policy, but it threatens to throw cities' skilled, middle-class, service-providing agencies into disarray.

This chapter has drawn attention to the contributions of bureaucratic accountability policies to exacerbating problems of the quality of service delivery. But there is more. Such policies set the stage for future management of service delivery and future conceptions of the role of human services. If current administrative practices erode workers' sense of responsibility for clients, then establishing nonmanipulative, responsive worker/client relationships will be that much harder in the future. If qualitative aspects of service delivery are neglected, cost reductions and volume receive more attention as workers and managers accommodate their behavior to agency signals of priorities. This contributes to the self-fulfilling prophecy of the ineffectiveness and ultimate irrelevance of social services, even though the human needs for nurturing, protection, support, and assistance remain unanswered. Thus the tones of the fiscal crisis may linger, even if the budgetary alarms of the current period are eventually quieted.

CHAPTER 12

The Broader Context of Bureaucratic Relations

In considering the potential for change in street-level bureaucracies it would be a mistake to restrict analysis to the coping dilemmas and adaptations of service workers, or the patterns of practice that develop among them. The resolution of contradictory tendencies in street-level bureaucracies cannot be understood without examining the role of these public agencies in the society and the ways in which the society impinges on the character of bureaucratic relations. As V. O. Key Jr. has observed: ". . . one of the great functions of the bureaucratic organizations is as a conservator of the values of a culture. In the purposes, procedures, ceremonies, outlook, and habits of the bureaucracy are formalized the traditional cultural values."[1] This observation actively translates into reciprocity between the larger society and the structure of bureaucratic institutions. For street-level bureaucracy it means that these agencies are embedded in a larger system that creates and fortifies working conditions. In turn, street-level bureaucracies help reproduce prevailing relations between individuals and government organizations.[2]

Societies differ in their bureaucratic relations, as they differ in many areas. Even such apparently similar societies as those of the United States and Great Britain exhibit sharp differences in bureaucratic interactions. In the case of police-citizen relations, for example, compared to their British counterparts American police tend to exercise control more informally, and American citizens tend to have less respect for the law, and to expect less considerate treatment from police.[3]

An important consideration in bureaucratic relations of a technologically advanced society is the extent and persistence of different subcultures and classes, particularly as expressed in clients' preparation and readiness for the impersonalism, hierarchy, and institutionalization of bureaucracy.[4] In this connection bureaucrat-client relations in the United States may be said to reinforce and be structured by the American system of persistent and cumulative inequalities experienced by subordinate groups, particularly as this system consigns people to poverty and low expectations of mobility, monopolizes the service function, and grudgingly provides for public services.

In stating this one must go beyond observing that the character of client treatment at the hands of street-level bureaucrats reflects and reinforces social class and racial divisions. While some may be tempted to view the character of U.S. social services as an expression of racism and of attitudes toward the individual in mass society, we cannot conscientiously stop there. This view does not explain the development of such an elaborate service and control apparatus. Nor does it account for the opportunities clients have to redress grievances, find support within the service network, and resist dehumanized services. Nor does it account for or comprehend the wide range of forms and structures affecting clients in street-level bureaucracies throughout the country.

Moreover, asserting that street-level bureaucracies reinforce social cleavages does not begin to account for the *content* of bureaucratic behavior. Coping behaviors and adaptive attitudes may be endemic in organizational life. But this says nothing about the nature of the coping behaviors, or the orientation of adaptive attitudes. Street-level bureaucrats do not fully invent responses to work stresses but instead at least partially reflect the culture in which their agencies are embedded. In other words, responses to work stresses arise out of the work situation, but their content or direction are colored by prevailing cultural assumptions.

In what ways do street-level bureaucracies reflect and perpetuate the values of the larger society? There are at least two respects in which the structure of relationships between workers and clients appears to be derived from the particular character of American society.

First, street-level bureaucracies are affected by the prevailing orientations toward the poor in the United States. These orientations include the deep conviction that poor people at some level are responsible for the conditions in which they find themselves, and that receiving benefits labeled "for the poor" is shameful. These convictions are epitomized in the observation that public programs for poor people are almost always treated in the press as costs to society, not benefits.

These attitudes toward social services for the poor amount to a general stigmatization of poor people. Stigma leads to a general reluctance to join the deviant group in the society on the one hand, and on the other hand provides subtle justification for patterns of practice that result in inadequate service provision. Prevailing attitudes toward the poor permit rationalization of patterns that result in client neglect, which would be more difficult to rationalize if clients were middle class and generally respected. The same may be observed in agencies of training and control. Some lower courts and public schools, for example, develop community reputations for dealing mostly with low-income clients, and they develop patterns of practice that process people less respectfully than similar institutions with middle-class clienteles.

Intersecting with attitudes toward the stigmatized poor are attitudes prevalent in the larger society regarding clients' racial or ethnic backgrounds. Racism also affects the extent to which public employees regard clients as worthy, and it affects the extent to which patterns of practice evolve that distinguish among clients in terms of their racial backgrounds.

Second, the politics of the larger society affect street-level bureaucracies and their clients in the dynamic relationship between the requirements of providing services and their perceived costs. Governmental initiatives for programs of social service and control expand or contract, grow more quickly or more slowly, in part depending upon the relative degree of concern over crisis or control. In periods of social turmoil or widely perceived crisis (the depression of the 1930s, the ghetto revolts of the 1960s, the "Sputnik" crisis in education in the 1950s) service benefits and/or funds for training and control functions increase. In periods of relative quiescence pressures are exerted to return the balance to a ratio of benefits to costs more favorable to costs. Social analysts may disagree on the precise dynamics of the dialectics of expansion and contraction of governmental social service and control policies. But there should be little doubt that public bureaucracies that normally process clients vacillate in their generosity toward client treatment. Street-level bureaucracies are alternately able to treat clients with greater degrees of latitude and forced to restrict options and more narrowly designate benefits.[5]

In the current period street-level bureaucrats are under pressure to develop more restrictive patterns of practice. They are under pressure to increase case loads and to be more formally accountable, and they are generally asked to expand or maintain coverage in the face of static or declining budgets. Talking to any social worker or public-school teacher, one discovers that over time the formal reporting requirements of the job have increased in response to managers' efforts to secure greater control. The opposite may be observed when programs are attempting to attract clients; then st et-level bureaucrats are encouraged to open more widely the categories of possible assistance and to render aid in more open and responsive ways.[6]

It seems apparent that American street-level bureaucracies must be understood as organizational embodiments of contradictory tendencies in American society as a whole. The welfare state calls for and requires social programs to ameliorate the neglect and insecurity of the economic system, to prepare people for roles in the economy, or to manage their deviation from expectations of appropriate behavior.[7] In the ideology of the welfare state humanitarian impulses are coincident with the requirements of system maintenance.

This, of course, begins to explain how people with humanitarian impulses can work for impersonal, paternalistic, or repressive public service agencies. Most people never question that the requirements of the state are congruent with the needs and interests of large numbers of people. Thus, teachers with compassion for children work in brutalizing schools and picture themselves as victimized by the same system that victimizes their pupils. Social workers with compassion for poor people participate in assigning inadequate benefit levels to welfare recipients and wish they could do more.[8]

The legitimacy of the political and economic system depends on the appearance of providing for those who cannot provide for themselves and responding openly and fairly to citizens' claims. Public service workers actively translate this requirement into programs. But government policy is not likely in fact to respond fully to the needs of citizens for at least two reasons relevant to this discussion.[9]

First, there is no agreement as to what those needs are. What it means to "respond fully to citizen needs" is a socially determined concept albeit defined by a process that gives more weight to policy elites than clients. As continuing controversies in such areas as health care, welfare, and legal services reveal, the demands of citizens are open-ended while program costs must be kept within certain bounds. Indeed, the definition of those boundaries is the basic issue in social welfare policy making.

Second, there is a powerful imperative to maintain private responsibility for social needs and to make dependency punishable by welfare, public hospitals, and inner-city schools. Granted that street-level bureaucracies exist outside of the welfare context, and that limitations on program expenditures must be encountered *at some point.* Yet it is not at all clear that the United States inevitably had to develop relatively low social service and benefit levels compared to other advanced industrial countries.[10] In an assessment of income and service provision an independent role should be assigned to a perceived need among policy-making elites to limit benefit and service provisions, allegedly to enhance individual and family self-reliance and to stigmatize the status of worklessness and poverty.

In short, this is a political system that, whatever its current levels of social welfare expenditures, must also symbolically project images of adequate and reasonably comprehensive social welfare programming to taxpayers and middle-class consumers, while in fact it limits support and assistance.[11] Such a system develops mechanisms to maintain legitimacy and deflect criticism that the society does not provide adequately for its citizens. Street-level bureaucrats mediate between citizens and the state in that clients' inability to obtain benefits or services and inequities of distribution may be understood by clients as personal malfeasance of street-level bureaucrats or administrative agency disarray.

The mediation of street-level bureaucrats helps structure the nature of urban conflict in several ways. First, as the deliverers of policy they personally must build into their work life responses to decisions made at the system level. Thus a teacher with a classroom of forty students must develop ways to cope with a high enrollment. Although the teacher did not decide to attempt education with this student-teacher ratio, he or she nonetheless must confront this condition. Parents and children, however, may perceive teachers' coping responses in their own terms and attribute the quantity and quality of educational services to teachers' abilities or their own capacities to utilize teachers' services. They may not look to the systemic decisions that relegate them to large classes, particularly as these decisions are usually screened from the view of the typical parent and student.

Street-level bureaucrats' needs to control their work situations force them to defend themselves and the current arrangements. Agency expectations and occupational norms preclude the excuse that working conditions prevent effective efforts on clients' behalf, despite private recognition that this is the case. This defensiveness separates street-level bureaucrats from their potential allies in improving working conditions for mutual benefit.

Second, the difficulty of controlling street-level bureaucrats is sufficiently understood by clients so that issues of service are translated into issues of controlling workers or holding them accountable for performance. Agencies may deflect potentially significant demands by directing attention to questions of individual service provision, without examining the structural basis for those relationships.

Third, it seems easier (although it actually may be harder) to change workers' behavior or approaches to their jobs than to affect the political system that structures the jobs. Clients and client groups appear to have a better chance to reorient (reeducate?) individual street-level bureaucrats in a single facility or field station than to affect the general patterns of recruitment, budget making, and policy establishment that condition the work. These other aspects of the work structure are determined far away in time and place from the grievances experienced by clients. How much easier it is to meet with workers and discuss changes in routine, procedure, and attitudes than to organize to work with others to change the policy system.

Thus street-level bureaucrats' mediating role functions beyond providing face-to-face contact and facilitating potentially flexible and appropriate responses among lower-level workers. It also helps define problems citizens have in dealing with public service agencies as conflicts associated with lower-level workers.[12]

In addition to absorbing conflict in their buffer roles, street-level bureaucrats in other ways help shape the general attitudes of clients and workers towards public services.[13] First, the structure of street-level practice has an impact on clients' conceptions of their capacity. Street-level bureaucrats' control of clients confirms for clients their dependency and subordination. In turn, this control more generally affects clients' self-respect and self-expectations[14] (see chapter 5).

Second, street-level bureaucracies discourage employees who seek to work as advocates. The process begins when the agencies provide an avenue for people with altruistic orientations to enter the work force. Although job security is a significant attraction, another important element in seeking street-level work is the opportunity to help people. Teachers, social workers, legal aid lawyers, and police officers all enter the work force at least in part with a desire to make a contribution to individuals or to the community. In some fields public agencies have a monopoly on jobs available to people in certain professions. Social workers may be able to seek employment in private as well as public agencies, but young adults aspiring to become police officers or teachers largely have to seek public employment if they want to work in these areas.

Once attracted to these occupations, however, the dynamics of street-level bureaucracies combine to persuade workers that they are destined to be ineffective in their chosen fields, that clients may not substantially benefit from their efforts, or that conditions of successful intervention are not likely to be available. These conclusions are all the more persuasive because they appear to be substantially true, at least in the short run. It is difficult to aid clients in ways consistent with idealized conceptions of assistance within street-level bureaucracies as they are currently structured, particularly when the least experienced workers are thrown into the most difficult work environments.

Thus, generations of thoughtful and potentially self-sacrificing people are disarmed in their social purpose. They come to believe that it is impossible to find conditions conducive to good practice, and that public agencies cannot be otherwise structured. Their choices appear to be to leave public employment for other work or to resign themselves to routine processing of clients while instructing the next generation of idealists that there is little sense in hoping for change or in rendering human services.

Similarly, the practice of street-level bureaucrats leads to the self-fulfilling prophecy that relations with clients cannot change. The actions of street-level bureaucrats confirm for clients that they will continue to be treated as they have always been treated. This perpetuates the cycle of the irrelevance of professional help and reinforces tendencies toward despair and inaction. This is the most painful part of the estrangement of workers from their original purpose. These orientations reinforce the tendencies originating in the culture toward enhancement of private interests and the abandonment of social purpose.

If the potential for a more humane practice were entirely negative, of course, these considerations would only be lessons in realism. However, the relevant experiences are not monolithic, and the impressions of hopelessness are as much socially constructed as they are rooted in fact. The potential for growth and change in street-level bureaucracy is dependent on both identifying the critical problems and recognizing that patterns of practice may be reconstructed as well as reproduced. With this in mind it may be useful to mention several other factors that contribute to the difficulty of reconstructing street-level bureaucracy.

First there is the problem posed by the apparent conflict between contending interests. Street-level bureaucrats have different interests from clients, organizational superiors, and the public to which they are nominally subordinate. The conflictual nature of these relationships is particularly apparent in the current fiscal crisis, which appears to call for taking one side against another. Conflict between contending interests may be inevitable (by definition), and in any event it may be socially productive,[15] but it is difficult to think about deliberately changing major institutions when it appears that the interests of one party conflict so fundamentally with the interests of other powerful groups. The more that contending interests appear to be fundamentally in conflict with others, the more hopeless social change appears to be for interests that are relatively weak.

If, for example, parents believe that changes they favor conflict with the interests of teachers, and that teachers are powerfully situated in the school system, they will be discouraged from attempting to make changes. Similarly, teachers who believe they are not supported by parent groups or by school authorities (or by the public-at-large) will be unlikely to seek changes in working conditions that go beyond those expected of normal labor-management demands. In short, the more different groups perceive themselves to be in conflict with others, the more narrowly they must choose among objectives and the less they can devote themselves to long-run goals.

A second difficulty is that the patterns of practice that develop in this work are rooted in the fundamental coping requirements of the job. These are not easily abandoned or changed because they are experienced by workers and outside observers as virtual job requirements. People do not readily give up survival mechanisms. This is one of the reasons it is easier to change articulated policy from the top than to change practice from below. Policy articulated from the top is not rooted in defense mechanisms developed to cope with the job, while the policy that emerges from practice is rooted in survival.

Curiously, a third reason it is difficult to think about changing street-level bureaucracies is related to the appearance of flexibility and innovation. Street-level bureaucracies are permeated with turmoil rationalized as change-related. The social service industry of managers, management consultants, public administrators, foundation officials, and academics whose business is to tinker with social service improvement insures that public perception of street-level bureaucracies is one of constant alterations in the structure of service delivery. The volume of pilot programs, demonstration projects, and innovations in management and personnel practices presents the image of frequent reconstitution of public agencies. This profligacy of reform confuses a public that cannot possibly assess the programs undertaken in the name of reform and rarely experiences results of such reforms directly. The pluralism of the social service industry tends to credit virtually any kind of change so long as it has its origins in a legitimate source (which rarely includes clients). Thus the currency of reform is debased. With so many reform proposals no one change seems better than any other change.

Finally, thinking about significant changes in street-level practice implies a commitment to altering or improving relations between individual workers and clients. Yet we are profoundly shy and inexperienced in talking about relations between and among people. We know much more about deploying resources than about affecting working relations. It is typical for community meetings to address issues of recruitment, procedures, incentive structures, chains of command, and so on, instead of confronting the problems that actually brought people together in the first place—incompetent or insensitive teachers, police officers, or social workers. It is easier to avoid these problems, the heart of community relations, and defer them as professional matters better left for professionals to handle. In any event it is difficult to measure the quality of relationships; better to stick to dimensions of the work more subject to administrative manipulation.

In sum, if bureaucracies mirror the society in which they develop it is difficult to change bureaucratic forms fundamentally without larger changes taking place. While superficial changes may frequently develop in bureaucratic organizations—for example, changes in the relative degree of administrative centralization—in a sense there remains a deeper structure of organizational relationships that are not likely to yield easily to administrative rationalizations. This provides an additional reason for insisting that policy implementation in street-level bureaucracy must be studied at the work place rather than tracing policy through the bureaucratic and interorganizational systems. Not only do street-level bureaucrats exercise discretion to such an extent that they are not easily affected by policy articulation from above (as I have previously argued). Also, the character of worker-client and worker-supervisor relations, no matter what the articulated organizational policy, is likely to continue to reflect the dominant bureaucratic relations of the society, no matter what the administrative guidelines provide.

Contradictory Tendencies in Street-Level Bureaucratic Relations

By their nature political systems are relatively impervious to change. To identify a set of social relations as a political system is to draw attention to the relative stability of the patterns of interaction that make it up. While it is useful to specify as clearly as possible the forces supporting the status quo, it is hardly surprising to discover that the prevailing structure of relations is deeply rooted.

However, just as the larger society establishes the environment in which bureaucracies operate and significantly affects bureaucratic relations, it also gives rise to contradictory tendencies that provide opportunities to challenge prevailing relationships. Going against the grain, these tendencies are more difficult to identify and more hypothetical, since their contributions are rarely dramatic. Nonetheless, consideration of the prospects for change in any political system requires specification of tendencies that potentially give rise or support to reformation.

Of the attributes that support change in street-level bureaucracies at least five should be noted. First, public programs of entitlement and control pro-· vide at least the potential for mobilizing clients and sympathetic publics toward greater accountability in implementation and administration.[16] One of the contradictions of the American service sector is that programs contributing significantly to the management and control of populations are supposed to be responsive to public preferences. This, of course, does not mean that democratic theory necessarily calls for the citizen-subjects of public agencies to control agencies. Agencies of service and control are theoretically accountable to a larger society, of which the client population is only one, and an often relatively powerless, constituency. Still, while public programs have many constituencies, they more or less present the potential for formal responsiveness to client preferences. The requirements of accountability in theory contribute to the actual capacity of client populations to organize to change public agencies as they strive to close the gap between accountability in theory and practice.

This consideration is likely to be important in proportion to the population covered by service. One possibility is that public agencies will simply differentiate among high- and low-status clients. But another is that service will improve for all if high-status clients are included in the population mix. As public-health care delivery becomes more and more generalized and less the concern of low-income populations, it is more likely that clients will be able to have an impact on service quality. Likewise, parents of children in an integrated school can have a greater impact on the quality of service than can parents of a segregated school whose needs can be more easily isolated.

The importance of this consideration increases as the public service sector in the society grows. As people are thrown more and more into the public sector for relief or entitlements they will be more able to make claims based on the discrepancies between programs that would provide for them adequately and programs as they actually exist. Government becomes more vulnerable to challenge as it assumes more responsibilities. This is why the service state, increasingly penetrating aspects of private life, contains elements that contradict the control it presumably exerts.

Second, professional norms of behavior toward clients provide a measure of resistance to bureaucratization. Street-level bureaucrats' claims of professional status imply a commitment that clients' interests will guide them in providing service. The implicit bargain between the professions and society is that in exchange for self-regulation they will act in clients' interest without regard for personal gain and without compromising their advocacy. In a word, according to professional norms professionals' interest as expressed on behalf of clients must be unalloyed.

This is not to say that street-level bureaucrats do not also confront organizational demands. On the contrary, the essence of their dilemma is that they are partly professional and partly bureaucratic. However, the potential for appealing to the professional dimension of these work roles means that there is an irreducible minimum consideration of the importance of respecting clients' individuality and acting accordingly.

Even in the roles of police officers and judges, where the concepts of client advocacy and representation might appear remote, we can see norms of appropriate application of sanctions that in these occupations are the primary ingredients of resistance to bureaucratic treatment of offenders. Although it is tempting to see teachers, social workers, and other low-level workers as constantly under attack for routinizing social services, one can turn this observation around by calling attention to their resistance to bureaucratization (to the extent that they have been able to resist), largely stemming from their recognition of the importance of this aspect of professional identity. (The role of professionals in reform of street-level bureaucracy is discussed at greater length in the next chapter.)

Third, street-level bureaucrats by definition interact constantly with clients. This provides the salutory condition that workers must continually attend to the people they are supposed to serve and their problems. However elaborate the defense mechanisms developed to shield themselves from the enormity of clients' needs, street-level bureaucrats at some level retain a sense that the people with whom they come in contact are not sufficiently served by the agencies designated to do so. Thus, one might speculate that street-level bureaucrats more than other organizational workers are able to retain a concept of the notion of need in relation to what is actually being provided. This residual awareness may provide a resource that can be tapped.

Fourth, lower-level workers maintain a degree of control over their work environment. Individually street-level bureaucrats exercise discretion to control the work situation. Collectively many street-level bureaucrats are able to have a significant say in the rules under which they are employed. Particularly at the individual level this discretion is not likely to be significantly eroded so long as street-level bureaucrats' jobs require them to make discretionary judgments that cannot be entirely programmed.

Finally, there is a distinct but neglected precedent for organized public employees championing the needs of clients. Teachers have included limitations on classroom size as an objective to be sought through collective bargaining. They have sought this objective not only to improve working conditions but also to create the environment in which they could function optimally as teachers. Likewise, social workers have struck on behalf of improved benefit levels for clients.[17]

The cynic may wish to point out the strategic advantage to public workers of couching bargaining objectives in altruistic terms (although managers are equally guilty, insisting that they act on behalf of taxpayers and the economic well-being of the community). Still, cynical or not, such alliances, the stuff of politics, may be exploited by client groups, particularly when, in collective bargaining in the fiscal crisis, wage gains are subordinated to improvements in working conditions.

The impulse to provide fully, openly, and responsively for citizens' service needs exists alongside the need to restrict, control, and rationalize service inadequacies or limitations. This is the central contradiction of social services. It is more than simply a tension between costs and benefits. It is critical to reassure mass publics that their elemental needs will be taken care of if they are not met privately and to rationalize service inadequacies by deflecting responsibility away from government.

Through street-level bureaucracies the society organizes the control, restriction, and maintenance of relatively powerless groups. Antagonism is directed toward the agents of social services and control and away from the political forces that ultimately account for the distribution of social and material values. Thus the American system of service delivery and control is shaped by the aspirations of the population and by the requirements of the larger political and social system. In this sense the United States, no less than other political systems, lends public bureaucracy its particular character.

CHAPTER 13

Support for Human Services:

Notes for Reform and

Reconstruction

I have argued that the determinants of street-level practice are deeply rooted in the structure of the work. Further, I have pointed out that street-level bureaucracies do not stand alone, but they reflect the character of prevailing organizational relations in the society as a whole. In turn, as a primary instrument of contact between government and citizens, street-level bureaucracies reinforce the relationships between citizens—both clients and workers—and the state. These observations contribute to our understanding of the stability of the institutions and their unlikely responsiveness to significant reform activities.

Nonetheless, it is important to address the potential for significant reform, however remote. To say that institutions are stable does not mean that they are inert, or that the possibility for movement is unavailable. Indeed, street-level bureaucracies continually confront proposals for change. Seeking efficiency, equity with flexibility, and appropriateness of intervention, from different perspectives public officials, client-oriented interest groups, organized public employees, and policy analysts perpetually engage in activities to reform the public services. A theory of street-level bureaucracy should help clarify the stakes in and potential for reform perspectives.

At any given level of public support we seek at least three values from service bureaucracies. We seek services or benefits appropriate to our situation or needs, equity tempered by flexibility in the distribution of public benefits, and respect as citizens receiving our due from government. Many of the criticisms of street-level bureaucracies focus on the extent to which people fail to receive appropriate, equitable, or respectful encounters. Taking these criticisms as points of departure, three major lines of analysis are discussed below.

1. Encouraging client autonomy and influence over policy.
2. Improving current street-level practice.
3. Helping street-level bureaucrats become more effective proponents of change.

There is a necessary and inevitable tension between the desire to have an impact in the short run, and the recognition that problems are not reducible to short-term incremental manipulations. Furthermore, significant changes in street-level bureaucracy are likely to be realized only in the context of social changes that support the relationships that must be forged. Short of such changes, these lines of analysis simply become points of dispute in an ongoing struggle over the relationship of citizens to the state.

Directions for Greater Client Autonomy

Proposals for greater client autonomy generally suffer from the fact that clients tend to remain relatively powerless. Clients accorded greater collective influence may not possess the bureaucratic skills necessary to operate in the policy arena, or they may inherit control over programs or facilities so bankrupt that they defy significant management improvements. Tenant management of underfunded and poorly maintained public housing, for example, may fail to improve service more for financial and structural reasons than for reasons of client capability. In this sense giving clients control over public facilities may contribute to social control, as tenants contest with other tenants over scarce jobs and project resources.

Nonetheless, proposals to increase client autonomy must be vigorously studied for their potential contribution to changing street-level relationships. One approach to change in street-level bureaucracy is to eliminate public workers as buffers between government and citizens. A class of proposals utilizing such an approach is represented by plans to issue service vouchers to citizens. By providing clients with claims on public or private service agencies, sponsors of voucher proposals hope that agencies would be more responsive to client preferences in order to attract their patronage.

Voucher proposals have gained support because they promise to introduce consumer sovereignty into the production of social services.

After considerable experimentation with educational vouchers the record suggests that it is extremely difficult to establish the conditions under which clients of educational services are fully informed about a wide variety of educational options. It is not so much the theory that is damaged by these experiences as it is the hope of creating the rudiments of competition on which the theory actively depends.[1]

On their face, voucher proposals are attractive because they evoke the model of a competitive market that develops products in response to consumer demand. Unfortunately, market models in service provision will not solve any problems so long as service providers monopolize the scarcely supplied skills of semi-professionals, dictate the conditions under which services will be supplied, or are allowed to limit information available to the service consumer. Moreover, even in theory market models can only be as appropriate as clients can be expected to have an opinion about service quality. This creates confusion in areas such as health and even education, where clients cannot always assess the appropriateness of service.

There is surely something attractive about the idea of providing people with money to purchase services on the open market. But so long as professionals control access to services prices will be bid up, and bureaucracies will be created to control eligibility and costs or insure minimum standards. Moreover, variation in location is a critical aspect of access to service, representing a substantial hidden cost to some service consumers. Segregation of clients by classes would likely continue to take place unless ways were found to overcome the costs of seeking services on a geographically diffuse basis.

Another set of reform proposals calls for eliminating mediating public workers from service contexts which, properly supported, might be handled by citizens with little or minimum assistance. Thus legal reformers encourage experimentation with community dispute resolution and simplified legal procedures in order to make the law accessible to citizens without lawyer mediation. Community dispute resolution mechanisms presumably free the courts and other legal institutions from cases that might be processed by other means. Similarly, home care programs in the health field represent efforts to permit people to avoid institutionalization and make maximum utilization of service personnel. On an experimental basis many school systems attempt to provide educational experiences through utilization of community resources. Citizen patrols have developed to end or supplement community dependence on the police.

Not all proposals to support indigenous efforts to provide service and eliminate mediating public employees will accomplish these objectives. They may spawn quasi-public agencies that have the potential for replicating the difficulties of the agencies they replace. They may develop entitlement, regulatory, or service bureaucracies that perpetuate bureaucratic experiences. Home care, for example, frees people to stay out of the hospital under certain circumstances, but it still requires a bureaucracy to certify eligibility, to promulgate and monitor standards for service providers, and to see that service personnel are hired to provide home care. In general, questions of supply and maintenance of standards remain in all service areas so long as the government retains ultimate responsibility.

These alternative perspectives on service provision suggest opportunities to define the relationship of providers and clients differently. However, they do not fundamentally reorganize the need for service in many instances and do not offer guidance where street-level bureaucrats remain in a controlling relationship. A sharp need continues to provide a better balance of power between street-level workers and clients. A better balance would be achieved if the following developments were encouraged.

Wherever possible, opportunities should be seized to demystify street-level bureaucracies and the practices in which they engage. Workers should be taught how to communicate with their publics in plain language, and clients should demand explanations they can understand. Client advocates should be sponsored and trained to guide clients through the bureaucracy, to obtain answers they are otherwise unable to get, and to represent clients to workers where they would otherwise be intimidated. Guides to clients' rights and maps of bureaucratic systems should be developed; more important, street-level bureaucracies should simplify procedures to make service systems more manageable without expert intervention.

Simple practices should be developed to make street-level bureaucracies more accountable to clients. Requiring workers to provide summaries of the transactions clients experienced but may not have fully comprehended would be a significant step forward in some places. Routine reviews to determine whether clients were receiving all benefits to which they were entitled would place the burden of programming for clients on public employees. Such details would modestly contribute to the development of more reciprocal relationships.

As a matter of public policy we should welcome investigations by public-interest law firms, legal services offices, government agencies, and others challenging prevailing practices where those practices entail responsible allegations of inhumane service or systematically neglected clients' rights. We should recognize that the discretion of street-level workers is uncertainly monitored at best and that governments that create these bureaucracies may properly oversee their direction by encouraging client as well as bureaucratic scrutiny.

The struggle of clients to organize and obtain some control over service provision should be respected and encouraged. Client involvement in governance of service agencies will help to insure that clients contribute to the way street-level bureaucrats define their roles. Service provision should be decentralized to a significant extent, so that the advantages of orienting practice toward local initiatives can be realized.

During the 1960s some communities experimented with client participation in governance of schools, neighborhood health centers, public housing, and other public services. From these experiences we should know better than to encourage citizen control without examining the conditions of transfer and the degree of control. More often than not, the experiments of the 1960s inappropriately discredited citizen participation by providing control over programs lacking financial viability or by narrowly circumscribing the scope or powers of client or citizen boards. While avoiding the problems of cooptation of community activists in financially unhealthy public enterprises, or of tokenistic participation, client control over service bureaucracies remains potentially critical in making the bureaucracies more responsive to clients.

Issues of client control over service bureaucracies are not separable from considerations of large-scale social changes or changes in the organization of public services. It is surely simpler to contemplate neighborhood representative councils governing outreach health centers, legal services programs, and local schools than it is to consider citizen participation in the governance of centralized health facilities, downtown legal services complexes, and consolidated schools. Yet, if client control represents a way of making clients more central to street-level bureaucrats' tasks and promoting further changes by fundamentally challenging the bases of service provision, then extending citizen control over complex systems and facilities should be encouraged.

Directions for Current Practice

TAKING DISCRETION OUT OF BUREAUCRACY

Managing discretion is at the heart of the problem of street-level bureaucracy. For the most part, society is not willing fully to circumscribe street-level discretion. However, there may be some contexts in which it *is* desirable to circumscribe it. It is hardly obvious that every discretionary role played by street-level bureaucrats should continue to exist. Where workers' discretion leads to unfair and unequal treatment of clients, with no compensating benefits, it should be desirable to reform systems by removing this unredeemed source of unfairness. If, for example, a teacher's right to strike pupils is judged to be undesirable in all cases, it is obviously appropriate to prohibit flatly this option.

Some situations may arise, or may develop from previous practices, in which the judgment must be made that intervention by street-level bureaucrats is harmful or wasteful. However, the judgment that street-level bureaucrats' discretion is inappropriate is not necessarily easily made.

The decision to separate social service functions from income-support determination functions in public welfare is an example of removing considerable discretion from street-level bureaucrats. The stated intention was to limit discretion of case workers in support determination and free them to provide services without the burden of client appeals or tactics designed to obtain more benefits. (Perhaps the primary appeal of this "reform" was that it also promised to reduce the number of welfare personnel.) This change in policy probably deserves support because the capacity of social service workers to provide meaningful assistance to clients had become so circumscribed that their interventions had largely lost whatever beneficial potential may have existed in the previous definition of social worker roles. Moreover, the paternalistic and degrading assumptions of the welfare system virtually guaranteed that social services would be provided in a nonreciprocal context. In this case the discretionary opportunities of case workers had already become so limited by the social context in which aid was provided that it was probably beneficial to further routinize the aid process.[2]

Still, some doubts linger. Questions remain concerning the meaning of this "reform." To what extent was this policy adopted in order to reduce the power of social workers, diminishing their role and also their numbers? To what extent was the transformation of support determination motivated by a desire to reduce support levels by eliminating client-oriented social workers from the process in favor of cost-conscious accountants? To what extent did this reform indeed eliminate discretion, or did it simply transfer discretionary powers to a new set of employees? Finally, by eliminating the social service provider at intake, to what extent did this reform represent an implicit decision to reduce service levels by restricting social workers' opportunities to pick up relevant problems at intake, when people are often most receptive to assistance?

Some of these questions arise generally in considering systems to routinize discretionary judgment. Hospitals attempt to develop elaborate protocols to help nurses determine medical priorities in emergency rooms. This is done in the name of optimizing the use of available resources. But the assigning of priority categories also restricts the observations that can be made about a patient. Responding to the most salient symptoms may mean neglect of the whole patient or overlooking other conditions requiring diagnosis.

Similar problems with categorization may be observed in legal services. To serve more clients legal services offices often train receptionists to discover quickly the reason for a potential client's inquiry, and then refer the caller to a trained paraprofessional. Systems are elaborated to help the receptionist do this reliably. For this system to work well the receptionist should precisely follow the guidelines for referral.

Two problems arise in such a system, however. First, it is extremely difficult to circumscribe all possibilities. Thus the receptionist needs a back-up to handle calls that are not easily categorized. Second, and much more difficult to resolve, the presenting problem may be only the client's most urgently felt concern. The client may have more pressing and perhaps easily resolvable legal problems, but he or she is not aware of them or aware that assistance may be available. The system of early categorization, dependent on nondiscretionary slotting by the receptionist, produces efficient use of paraprofessional resources at the possible expense of serving the clients holistically.

On balance the judgment may be made that the costs of categorization are more than compensated for by the benefits of standardization. But it is a judgment that must be made with recognition of the liabilities involved. The logical extension of this way of thinking is to eliminate people from these judgments entirely. It is technically possible to program computers to make categorical determinations and even to advise people on, say, errors they may have made on their applications. This way of thinking similarly motivates adherents of computer-aided teaching machines, which may be programmed to provide the closest thing to a warm hug that machines are capable of (talking to students in a friendly tone, asking them personal questions, providing verbal encouragement). We can make teaching machines and diagnostic machines. At issue is the importance of seeking aid through other people. It is likely that when this technology is highly developed the rich will choose to pay for teachers and doctors, while the poor will be taught by machines and will obtain medical advice from a computer terminal.

ENHANCING CAPACITY OF STREET-LEVEL BUREAUCRATS

Embedded within the critique of street-level bureaucracy appear to be piecemeal formulas for reform. If discretion were constricted street-level bureaucrats would have less need for routines and simplifications to deal with uncertainty. If goals were clearer, workers could direct their energies with less ambivalence. If appropriate performance measures were available, street-level bureaucrats could be made more accountable for their behavior.

Within limits these observations are probably correct and sometimes may form the basis for action. However, ultimately they are likely to be quite limited for several reasons.

First, conditions of street-level bureaucracy comprise a syndrome. Except for those instances in which client-worker interactions can be eliminated, the conditions affecting the work context occur together and cannot easily be rationalized or simplified. Goals are ambiguous, performance measures are difficult to obtain, and discretion is required by virtue of the need for human interaction. It is unlikely that the apparent looseness of the bureaucratic context can be tightened up. If the organization could be tightened up, it is likely that it would have been tightened up before. To say that human interaction is required in service delivery is to suggest that judgments must be made about potentially ambiguous situations. Reciprocally, to say that the conditions of street-level bureaucracy exist is to say that the situation requires human judgment. It is quite unlikely that a part of the street-level bureaucracy syndrome can be transformed without a change in the basic assumptions underlying the service policy.

Second, even if it were possible to clarify lower-level workers' decision-making contexts, it is uncertain whether improvement in one aspect of the syndrome would alleviate problems arising from the whole. This would be different if the problems of street-level bureaucracy were additive so that every diminution of an aspect of the problem would result in a corresponding benefit.

The desirability of increasing or improving the resources of street-level bureaucrats also seems implicit in the critique. However, as suggested in chapter 3, we should be extremely skeptical of proposals for additional resources as a solution to problems of street-level bureaucracy. More resources are likely to reproduce problems of service quality at a higher-volume level. More clients may be served—a valuable objective—but this may be an achievement comparable to accommodating more cars going nowhere during rush hour on the Long Island Expressway. Furthermore, if for some reason agencies are able to hold the line on volume and apply increases to current client loads, additional resources may not enable street-level bureaucracies to cross over a hypothetical threshold level whereby such resources would begin to have an impact. A reduction in class size from 30 to 25, for example, would require a tremendous commitment of resources for a large city school system, yet reductions might only begin to be effective when class size reaches 15 students.[3]

On the other hand, maintaining current resource levels may be an important objective simply to prevent further erosion of client-worker relations. To this end the Denver Plan appears to be justified. Under this plan children are assigned numbers based on the presumed difficulty of teaching them. Teachers are guaranteed through contract that class size will not exceed the equivalent of teaching 25 normal pupils.[4] In this way teachers are rewarded rather than punished for having challenging pupils in their classes. Case loads in other bureaucracies could be meted out in the same way.

Second, additional resources might not improve working conditions but instead might increase the number of clients served, dilute the services provided, or be allocated to the incomes of employees. In the public services it is currently difficult to hold the line for service quality when there are clients who remain unserved, demands for more services, and organized employees who feel aggrieved. Moreover, to the extent that additional resources mean additional worker training it is questionable whether this investment can overcome the impact of working conditions. Worker training is less important for practice than the nature of the working conditions themselves.[5] Without a supportive network of working peer relationships, training to improve service capacity of workers is likely to wash out under the pressure of the work context.

The best chances of affecting work performance through job enhancement come when the system of service delivery supports workers in maintaining high standards of service quality. It is likely to be helpful if proposals for supporting practice are specifically job related, that is, helpful in solving specific challenges experienced by workers. Thus on-the-job training is likely to be more effective than classroom learning experiences because the training is provided in the context of actual problem-solving situations. Generalizations about police training apply to other street-level bureaucracies as well. Instruction relating to experiences police officers are likely to encounter is retained; instruction unrelated to direct problem solving is subject to erosion because it is irrelevant to officers' needs. In the short run, assistance in job problem solving is likely to be the most effective way of improving street-level performance.

This suggests some of the limits to direct job training. If street-level bureaucrats are likely to retain only that counsel relating to current job problem solving, then training oriented toward transforming jobs into something else is likely to be ineffective.[6] Thus one would be skeptical about developing new kinds of street-level bureaucrats primarily through instructional efforts.

The Prospects and Problems of Professionalism

These reform orientations have their limits. Most street-level work is not open to meaningful revision by limiting discretion, removing public employees from interaction with clients, or modestly altering bureaucratic structure. In street-level bureaucracies there is an irreducible requirement that public employees interact with citizens to determine the nature and extent of public services they should receive and to provide those services through interactions with them. If this is the case we are challenged to obtain accountability when bureaucratic mechanisms are inadequate and inappropriate.

The limits on bureaucracy in this area draw attention to the argument that street-level bureaucrats should be professionals whose relatively altruistic behavior, high standards, and self-monitoring substitute for what the society cannot dictate. Who will watch the watchmen? The watchmen will watch themselves. The argument for professionalization comes down simply to the realization that control of occupational groups must come from within the individual members of the group if it cannot be dictated from outside. If street-level bureaucrats cannot be restricted in everyday functioning, then self-monitoring must substitute for bureaucratic controls. To this extent, the advocates of greater professionalism in street-level bureaucracies appear to have an unassailable point. There is a powerful coincidence in our apparent need to have street-level bureaucrats monitor their own performance and in the aggrandizing claims of street-level bureaucrats that they are indeed sufficiently autonomous and self-policing to be granted at least a degree of professional status.[7]

The professionalization of street-level bureaucracies is commended by some analysts because standardized formal training in universities, seeking training to get credentials, and control over occupational entry is already far advanced in teaching, nursing, social work, and other street-level occupations.[8] In addition, it appears possible to influence the professionalization of these occupations. Public policy to influence the direction of professionalization is typically directed toward paying higher salaries to make these occupations more desirable to a more educated class of people, improving and subsidizing preprofessional training through universities, overseeing certification through professional boards to insure minimum standards, and making promotion and advancement dependent, at least superficially, on meeting professional standards of performance.

There are some attractions to focusing on professional development for solving service dilemmas. As discussed above, professionals are theoretically committed to a service orientation. The professions constantly receive recruits who to some degree are initially committed to realizing these ideals. Not only do professions embody a service ideal in theory, but also some people, believing the theory to apply in practice, seek to enter the professions in order to have a vocation consistent with ideals of service and sacrifice.

The problem with the "professional fix" in solving dilemmas of street-level accountability lies in the great gap between the service orientation of professionals in theory and professional service orientations in practice. The leading professions of medicine and law have not measured up well to their own standards, which call for providing service to those in need, dictating the primacy of the client over the needs or preferences of the professional, and recognizing that, in light of their monopoly over service, professionals need to develop practices that meet community requirements. On the contrary, studies of professional practice suggest that doctors, lawyers, and other professions tend to seek out higher-status clients at the expense of low-status clients, to neglect necessary services in favor of exotic or financially rewarding specialities, to allow the market for specialists to operate so as to create extreme inequalities in the distribution of available practitioners, to provide only meagerly for the professional needs of low-income people, and to respond to poor people in controlling and manipulative ways when they do serve them.[9]

These are broad generalizations to be sure, and they undoubtedly ignore contradictory evidence to some degree. Still, one can hardly claim familiarity with professional practice or read the literature on the response of the professions to social problems without recognizing these observations as central tendencies. At the very least these observations caution us to be quite skeptical of proposals to solve problems of street-level bureaucracy through increased professionalism.

Undoubtedly many people enter the professions seeking primarily the high status and income that they have been led to believe they would enjoy. But what about those who originally aspire to work with a degree of service orientation and are unable to maintain that direction? Whether they drift away from a service ideal or abandon it after protracted struggle with themselves or others, the careers of idealistic professional recruits are usually abandoned to processes that insure their socialization to the dominant professional values. There are at least three areas in which the professions as currently organized help to erode the service orientation.

First, professionals by definition are accountable only to peers. While the peer orientation protects professionals from the criticism of untrained and inexperienced outsiders it also insulates them from the criticism of clients and people who would speak on clients' behalf. Professionals are notoriously reluctant to criticize each other and at best direct attention only to the most extreme violations of ethical norms. Informal peer review is normally avoided and formal peer review focuses on immoralities unrelated to professional performance or to narrowly defined technical capabilities. Formal peer review is irrelevant to guiding the normal routines of practice or the directions of the professions.[10]

Of greater impact overall are informal peer pressures (as opposed to reviews) that guide professional development. Here, as in other social groups, professional novices are initiated into the rituals of practice through encouragement to develop amiable relations with peers, to protect fellow members of the society, and generally to appreciate the problems of other professionals, even at the possible expense of clients. Thus the doctor's advocacy of patients' medical needs is tempered by the requirement that he or she appreciate the organizational needs of the hospital. Thus the lawyer's advocacy of clients' rights is tempered by his or her need to appreciate the norms of the court. Untempered peer definition of professional norms thus effectively erodes the client orientation to which professionals are theoretically committed.

Second, a major problem with professionalism as a model for street-level bureaucracy is the tendency of professionals to work in isolation. Effective professional norms call for mutual deference and shows of respect except when other professionals grossly violate these norms or threaten to embarrass the profession. It is not that well-qualified professionals actually respect the bumbling fool in their midst. However, it is unlikely that they will take steps to help the fool improve (or, for that matter, to aid the eager but inexperienced novice) except when pressed by matters of self-interest. Looking at the same problem from the viewpoint of the professional who could use help, the norms usually inhibit professionals from seeking guidance in solving problems or providing services to clients, since to ask for help would be to admit a degree of incapacity. It is instructive that police officers who feel themselves dependent on their partners for personal safety are extremely intolerant of a partner's operational defects. But in street-level bureaucracies in which co-workers' defects do not so directly impact on others' well-being (for example, building inspectors), deficiencies may be tolerated for a considerable period of time.

Third, the most powerful agent in professional socialization is the work setting. Thus it is the extremely rare newcomer who is able to assert unpopular or unsanctioned values. The education of new recruits as to what is acceptable, what is appropriate, and what will enhance one's career is an extremely powerful determinant of future professional behavior.

In summary, although there are both theoretical and practical reasons for looking to professional development as a way to improve street-level bureaucrats' performance, the record of the professions suggests that the model they provide in practice is not necessarily an auspicious one for increasing responsiveness to clients.

Keeping New Professionals New

During the 1960s the service occupations and professions appeared to experience a degree of revitalization as an influx of idealistic recruits joined with like-minded members of the profession to dedicate themselves to practices based on different principles from those that were dominant at the time. These principles included placing their skills in the service of those people who most needed them (the poor, ethnic, and racial minorities), committing themselves to respecting client autonomy, turning the power of the professions to helping achieve greater social and economic justice, and eschewing personal status enhancement when it conflicted with these principles. These "new" professionals were radical in the classic sense of seeking a return to first principles.[11]

The surge of idealism during this period differed from other times only in volume and attention paid by others. In every era people sympathetic to these principles have entered the professions only to be ground down by the social structure of their jobs. If there was a difference in kind in the 1960s it stemmed from the greater numbers, which provided a critical mass to articulate these ideals, and from the social movements that provided the setting in which these ideals were stimulated and received notice and approval.

In every era, there is a propensity among at least some members of street-level bureaucracies to work according to the ideal standards of their roles. If we must depend upon a core of street-level workers who will strive to maintain integrity in the exercise of discretion, we may well ask what can be done to support and enlarge this core? Where such a core does not presently exist, we may ask what can be done to bring it into being? What can be done to keep the new street-level bureaucrats flexible in their response to clients and zealous in their commitment to client rights while delivering public policy? While pursuing these objectives, what can be done to insure that the new street-level bureaucrat possesses the skills to intervene with clients effectively? It is helpful to ask these questions in these ways because they direct attention to building on opportunities that currently exist. They guide analysis of one possible direction of street-level reform without directly confronting the enormity of attempting to think through fundamental reforms for the totality of street-level bureaucracies.

The new street-level bureaucrats already exist in public agencies, trying as best they can to maintain high standards and resist the routinization that they fear is their fate. The new street-level bureacrats already exist in professional schools, searching for positions that will permit them to develop careers consistent with the objectives that motivated them to consider public service in the first place. The new street-level bureaucrats exist in the reservoir of young people who would commit themselves to public service if they had effective service models which they might follow.

What is needed to develop this potential?

Financial support for the human side of street-level bureaucracies is a necessary although insufficient condition. Although additional resources cannot overcome the patterns of routinization and simplification that are currently endemic, teachers, legal services lawyers, police officers, and other street-level bureaucrats will not have the slack to organize themselves for more responsive interactions with clients unless they have adequate material support. It is particularly important to reverse the current decline in support for the human services, since workers' impressions of harassment and resource inadequacy are probably as important as the fact when it comes time to organize client processing. Public agencies must provide an atmosphere of deliberation or workers will not be able to escape the conviction, rooted in coping needs, that they must routinize client processing. This is part of the reason that incremental reductions in case load often fail to show an effect, since the feeling of harassment remains when case loads are marginally reduced, say, from 50 to 45 cases.

Financial resources are also necessary to provide the incentives necessary to make possible career commitments. It is not that a new street-level bureaucracy needs to provide the same financial rewards as careers in the private sector. However, the substantial material (and purposive) uncertainties of this public service work are detrimental to building a cadre of committed human service workers.

This is less of a problem in the established semi-professions, such as policing and teaching, where civil service systems and collective bargaining have resulted in reasonably high salaries. In these areas the competition for places and current reductions in work forces are larger obstacles to revitalization.

The problem is somewhat different in professions with extremely high status. Legal services, for example, has only a very few positions at the top. Thus young lawyers quickly must determine whether they are going to stay in this line of work at the considerable risk of a dead-end career or shift to the professional mainline where financial opportunities are much greater.

It is easier to discuss career ladders and mobility opportunities in periods of system growth than in periods of contraction. In the current period it is thus easier to consider molding career opportunities in legal and health services than in education, since the work forces in the former are likely to expand while those in the latter are likely to shrink in response to declining enrollments.

The new street-level bureaucrat needs rewards for effective performance. Currently professional associations and public employee unions discourage performance rewards based upon "soft" evaluative measures. They prefer so-called merit increases only where the majority of members have easy access to achieving the rewards. The lockstep of advancement in civil service systems must begin to yield to assessments of ability based on recognizing not only the volume of work but also the appropriateness of response and quality of the interaction with clients. In turn, this will mean seeking out and crediting citizen reports on street-level workers (with due recognition of potential bias, as is the case of all assessments). It will also mean development of peer assessments in the provision of services and worker contributions to determining assessment criteria. Above all it will mean developing ongoing consultative interactions of workers and supervisors to provide systematic qualitative evaluations of case handling.

But breaking down the isolation of individual street-level bureaucrats will be mostly destructive if it is done simply in the name of higher degrees of scrutiny. The hardest reform of all will be to develop in street-level bureaucracies supportive environments in which peer review is joined to peer support and assistance in the working out of problems of practice. Currently peer review takes place in the unsystematic culture of lunchroom chatter, casual observation, and third-hand reputational assessment. Peer instruction takes place in the schooling of rookies in how to survive on the street, with supervisors, or in the face of client harassment. In other words, peer review and instruction currently do take place, but in ways that force workers either to be extremely circumspect or to promote routine processing rather than responses appropriate to individual clients.

The development of peer support mechanisms can and must be related to work processes. Street-level bureaucrats need to receive recognition for good work and to be free to seek help when they encounter work-related difficulties, without feeling that their reputations are in jeopardy. Perhaps outside specialists should systematically review the work of street-level bureaucrats with their clients. Perhaps agencies can develop this capacity without such assistance. Whatever the mechanism, those street-level bureaucrats who continue to aspire to provide appropriate community service will welcome the chance to grow in their jobs without being judged and placed at risk in the process.

A street-level bureaucracy that has developed processes of staff growth and development will also develop processes for small group decision making. Small group units for street-level decision making (for example, grade levels or departments in schools, subprecinct units in police departments, neighborhood service offices in legal assistance and health maintenance) are probably best suited to determine which aspects of social services should be routinized and which aspects should remain unprogrammed. Routinization in social life may be inevitable, but it is not inevitable that routines should be imposed from above or by authorities that do not directly confront clients. Decentralized units would be far more likely to develop routines consistent with responsive and efficient client treatment than authorities removed from the scene, particularly if outside audits are continually able to draw attention to issues of service quality.

Fundamentally at issue is making the most of the reality that street-level bureaucrats primarily determine policy implementation, not their superiors. If the bureaucratic connection between lower-level workers and the reins of authority are indeed tenuous, as I have argued, perhaps it is better to flow with the organizational dynamics of policy delivery in these organizations rather than resist them by insisting on bureaucratic solutions to problems defined as worker deviation from preferred performance.

In reality, decentralized units given full responsibility for practice would have to resist the tendency to drift toward recentralization of routine functioning. The pull would be strong to let higher authorities make critical decisions, thereby absolving lower-level workers of responsibility. However, even creating the opportunity for self-determination of small units provides a context for considerable learning and the potential for achieving a more client-oriented practice.

Even if it were possible to restructure street-level bureaucracies in these ways, what would keep people from drifting into the old patterns? This is a particularly significant question if we believe that bureaucracy to some degree reflects as well as reinforces and perpetuates the prevailing social structures. Three considerations conducive to workers' exercising effective and responsible control over the work situation may help consolidate changes in street-level bureaucracies in ways that limit the likelihood of retrenchment.

First, the clients of service must become a more potent force in the reference groups of street-level bureaucrats. Ways must be discovered to make visible and accessible the behavior of lower-level workers, and clients likely to be affected by their actions must become more involved in the definition of good practice. To the extent that peer relations are the primary source of the expectations and values promoted within the occupational sector, there will remain a temptation to develop esoteric criteria of practice judgment. Street-level bureaucrats' performance has not been so good nor our confidence in their work so well established that great harm would come from creating regular mechanisms to expose street-level work to the scrutiny of clients. Even if clients are overwhelmed by the trappings and rhetoric of professionalism or are limited in their understanding of the ramifications of decision making, exposing the decision-making environment to clients should anchor street-level bureaucracies more firmly in a client orientation. Moreover, street-level bureaucrats should undertake to develop techniques to educate clients toward making better judgments about seeking service and better assessments of service provision. Studies and observations concluding that clients are overwhelmed by professionals caution us about involving clients in decision making, but they do not reflect experiences in which client involvement has been systematically nurtured.[12]

Client contributions would be enhanced if street-level units accepted responsibility for group case loads rather than incorporating clients as the case loads of individual workers. In many street-level bureaucracies, a primary contribution to workers' isolation and pressure is the fact that workers are individually positioned to be fully responsible for clients, are unable to seek assistance or advice, and must compete with other workers for advantage so as to minimize their load. So long as street-level workers are individually responsible for their sector of client services they are likely to be defensive in developing cooperative and supportive relations with fellow workers or clients. Without abandoning the efficiencies of specialization or the accountability that individual case loads minimally provide, it is possible to develop conceptions of group or office case loads that make clients the responsibility of the staff, not individual workers.[13]

A second requirement in sustaining the new street-level bureaucracy is the zeal and leadership of people committed to the new orientation. Reform orientations are not self-implementing. They can only survive in a context in which people are dedicated to public service and receive support from client groups, fellow workers, and the community. The nurturing of such leaders is a process that would well begin in the training grounds of universities, where relatively visionary orientations are sometimes rewarded, and would continue through a public policy that valued such leaders for their commitment to a client-oriented service. Without the development of such a reward structure it would be reasonable to conclude that there was no constituency for these reforms.

Traditionally universities have provided strategic sanctuary for some of the most important dissenters from contemporary practice, but they have often been rendered ineffective because their lessons come from the ivy tower rather than from the streets. This is particularly regretable because such teachers may inspire young professionals to go into their work without experiencing the dilemmas of practice or helping to prepare the environment into which students insert themselves. The new street-level bureaucracies would be significantly assisted by policies in which supporters of this orientation circulate between the teaching of young professionals and the practice of public service. Some of their teaching ought to be done not in universities but in the field, where there is opportunity for constant confrontation with the realities of practice. A police academy in which students worked half-time as apprentice officers, or a social work institute in which students received training from teachers who shared an office practice with their students, might provide the reality-based environment in which staff and students would find an appropriate balance between experience and detachment.

A final aspect of support for maintaining the client orientation of street-level bureaucracy rests in the development of ongoing processes of supportive criticism and inquiry. Built into every week of practice should be opportunities to review individuals' work, share criticisms, and seek a collective capacity to improve performance. The orientation should be skeptical, for the objective of such sessions would be to resist *where appropriate* the early closure of possibilities that accompanies the inevitable routinization of practice. Some police departments hold an inquiry every time an officer draws a weapon. Hospitals ordinarily inquire into circumstances accompanying deaths. These inquiries become defensive because the consequences of malfeasance are so grave. What is called for is introducing a norm of inquiry into routine practice, to keep alive the potential of client services and contradict the neglect that results from ordinary inadvertence. At the same time, the staff would be more receptive to learning when the potential consequences were less grave and all staff were in turn the objects of attention.

This general thesis assumes that people who are constantly engaged in planning for group practice, who have some control over their work processes, and who regard clients not as units to be processed but as people, will discover the rewards of doing a good job gratifying and renewing. The service sector of the society will be substantially transformed when teachers find (or rediscover) their rewards in the education of children; police officers take pride in doing a difficult job strictly on the merits of individual encounters; and social workers have the resources and the untrammeled commitment to help clients find solutions to their own problems.

There are obvious intellectual hazards in sketching an outline of new approaches when confronted with the enormity of the present distress in social services, the ambivalence toward improving social services born of personal encounters, and the bureaucracies' apparent resistance to responsive reforms. I will consider it a measure of accomplishment if these notes toward a new era for street-level bureaucracies are taken as not so ungrounded in reality that they seem drawn from thin air and not so remote from human potential that they seem farfetched.

In recognition of the magnitude of the task I have framed this discussion in terms of building on the commitments of new professionals. But the reconstruction of street-level bureaucracies is unlikely to take place in the absence of a broad movement for social and economic justice. Precisely because reform of mass client processing involves more equitable distribution of services as public goods, valuing more highly the status of individuals in society, and challenging the control and mystification of public services, it is difficult to achieve and requires general political support. If street-level bureaucracies indeed play critical roles in the political structure, isolated reform efforts cannot plausibly be expected to bear the full weight of social change.

Current reform interests are fragmented among the three parties of the buffer relationship. They are divided among administrators who seek to improve efficiency and effectiveness through management tools; unions that seek improved working conditions but are constrained to protect job benefits; and clients and client interests that seek service improvements but lack legitimacy in policy arenas. The quality of street-level practice will change only when an effective coalition develops that harnesses public concerns for service costs and effectiveness, respects client involvement in service procedures, and recognizes the needs of the work place, where the fate of innovation will ultimately be decided. This is not likely to occur in this society of protected interests unless this social and political movement brings the priority of more humane service provision to the forefront of concern. If such concern is likely to be evident in the future it will be because place by place and issue by issue, people effectively demand respect for themselves and their proper claims on government, while at the same time they are able to explore ways to support street-level bureaucracies in their struggle to do a decent job under adverse circumstances.

CHAPTER 14

On Managing Street-Level Bureaucracy

Street-level bureaucrats, by definition, have an autonomous core. In a limited sense, they are the authors of the policies that are finally delivered. But if the public wants to affect public service policy delivery, it must look not to the behavior of individual workers but to managers and policy makers. Throughout the book, particularly in chapter 11, I emphasize the various ways that street-level bureaucrats are able to undermine or evade efforts to bring them to account. In this new concluding chapter, written especially for the thirtieth anniversary of publication, I gather a number of thoughts on managing street-level workers to bring public services in line with expectations established, ultimately, through the political process. In doing so, I comment selectively on developments in the field that inform our understanding of the key issues.

I start by treating the origins of the concept of street-level bureaucracy. I review how the political environment has changed and why it is particularly timely to learn how teachers, police officers, social workers, and others may be managed to achieve greater policy responsiveness.

An Evolving Policy Environment for Street-Level Bureaucracy

Street-Level Bureaucracy was written at a time when the United States was adjusting to the civil rights movement for social and political equality. It was written as African Americans and their allies sought to bring into reality the promises of equal rights. In the early 1970s, when the structure of the book was being worked out, the ripples of the civil rights movement included conflicts over schools, the police, and paternalistic welfare administration. These institutions were the places people encountered or confronted government, the places unequal treatment would be manifest. In general, they were populated by white workers and administrators who became the focus of contentious race relations.

Since the early 1960s I had been personally and professionally committed to advancing the objectives of the civil rights movement, as I understood them. But this did not include sympathy for characterizations of public sector workers as indifferent to the experiences of the people they dealt with. A crude racism could not explain on-the-job behavior. Nor did the many interviews and observations of street-level bureaucrats my collaborators and I conducted support the proposition that personal attitudes or indifference of street-level workers could explain the experiences of citizens with these agencies.

I wanted to understand the performance of critical public services that were either at the heart of community conflict or were central to providing for citizens in need—the panoply of institutions that focus on citizen welfare: income supports, housing provision, social services, and the justice system. I came to believe that the experiences of citizens with public services were the predictable consequences of the structure of particular kinds of publics sector work. This belief was based on the recognition that the work of police officers and then, I realized, other frontline workers, consisted of layers of coping mechanisms that guided them through complex interactions with the people they served, and allowed them to salvage at least a portion of their work as authentic and worthwhile. My primary concern became reconciling the human dimension of street-level positions with the often problematic outcomes of the systems in which they worked.

Another influence was the emergence in political science of studies that analyzed what actually happens when public policies are enacted—work that later became known as implementation studies. It was only in the mid-1960s that political scientists began to focus on the now-obvious point that the passage of laws and the promulgation of regulations did not fully encompass the policy-making process. On the contrary, as we now take for granted, policy is only finally made when laws or regulations are fully implemented, through subsequent processes that cascade from the initial declarations.

At least initially, studies of implementation were part of a discourse that sought to confront the contradictions between American ideals and American policy in practice. In 1968, as the issues contested in the streets began to engage academics, James Davis and Kenneth Dolbeare published a study of the Selective Service System that asked whether the military draft fairly apportioned risk among potential recruits, as it was supposed to do.[1] They found that the implementation of the military draft laws led to systematic overrepresentation of young men from lower socioeconomic backgrounds, despite elaborate propaganda to the contrary. Studies followed that sought to understand why substantial plans to enhance economic development came to grief in Washington, D.C.,[2] and Oakland, California.[3] These early studies were products of a broad skepticism about the capacity of government shared by many elements in society in the decade deeply influenced by the "discovery of poverty" amidst plenty, the civil rights movement, ghetto uprisings, and the antiwar movement.

Imbedded in the early works on implementation is an implicit critique of American democracy and an appeal to close the gap between public promises and performance. Thirty years later, concerns about access to public services, and of the relationship between public promises and policy implementation, continue to be valid. But they are joined by another compelling issue. We now live in an age in which support for government has been eroded, and the very purpose of government is deeply contested. The times require advancing an understanding of the critical roles of government on which successful modern societies depend: social welfare provision, environmental and consumer protection, public goods such as schools and highways, and planning and investing for the future. Appreciating the complexity of public services through which citizens engage government on a regular basis should make a significant contribution to this agenda.

The new reality results from several trends that have been well-rehearsed elsewhere but bear mentioning here. For one thing, today we confront limits that were hardly on the horizon thirty years ago. In the post–World War II period, an era of "easy financing" facilitated the expansion of public programs with only limited concern for whether revenues could be found to support them.[4] That era is long over. In state governments that by law cannot run deficits, public budgeting has always been about playing zero-sum games. Now this is the case at the federal level as well, as federal officials are under increasing pressure to match any new expenditure with a corresponding budget cut or tax increase.

Another major development has been the sharpening of the tools of government and the invention of new tools. In contrast to earlier times, when the distinction between governmental and nongovernmental was reasonably clear, public policies today are coproduced with individuals through tax breaks, credits and vouchers; and with private organizations through tax expenditures, subsidies, public-private partnerships, and contracting for services.

Separate from these developments but related to them are two additional trends that shape the future of street-level bureaucracy. The rise and persistent strength of the conservative perspective on public policy, through academic and scholarly outlets as well as the pronouncements of political leaders, has promoted the view that government is intrinsically inefficient and inherently wasteful. According to this perspective, government should be small and taxes low. In addition, markets and market mechanisms, in contrast to government, are said to produce optimal outcomes and lead to innovation and lower costs.

In hindsight I see that in the earlier edition of *Street-Level Bureaucracy* I took the existence of government and critical public services for granted, as most commentators still do today. I assumed that government services, though they might change to some degree, were fundamentally enduring in their basic structure and support. With the passage of time those assumptions seem more tenuous, for several reasons:

1. Contracting for services and other new approaches to service delivery, which appear to introduce market-like mechanisms into public systems, have been hastened onto the public stage by the conservative challenges to existing forms of service delivery.
2. At the national and particularly the state and local level, where education, policing, income supports, and other social policies are administered, governments are more or less in permanent fiscal crises as they constantly struggle to match revenues with the cost of meeting existing obligations.[5]
3. Implacable criticism of intrinsic government capacity, when combined with the public's historic reservations about government, lead to heightened attention to government effectiveness.

CONTRACTING FOR SERVICES

The widespread government use of contracting for public services with nonprofit organizations illustrates some of the challenges in the convergence of these trends. In the last several decades, American governments have abandoned direct service provision, such as state homes for delinquent youth, and substituted instead decentralized service provision through contracting with nonprofit service agencies. Governments subsidize community-based organizations providing a range of social services, such as shelters for battered women and supervision of mentally ill homeless people who can live independently with assistance. By making funding available, they have spurred the emergence of flexible and innovative nonprofit organizations by building into the design of work training and other policies the assumption that they would be delivered by private contractors. Contracting for services is now the default approach in many areas, and a new kind of street-level workforce has emerged to serve citizens in the social services, welfare placements, mental health facilities, and many other service areas.

Although they do not directly work for government, we can expect these workers to fit the street-level bureaucracy profile, for several reasons. As the contracting regime has gone from essentially underwriting the policies of traditional private organizations, such as service agencies, to demanding that the contracting agencies conform to high standards of accountability, work patterns on the public side and the private side converge. The controls, performance measures, and agency review procedures imposed on private agencies by public authorities have become increasingly rigorous, tending to drive out whatever differences in the treatment of clients attributable to public or private status that might at one time have prevailed.[6]

Also, in many street-level bureaucracies, workers' perspectives strongly reflect professional rather than administrative norms. Thus a social worker in a contracting agency may process clients very much like a counterpart employed by a state agency. In some jurisdictions, such as Alameda, California, indigent defendants in criminal cases may be served by attorneys who work for local government. In others, such as Brooklyn, New York, they would be served by attorneys who work for nonprofit agencies. Attorney practices might vary, but it would be surprising if the variations reflected their status as employees of government or nonprofit entities. [7]

Every public program administered by private organizations under contract is in essence a government program. However, though the contracting regime has facilitated the growth and greater flexibility of the public sector by linking it with private community groups, these developments are rarely treated as public achievements. The transformation of the nonprofit service sector into what amounts to an arm of government is not credited as an achievement of government, acknowledged by the sector, or claimed by public officials.

FISCAL STRINGENCY

Because state governments cannot run deficits and their tax revenues vary with employment, wages, and consumer spending, they are subject to budget fluctuations as revenues rise and fall with the business cycle. Consequently, they periodically need to cut budgets as revenues decline in economic downturns. Over the years, as the anti-tax, small-government perspective has taken hold, state governments have been thrown into more or less permanent budget crises. They have legislated spending limits and passed laws making it difficult to raise taxes, or have just cut taxes when there have been surpluses, and cut programs when revenues declined.[8]

It has been in the context of continual pressure on limiting the growth of their budgets in relation to need that the states began to experience the Great Recession in 2008. One year into the recession, states overall have had to cut almost one out of every four dollars in their budgets, with more cuts anticipated for the following year.[9] Such cuts take enormous tolls on the services that provide for or protect people in need through street-level bureaucracies.

In Ohio, to take one set of examples, a series of tax reductions and a refusal to raise taxes in a recession led in 2009 to the elimination of the state's early childhood education initiative, and to deep cuts in subsidized childcare, mental health services, and protective services for children and adults.[10] In October 2009, the eminent economist Paul Krugman calculated that over the previous five months the United States had fired more than 143,000 teachers in reaction to the recession, with undoubtedly tens of thousands more on the block as state revenues continue to be in crisis.[11]

No politician wants to reduce the number of teachers, and few want to reduce the number of other public employees—recreation workers, nursing home attendants, and the like. These people work in services of which the public generally approves.[12] Instead, politicians target the size of government overall, making cuts in programs the inevitable consequence of reduced revenues. Writing about public benefits at the national level, political scientist Paul Pierson observes this dynamic: "There is a fundamental asymmetry between the organized advocates of public spending, who favor particular governmental initiatives, and their opponents, who (at least rhetorically) criticize government spending in general and on principle."[13]

CRITICISM OF GOVERNMENT

Casting a long shadow over the provision of public services is the rise and influence of the conservative movement, supported by well-funded think tanks and university centers. Since the 1970s and accelerating in influence during the Reagan era, conservative theorists and political figures have relentlessly promoted a set of linked ideas to support their version of a better society: small government, low taxes, reliance on individual initiative (except for subsidies and tax breaks for favored interests), and reliance on market mechanisms to achieve efficiency and innovation. Over these years the conservative perspective has contributed to the development of the new tools of government that include vouchers, contracting for services, and reducing the range and capacity of public institutions. More important, the conservative world view has greatly amplified resistance to public institutions as such.

There has always been an antigovernment streak in the American psyche, and properly so. The country was founded in opposition to an imperial power, and its constitution was designed in part to limit government's reach. Moreover, the complex narrative of American history includes government-sponsored episodes of great cruelty, the tolerance of unjust private behavior, and the use of public authority to advance the ends of privileged sectors.

However, starting with the New Deal of the 1930s, and despite inconsistencies, government has become the primary instrument for achieving greater equality and offering shelter from the insecurities generated by people's inability to participate fully in the market economy. Government also establishes the basis for a sound economy by creating the framework under which businesses operate on a competitive basis without unacceptable costs to individuals' well-being and the environment. It is this broad understanding of the social purposes government serves today that bear the brunt of the conservative critique.

In principle, a debate between defenders and critics of an expansive state can be healthy. That debate is rarely engaged, however. True, particular policy issues may be roundly debated, but the defense or advocacy of particular policies is not the same as defending the role of government as such. One reason government is in disrepute today is that it has many critics but few active champions or defenders. The critics include not just ideologues and sincere believers in the view that government is intrinsically flawed or that taxes are too high, but as well advocates for various interests who agree with government's objectives but believe it can and should do more. Advocates with an interest in an expansive government role typically focus on the shortcomings of the sector in which they take an interest, rarely pausing to note its accomplishments. If they defend anything at all, they defend the programs they support, but not the set of collective interests of which their favored programs are a part.

Another source of criticism unredeemed by balancing positive commentary is the tendency of communications media to report on government failures but ignore government successes. This ensures that when government comes to public attention it is in a negative light. Moreover, elected officials rarely praise government, possibly because they fear being regarded as self-serving. They almost never draw attention to government's essential role. With conservatives opposing government programs in principle, liberals opposing them in practice, and news about them focusing only on their failings, it is hardly a wonder that the reputation of government is low.

Of course, even democratic governments, like all human endeavors, are sometimes flawed, just as some churches are run by people of questionable morals, and some corporate leaders bring their companies to bankruptcy or breach the public trust. But of the major institutions in society, only government sustains attacks without effective rebuttal or even measured assessment of the charges.

The good news, I suppose, is that public programs typically enjoy popular support and are relatively stable over time. New programs are introduced as the range of problems deemed to require public action expands, and as new populations are included in the broad consensus of who deserves assistance. Although recent decades have witnessed vigorous efforts to cut back the state, the basic composition of the broad social compact remains intact.[14] Unfortunately, although members of the public consistently affirm their support of the programs government sponsors, their initial reaction to government in general indicates broad acceptance of the antigovernment perspective. A striking illustration of this was revealed in a 1997 Kaiser/Harvard poll. When asked their opinion about a health plan hotline, 70 percent were strongly in favor. The number dropped precipitously, to 43 percent, when the question asked about a *government* hotline.[15]

The shift in the political discourse opens several new paths to what, how, and whether government will respond to social problems and closes off others. The strong antigovernment perspective throws advocates for public services constantly on the defensive. Drawing the skirmish line in a public debate at whether something is "governmental" at the least ensures that policy debates will be ideological (what are the universal principles and values in terms of which the policy should be assessed?) rather than pragmatic (what are the best ways to solve this particular problem?).

One reason public managers have been put on the defensive is recent critiques of government effectiveness that draw on a narrow reading of business practices. Demands for accountability often seem to be attacking government programs even as they profess interest in improving them. To paraphrase Murray Edelman, the insightful guide to politics as symbolic action, to insist that one needs greater accountability is also to caution that accountability is lacking.[16]

A case in point is the movement to demand that social programs be subject to the highest evaluation standards, of which controlled experiments with randomized assignment of subjects is the gold standard. Every policy analyst recognizes that such research, when appropriate and properly executed, yields unimpeachable results. Within a certain range, the approach has unquestionable value.[17] Such research is often not appropriate, however. Experimental design with random assignment cannot carry the weight of assessing public programs across the board.

Applied as adherents appear to advocate, one result would be to recommend or insist on random assignment experiments even when they are inappropriate. For example, if the experiment involves mediation of street-level bureaucrats in the provision of a benefit or service, the results would likely be affected in unknown ways by variable implementation of the program. In such an example, a modest finding might reflect that the intervention was not particularly useful, or that a useful intervention was erratically implemented.

A second result would be to discount as unproven promising administrative reforms that cannot meet the test of random assignment experimentation. A third result would be to discount other approaches to sound policy making that are based on the best available evidence, but also on judgment, experience, and expert insight. At the symbolic level, insistence on policies that can meet the test of random assignment radiates the message that other ways of knowing and deciding are weak and illegitimate.

Governments and foundations, seeking to emulate what they believe are effective business practices, increasingly insist on evidence standards that are often inconsistent with needs of public and nonprofit agencies that help individuals and work with communities. At a certain level, these practices make eminent sense. At another, they seem intent on creating an evaluation environment that will markedly limit reasoning about public policy.[18]

It is extremely difficult to dislodge the antigovernment perspective. Neither the debacle resulting from the government's slow and uncoordinated response to Hurricane Katrina, nor the recent turmoil resulting from the extraordinary failures of financial regulation, resulted in more than a short-term boost in public appreciation of the importance of investing in public institutions. To be sure, President Obama has regularly reminded the public of the importance of government, providing welcome relief from the negative rhetoric of the past.[19] But to judge from continued opposition to government intervention in the health insurance industry and financial institutions—the pivotal policy issues in the United States in 2009—it would seem safe to conclude that antigovernment perspectives are an enduring feature of the landscape.

Recognizing that the early twenty-first century is characterized by deep skepticism about government, efforts to improve government performance take on new meaning. Improving schools or the welfare system or policing are not just narrow matters of achieving more effective public services at the appropriate cost. They may also be understood as contributing to a more substantial agenda in which government, by improving its public services across all the divides of race, ethnicity, and class, is perceived as fair and trustworthy.

In the next section I treat the central question of whether and how street-level bureaucrats can be managed when their work is defined as exercising discretion. I then take up the challenge of improving the capacity of street-level bureaucrats to make sound judgments when relatively standard approaches to management are insufficient in achieving public purposes.

Shaping Street-Level Bureaucrats' Performance

DO STREET-LEVEL BUREAUCRATS "MAKE" POLICY?

The logic of democracy requires that citizens and lawmakers alike have a high degree of confidence that enactment of a law will be followed by reliable implementation. As we know, however, accountability is complicated in street-level bureaucracies because workers in these organizations by definition cannot be fully controlled. Agency policies are not entirely comprehended by their authorizing statutes, regulations, budget allocations, and official procedures. Nor can discretion in these jobs easily be eliminated. From disability assessments of people with lower back pain and other ambiguous conditions, to police encounters in which the right thing to do must be constructed on the spot, discretion is required of those who deliver policy. [20]

Nonetheless, although street-level bureaucrats are widely expected to exercise discretion in the course of their work, managers must design ways to insure accountability at the street level. Earlier in this volume I observed that the actions of teachers, police officers, or welfare workers "become, or add up to, agency policy," and that their actions effectively "become" the public policies they carry out."[21] For a great many of the readers of the original edition, these conclusions were the primary and sometimes the only lesson of *Street-Level Bureaucracy*.

This interpretation is clearly too limited. Street-level bureaucrats may indeed "make" policy in the sense that their separate discretionary and unsanctioned behaviors add up to patterned agency behavior overall. But they do so only in the context of broad policy structures of which their decisions are a part. Street-level bureaucrats do not articulate core objectives or themselves develop mechanisms to achieve them. For any given public agency or any policy reform, we need to look into the entire policy environment in which street-level bureaucrats function.

The transformation in 1996 of the basic American welfare program was obviously a critical policy decision that took place far beyond the interview rooms of local welfare offices. The new program ended welfare as an entitlement and made eligibility depend on work effort and job-seeking. Street-level bureaucrats, who only a few weeks earlier were focusing on monitoring the accuracy of applications and applying eligibility rules, were now required to learn the vocabulary and ways of a system that expected clients to look for work and find it. And, ideally, they would have to learn how to apply that vocabulary to welfare applicants as they presented themselves, and strategize about the most appropriate path for clients to enter the workforce. These changes reflected policy making at higher levels. In addition, options available to workers in processing their caseloads were heavily influenced by several factors.

1. Work opportunities in the welfare agency's catchment area, including the kinds of jobs available, entry level wages, and clients' access to public transportation.
2. The availability of child-care services and health care (particularly for single parents whose reliability at work depends on the health of their children).
3. Client training and placement opportunities.

These (and other) factors shape the decision making of today's welfare workers. As Evelyn Brodkin observes, "the quality of choices about help [available to workers] depend[s] in part upon the 'helping resources' to which street-level bureaucrats have access."[22] As always, they depend on caseloads and other work circumstances that impinge on conditions of work in the welfare system. But since welfare reform they also depend on some new factors—especially the local employment situation—that are beyond their control.

Consider the *New York Times* report in 2009 that "more people were being turned down for welfare benefits because of overly stringent or confusing requirements."[23] It may be that welfare workers were exercising excessive discretion in discharging their responsibilities, but it also could be that the rules in New York really were overly stringent or confusing.

In short, in the new work and welfare systems, workers categorize applicants and deploy available resources according to routines and simplifications they develop, even as they exercise judgment and make unsanctioned responses. The content of these discretionary acts will not be random, and they will not only be related to the coping needs of the workers. On the contrary, they will be structured by the choices available to the workers as options (such as local funding for daycare) provided by the policies.

To understand worker behavior we need to pay much more attention to the overall structure of the policies. A study of nurses' preferences for public versus private hospitals in Australia concluded that the shortage of nurses in public hospitals might be attributed to their having less autonomy than their counterparts in private hospitals. The hypothesis is plausible, but other important factors, which the study did not investigate, might have accounted for the nurses' job preferences, including whether the private hospital nurses were paid higher wages, worked better or fewer hours, served a more congenial clientele, or had lower caseloads.

CAN STREET-LEVEL BUREAUCRATS BE MANAGED?

Over the years, some readers of *Street-Level Bureaucracy* have also concluded that street-level bureaucrats cannot be managed. It is true that earlier in the book I elaborate on the resources lower-level workers have that allow them to resist directives from supervisors. Managers of street-level bureaucrats are limited in the ways they can exercise authority, but thirty years of experience have shown that managers can surely narrow the gap between the performance of street-level bureaucrats and the desired policy results.

One approach is to minimize the mediating role of street-level workers in citizens' accessing services.[24] Administrators can radically reduce discretion by narrowing the job, as in the case of welfare departments converting the job of social worker from counselor to greater emphasis on the clerical.[25] In Britain in the 1990s, introduction of principles of the "new public management" resulted in administrative reforms that narrowed workers' discretion but also focused the objectives of the policy more sharply. In the case of teachers, school managers gained greater control by emphasizing clearer standards. In the case of geriatric social workers, policy makers placed greater emphasis on social workers' roles in structuring services for the elderly as they reduced their focus on counseling. Predictably, the reforms shifted and constrained discretion, but did not eliminate it. Workers often reported positive results because the requirements of the jobs were clearer, although many were dismayed by what they considered a loss of status and authority. [26]

Partly to reduce workers' discretion when unnecessary for effective agency functioning, but mostly to increase productivity and reduce costs, people-processing agencies have more recently devoted enormous resources to automated information gathering and intake functions, a trend accelerated by the Internet and the widespread availability of computers. The application of information technology can lead to extraordinary productivity gains. To take one example, the much maligned departments of motor vehicles, the agencies that have been poster children for government inefficiency, have expanded services, reduced waiting times remarkably, and kept costs down through data processing innovations and the use of the Internet. In Virginia in 2008, for example, the DMV reduced the average waiting time in customer service centers over the year from a tolerable thirteen minutes to eight. Although the number of drivers, vehicles, and agency responsibilities have increased steadily since 2002, the DMV workforce in Virginia declined by 3 percent.[27]

Like any tool, extensive use of information technology can be well-used or used irresponsibly. When the state of Texas attempted to reduce the number of welfare workers by contracting with a private provider to receive applications online, the misguided innovation deprived people of coverage. Enrollment in the Children's Health Insurance Program, for example, declined by 127,000 children in a five-month period.[28] This is a dramatic case of a general issue with streamlining intake through self-service: the costs for citizens and potential service claimants of being left on their own go unrecorded, and thus do not register as agency failures.[29]

Automated information systems do not eliminate concerns over responsiveness—treating people as individuals who may present unique circumstances—even in innovations such as providing or seeking fairly straightforward information from citizens. In 1997 the Australian government instituted a computerized system to provide assessment and referral functions to the unemployed. The scheme was touted as offering more finely tuned assessments about individual capacity and potential, but was also intended to enforce harsh financial sanctions that frontline workers could not be trusted to levy. According to researcher Greg Marston, the system failed in helping job-seekers with fine-grained decisions, and the task fell to the cadre of counseling and training organizations charged with actually helping people find work.[30]

Other concerns with automated service systems include ensuring that databases are kept up despite pressures to reduce costs, and maintaining systems even when increased access to an agency may result in higher demand to which it would be costly to respond.[31] Information systems must make sure that assistance is still available to those who do not have computers or cannot use them, and that language barriers and other issues of citizen access are addressed.

RESTRUCTURING INCENTIVES AND SANCTIONS

Aside from simply reorganizing the problem of street-level discretion by reducing it, the more significant way managers influence street-level bureaucrat discretion is by restructuring worker incentives and sanctions. In such restructuring, street-level bureaucrats' actions may still "add up" to the policy the organization produces, but the policy in fact conforms better to managers' expectations. Essentially, managers increase the probability that outcomes will shift in the preferred direction.[32]

Five examples illustrate this approach. Of these, the first four recount efforts to alter the behavior of street-level bureaucrats toward clients, in the first three reducing workers' generosity, but in the fourth expanding their helpfulness.

Diagnostic related groups. In an attempt to control medical costs, since 1983 the Medicare program has required hospitals to assign most new patients to diagnostic related groups (DRGs). The DRG system provides a basis for standardizing treatment and controlling cost by assigning a previously calculated payment level for the treatment of the diagnosed condition rather than paying for every procedure. Hospitals have a strong incentive to eliminate procedures that might result in costs that exceed the reimbursement rate. Although DRGs can be and are gamed (by assigning ancillary diagnoses to cover unexpected costs, for example), this and similar approaches have gained wide approval in the health care field as a way to rein in expensive outliers without intruding on doctors' medical decision making. In essence, the use of DRGs leads to convergence around a norm of treatment and payment, but without appearing to tell doctors what to do or threatening the sacred doctor-patient relationship.

Quality control in welfare administration. Every substantial enterprise, public or private, is concerned with maintaining standards and insuring against the degradation of products or processes. In welfare administration, quality control essentially means that welfare agencies, down to the office level, collect information to ensure that they correctly administer state and federal policies. In the 1970s, but particularly in the early 1980s, federal welfare officials sought to use the quality control system not just to ensure conformity with the law, but also to curb what they regarded as excessive welfare expenditures. The mechanism for reducing expenditures through quality control was engagingly simple. The federal government would penalize states for excessive errors in wrongful spending—admitting ineligible people to the rolls, or authorizing excessive payments. But in determining sanctions they would not count errors of stringency—that is, errors in which workers denied eligible applicants, or authorized payments that were too low.

As a result, state campaigns against error focused exclusively on inducing workers to be tougher, and to lean in the direction of refusing claims if there were any uncertainty. Ambiguities in the law were resolved in ways unfavorable to clients. Recipients already on the rolls were burdened with additional behavioral costs as demonstrating compliance with eligibility requirements became more onerous. Quality control appears to be an unobjectionable neutral administrative mechanism. As designed in this case, however, it had distinct distributional consequences.[33]

Reining in disability insurance determinations. Excessively liberal results in the Social Security Disability Insurance (SSDI) program were the subject of similar concerns in the same period. Federal administrators believed that many of the independent administrative law judges (ALJs) were not strictly applying the SSDI rules. In response they mounted a campaign that focused on the rulings of those ALJs whose records suggested that they tended to favor claimants.

Among the tactics to redirect the tendencies of judges deemed to rule excessively in favor of claimants were developing a protocol that tried to routinize the decision process; tracking and publicizing individual judges' reversal rates to draw attention to those who were deemed to be excessively generous, and then 'counseling' those judges who deviated most from the norm; subjecting judges' decisions to quality control protocols; and subjecting judges' decisions to a time limit, which constrained judges from gathering additional evidence that might be favorable to a claimant's case.[34] Again, these administrative changes focused on changing the choices ALJs made without challenging their right to make judgments on any particular presenting case.

Transforming welfare worker orientations. The three examples given illustrate administrators' efforts to increase the probability that discretionary judgments would be made to withhold benefits to potential recipients. Something of a contrary example is provided by the transformation of the Massachusetts Department of Welfare in the 1980s from an agency primarily focused on income support activities and monitoring the eligibility of recipients for cash payments, to one devoted to placing welfare recipients in jobs.

In 1983, the new welfare commissioner, Charles Atkins, adopted the then-unprecedented objective of placing recipients in jobs or preparing them for work with the goal of helping them get out of poverty. Employment and

Training Choices (ET) was one of the first programs in the nation to take seriously the importance of placing welfare recipients in jobs—a prescription that would dominate discussions of public welfare over the next decades. The ET program would offer welfare recipients three main services: assessment and career planning, training and placement, and further education in support of work preparation. Because the program would be voluntary, case workers would have to persuade recipients to enroll, counsel them as to the best options, and encourage them to persist if the experience was not satisfactory at first. These were the same case workers who just months before were focused exclusively on assessing eligibility and determining welfare award levels.

It was no easy matter to induce welfare recipients with low self-esteem, little work experience, and few employment-related skills to believe that the new program could help them succeed and was worth the personal and financial risks. Nor was it an easy matter to persuade DPW workers to believe in and adopt the new objectives. Workers would have to establish rapport with recipients, engage them in discussion of matters not directly related to the recipients' primary concerns of getting on welfare, and persuade them to investigate the program's options. This persuasion would have to be done by social workers who were not trained for such work and who, a short while ago, had been focused on an entirely different set of priorities.

In 1987, both the department and the independent Massachusetts Taxpayers' Foundation agreed—though they differed in the details—that ET had placed tens of thousands of people in jobs, reduced welfare rolls, and saved taxpayer money. Although some critics regarded the ET claims as unproven because the state resisted, on sound grounds, subjecting welfare recipients to an evaluation with random assignment, there should be little question about the transformation of the state's welfare staff. [35]

In his study of ET, Robert Behn summarizes how managers radically reshaped the behavior, motivation, and production of these street-level workers.[36]

1. They established a clear mission for the agency, and developed a wide range of vehicles and events to communicate it throughout the ranks.
2. They set specific goals for individuals and for each work unit leaving no doubt about the agency's highest priorities.
3. They monitored performance and rewarded workers' success at the individual and unit level.
4. They were personally involved in monitoring agency performance.

ET established a new mission for the welfare department and recruited its workers to support the mission by relentlessly promoting indicators of success, keeping track of performance, and conveying to workers that they were critical to the new mission of the agency.[37]

CompSTAT. A successful and widely imitated initiative that appears to embody these principles is CompSTAT, the police administrative reform begun during the administration of Commissioner William Bratton in New York City in 1994.[38] CompSTAT takes advantage of high quality data collection and reporting of crime statistics at the precinct level to hold precinct commanders accountable. Precinct commanders, like the welfare administrators subject to quality control initiatives mentioned earlier, in turn engage police officers to achieve the desired results.

In monthly meetings with the Police Department's high command, administrators require all precinct commanders to be ready to defend their performance and explain trends in their districts that require attention. If there has been a spike in reported burglaries, for example, the commander can expect to be interrogated on why this trend is occurring, and what he or she intends to do about it. The system works when precinct commanders, with clarity about their priorities based on the precinct data, and urgency deriving from the monthly meetings, design strategies to improve the performance of their units. At a certain level the critical elements present in the ET case are present here as well: clarity of mission, close tracking of performance, and keen involvement of the organization's leadership.

In evaluating these reforms a key question is whether focusing on a specific aspect of the mission pulls street-level bureaucrats away from the full range of their responsibilities to a detrimental degree. Does monitoring and evaluating performance on a particular measure improve job performance overall? Or does focusing on a single dimension of the job subtly change the job itself in negative ways?

In CompSTAT, police are not relieved of responsibility for law enforcement outside of departmental priorities, and in any case, if new crime trends emerge, they also can be targeted. In the ET experience, job placement was only one of many departmental priorities that received attention through monitoring and feedback from the high command. For example, in ET maintaining a good record on quality control remained a specified agency priority even though the first priority was recipient employment. CompSTAT has been widely emulated in other police departments, and its principles have been widely adopted in efforts to improve accountability in other agencies and—in the cases of Baltimore and Washington State—government-wide initiatives. As with any replications, success in these efforts depends on how faithfully the model is actually reproduced.[39]

These reforms of street-level bureaucracy seek to harness measurement of performance with appropriate sanctions and rewards. Their success appears to depend upon the alignment of the new approach with the core values of the agency, the clarity of the mission, and the extent to which street-level bureaucrats can in fact improve their performance in pursuit of the mission.[40] These examples demonstrate that managers can influence the behavior of street-level bureaucrats by strategically choosing the data they collect about workers' performance, and the incentives with which they respond to the data.

Investing in Street-Level Bureaucrats

A paradox of public service provision in democratic societies is that policies must be administered fairly; similarly situated people must be treated alike. And yet, as James Q. Wilson emphasized many years ago, we also want our public services to be responsive to the presenting case.[41] Although responsiveness to each case in practice would be a nightmare, at least in principle we want public services to recognize important and relevant differences. In pursuing responsiveness, managing street-level bureaucracy by manipulating measures, incentives, and sanctions is of relatively little use.

Public service bureaucracies must emphasize responsiveness in two circumstances. First, studies of street-level bureaucracies and everyday experience remind us that we want and expect public officials to be flexible and helpful. Consider the following examples.

1. The social worker, subverting strict rules, retains a welfare recipient on the rolls while she acquires necessary documentation.
2. An intake worker coaches the job training applicant on how to present his case in order to qualify for a benefit.
3. The hospital team tags a patient with a reported medical condition that allows her to stay in the hospital a day or two longer while team members shape a better discharge plan.
4. The teacher spends extra time with a new student.
5. The police officer accompanies the speeding motorist to the hospital as the motorist's wife is in the throes of childbirth.

In all these cases, the caring displayed by the public employee captures our imagination and confirms our belief that public structures are capable of treating people as individuals and not just as units to be processed.

When those with authority go out of their way to respond generously to people in need despite rules to the contrary, they join what sociologist Lisa Dodson smartly calls "the moral underground."[42] Members of the moral underground do not blow up rail lines. What they do is ignore rules that they are supposed to enforce but seem excessively rigid, in order to help people in need, at little overall cost to society.

Acts of flexibility not only benefit the recipient of compassion but also have larger implications for society. After presenting a case in which a vocational rehabilitation counselor cut through red tape to obtain a computer for a client, Steven Maynard-Moody and Michael Musheno describe the counselor as engaging "in an act that redeems the state by breaking through the bureaucratic labyrinth."[43] In addition, they suggest, such an encounter provides a context in which community values that coexist and sometimes conflict with bureaucratic rules find expression. Many administrative systems allow for such flexibility under certain circumstances, though flexibility can be misused and can result in wholesale undercutting of intended policy. Like so many matters in policy analysis, the proper degree of flexibility is a matter of balance.

Treating everyone alike is a requisite of building popular trust. But good rules allow for appropriate exceptions. How, then, can a society tolerate benign exceptions when universalism is so important? Exceptions that favor people because of their social ties or ethnic backgrounds undermine popular trust in government's fairness. We cannot specify where the lines should be drawn, but we can acknowledge that responsiveness within a norm of universalistic rule application can be consistent with fair and effective public services, even if it requires departure from strict mechanical accountability. The exceptions that mark the superior public agency must be those that would pass a test of deserving popular approval on the basis of the presenting facts and local values, and are not tainted by implications of favoritism based on the identities of those favored.

A second circumstance in which public service bureaucracies must emphasize responsiveness is when public services requires individual initiative, the cultivation of experience, and a degree of empathy that cannot be reduced to administrative guidelines. Thus there is another "problem" of street-level bureaucracy that is entirely different than the one we have considered up to now: how to insure that people employed by the state to teach, judge, evaluate, and counsel have the necessary skills, experience, and training to exercise discretion properly and most effectively. For some street-level occupations more than others, it is essential that decisions are made fully in response to the individual case or situation, deploying deep knowledge of the field with commitment and a common sense that cannot be codi-

fied. As Michael Hill and Peter Hupe put it, "[e]nhancing street-level discretion may, under certain conditions, be more functional for the implementation
of those policies than curbing it."[44]

NO CHILD LEFT BEHIND

These issues are reflected in the drama that has been playing out in the
United States for most of the current decade in educational reform. The
George W. Bush administration's legacy legislation, The No Child Left Behind (NCLB) Act of 2001, aspires to improve educational outcomes for all
children, and particularly to close the achievement gap among young people
of different socioeconomic groups. To accomplish its goals, NCLB requires
all states to test all children in certain grades in math and English and to
sanction schools that fail to make adequate progress. In essence, it is an
enormous exercise in performance measurement, with individual schools as
the units of analysis.

The theory of NCLB is that the reality or the threat of poor performance
ratings and the prospect of severe sanctions for poor school performance will
mobilize school administrators and their communities to improve the
schools. Whether the act has produced measurable progress is disputed, but
there are some indications of improvements in school performance, particularly in schools with high proportions of students from disadvantaged racial
or ethnic backgrounds. Educational reformers now rally behind a substantial
reform scenario rather than reject the new approach outright.[45]

One obvious problem with the law, identified by many observers, is that
the emphasis on testing skews the curriculum in the direction of test achievement to the neglect of other concerns that do not directly contribute to
higher test results. The task of schools has never been exclusively to convey
information. Mass testing does not assess the ability of students to manipulate knowledge in ways they will need to in later life, to say nothing of stimu-
lating creativity, coaching young people in how to get along with others, and
cultivating civic virtues, to name only a few of the qualities of mind reflective
of a good education.

There is wide understanding in the research community that "teaching to
the test" has several drawbacks. It drives out of the curriculum subjects on
which students are not being tested, such as art, physical education, and cultural studies.[46] It also distorts and excessively simplifies the subjects that are
tested. More broadly, the tests ignore the demand from all segments of society that children "become competent problem-solvers and critical think-
ers."[47] In principle, states could improve their tests, but such efforts are
costly, and in any case states have a perverse interest in reducing the rigor of

the tests in order to ensure that more schools meet the minimum standards.[48]

A deeper problem with NCLB, and one that generally confronts performance measurement reforms, is the failure to address the strategic question of how to improve achievement. In principle, performance-based accountability leaves open the question of how results are achieved; encouraging flexibility in achieving goals is more or less the point of these approaches. However, if the construction of a performance-based regime absorbs excessive resources and the attention of administrators, creating ways to achieve better results may suffer. This point is particularly relevant to NCLB, given the substantial evidence that improving the capacity and training of teachers is one of the most powerful paths to improved educational outcomes.[49]

NCLB requires the states to employ "highly qualified teachers," but to do so schools need only hire educators in core academic areas who are licensed, hold a bachelor's degree, and have taken courses in their subject area (as evidenced, say, by their undergraduate major). This is a decidedly shallow standard of what constitutes "high qualification" of a good educator. Higher expectations of teacher training and preparation would yield much better results. Recommending the approach of the National Board for Professional Teaching Standards (NBPTS), Mary E. Dilworth and Joseph A. Aguerrebere suggest that highly qualified teachers must meet the following criteria.

1. They are trained in their subject areas and broadly grounded in the liberal arts so as to be able to help students make connections across issue areas.
2. They command a variety of approaches to learning and are able to adapt their approaches to students with different learning needs and styles.
3. They are committed to teaching and the belief that all students can learn.[50]

The last is not a small matter and is separable from subject area knowledge and teaching methods. Good teaching depends on dedication and on the teacher's conviction that students will be able to succeed. Students who are taught by teachers certified by NBTPS, in 2009 numbering almost 83,000, achieve at a higher rate than those taught by uncertified teachers, as measured by evaluations in North Carolina, Arizona, and Florida.[51]

In principle, all street-level bureaucrats, from health-care workers to police officers, must be able to assess the presenting situation or client freshly. Equal treatment may require treating people differently to achieve equal results, particularly when responding to diverse populations. In the case of teachers, according to Dilworth and Aguerrebere, this means that teachers should know their students well, both as individuals and as children from shared but varying backgrounds. Teachers who apply "culturally responsive pedagogy" will understand, for example, "what types of errors a student who is learning English is likely to make based on patterns that exist in their native language."[52]

Accountability systems with single indicators are magnets for criticism because public sector services rarely have unitary goals.[53] The challenge for critics and supporters of No Child Left Behind is whether reducing the mission of the schools to achievement on the current tests is an acceptable reconceptualization of our expectations for schools. A generous assessment of NCLB is that it has placed achievement of every student at the center of a national debate, and located the problem at the level of the individual school. As mentioned, the law is distressingly simplistic on what constitutes a good education, and it is also more or less silent on how to achieve better results. Despite substantial criticisms, the law will have proved valuable if future iterations lead to support for substantial investments in teacher salaries, working conditions, standards, and training.

THE CASE OF CHILD PROTECTIVE SERVICES

Another occupation that cries out for greater investment in training and preparation for encounters with citizens is child protective services. Child protection workers are in some ways the ultimate street-level bureaucrats. They exercise police powers in their mandate to remove endangered children from their homes, but, in the name of supporting families, are expected to exercise this authority as infrequently as possible. Although their presence in a family situation always suggests that they may decide to separate children from their families, CPS workers are nonetheless expected to use their interpersonal skills and agency resources to help families cope with crises. Like police officers who live with the knowledge that a wrongful shooting may result in the loss of innocent life, and on a personal level may lead to severe discipline and public notoriety, CPS workers are vulnerable for the fateful judgments they must render.

There is no decision more fraught with potential for serious errors of omission and commission than those concerning whether children should be removed from their families. Removing a child from a home can be heartbreaking and often leads to results from which it is hard to recover, even if the child is returned home after a period of separation. Yet leaving a child in a home where violence or neglect may occur can be even more dangerous for the child, and in a different way, for the worker. Rarely are the choices clear cut.

Yet who is typically called upon to render judgments of such consequence? Here is how Harry Spence, commissioner of the Department of Social Services in Massachusetts in the early 2000s, described the workforce he oversaw:

We entrust the basic work of ensuring the safety of children to individual social workers, generally between the ages of 23 and 30, with an average tenure in the Department of 1 year and 11 months, with one month of training. We ask them, with only one set of eyes and ears, to observe each of at least 18 families for a few hours each month, often in circumstances of considerable tension and even danger. We require that they then predict the future behavior of that family, and make gut-wrenching, life-shaping decisions on the basis of those scant observations. They live with the constant knowledge that if they are wrong, a child may die, and they will be fired and publicly excoriated.[54]

The challenge for the Massachusetts Department of Social Services (DSS) was not to develop accountability mechanisms to secure compliance with agency objectives. Those already existed in such indicators as the number of home visits and supplemented with extensive case reporting requirements. In any event, the operative or tacit performance measure was whether a worker's cases stayed out of the newspaper.

In considering whether he should take the job, Spence saw in the Massachusetts DSS an ultimate public administration challenge: inexperienced and poorly trained workers practiced defensive social work and had little support from management if they erred. To make sound decisions, the work of DSS had to become better work.

With respect to workers' preparation, Spence invested in worker training, establishing an institute for protective services workers at a state college near Boston. Like the approach to teacher training mentioned earlier, he also emphasized the empathic requirements of the work. Social work was as much an "art" as a skill set, he wrote, consisting of "an open and sensitive emotional connection to the family and child," and a "habit of self-reflection" that were supported by a "community of self-reflective practitioners."[55] These observations are notable because in the public mind child protection workers are not seen as empathetic professionals but come to attention only when a decision or a nondecision has gone fatally wrong.

Reflecting an understanding that protective service work required rethinking the structure of decision making in the field, Spence introduced two unusual reforms designed to overcome the paralyzing, fear-driven model of child protection practices.

One innovation was to introduce into the department's routines the medical model of error prevention. In the past, workers who experienced even near-disastrous outcomes were afraid to talk about them or seek help for fear of being reprimanded. The consequences of making a mistake were so great that workers who had committed "near-errors" never discussed them openly or sought advice about how they might have handled situations differently. DSS lacked the cultural norm of being able to ask for help or advice.

In response, Spence introduced a version of no-fault case review widely adopted in U.S. hospitals after being pioneered in the Veteran's Administration.[56] Under this model workers are encouraged to bring up troubling cases for review. The model rejects the "error and blame" approach to accountability in favor of a culture in which it is safe to discuss and acknowledge error the better to encourage organizational learning. The no-fault model works by making it safe to bring up problematic situations on the assumptions that no sanction will result from bringing up problems in the field, and that such discussions are the basis for workers' and the organization's continuous improvement.

The second innovation was to introduce the team approach to case work. Two workers rather than one would be responsible for each case. This approach would directly confront a critical imperfection in the existing system, in which a single worker, with little experience and few resources to cope with the tensions of the visit, would call on a distressed family. Family members were often hostile or unresponsive in these settings, and often withheld critical information about the functioning of the family.

A team approach might be better. No longer would an individual worker be the solitary judge making a momentous decision alone. Workers could share notes and consult with one another on a course of action. Families were more forthcoming, perhaps because they believed they could appeal to another worker if one did not seem sympathetic, or because the team approach conveyed to clients that the agency took their case more seriously. In any event, the team approach found favor with workers and clients alike.

No outcomes in protective service interventions are certain, particularly when the philosophy of child protection toggles between removing children from the home and maintaining family integrity. Children die or are hurt while families are under protective custody orders, just as they die or are hurt in families not designated as requiring state intervention. In the new approach to accountability, Spence promised never to scapegoat workers when a child died in the care of the department—if the worker had made a good-faith effort to execute agency policy. He acknowledged that the work was fraught with danger and uncertainty, and said he would protect workers when misfortune occurred, as it inevitably would.

This approach to reforming protective services recognizes that human judgment is essential for effective public policy, and that the central chal-

lenge for management is to improve workers' capacity to render that judgment dispassionately, as much as possible based on the presenting case, and
as little as possible on extraneous fears or the instinct to take the easy way
out.

The case of protective services is a dramatic one, but the principles are
not unique to this policy arena. They apply, for example, to the case of children's mental health services, in which professionals must recommend a
drug regimen and referral to supportive programs with relatively little certainty about whether the client will respond positively, but with the knowledge that the referral will be consequential for the client and the family or
the placement environment.

Street-level bureaucracies such as child protective services, mental health
assessments, and the police are actors in arenas in which issues of public
trust are particularly mediated. We have some reason to believe that citizen
trust in society is related to the effectiveness of street-level bureaucracy,[57]
just as we have confidence that one of the components of public trust is fairness in the application of the law and the administration of public policy.[58] In
the case of street-level bureaucracies with episodically high, negative pro-
files, much more attention should be paid to helping citizens appreciate the
complexity of efforts to achieve public purposes and the futility of banishing
all mistakes. As Murray Edelman observed, it is "the routine functioning of
. . . street-level bureaucracies without too much controversy [that] confers a
reputation for leadership upon their immediate heads and also upon the
highest officials of the regime."[59] Our knowledge of the linkages between the
actual effectiveness of public services and support for an expansive public
sector includes considerable speculation, but it is a subject worthy of greater
attention.

Conclusion

In the 1970s, as I noted in chapter 1, some 3.7 million people were employed in American public schools, most of them teachers. Now that population includes more than 5.3 million teachers. Then, more than half a million
people were employed in police work; now close to 1 million are. Then,
300,000 worked in public welfare; now more than 540,000 do, with many
more working in nonprofit agencies performing welfare functions.[60] These
public sector jobs increase with the population, are relatively impervious to

automation, and will not be relocated overseas. By reasonable societal standards, they pay well.

These and other public services employing street-level bureaucrats have weathered the storms associated with racial integration of their members, and of the communities they serve. Immigration has introduced new cultures, styles, and languages to the streets, classrooms, and waiting areas where people still receive what the state has to offer or imposes on them. They have been transformed by new ways of communicating and record keeping. Many have been challenged by new ways of organizing services, including vouchers, charters, and contracting with nonprofit agencies.

Ultimately, the work of street-level bureaucracies comes down to relationships established in single encounters, or over time, between citizens and the people whose job it is to render services, provide support, or make judgments about how citizens fit the laws and practices of public agencies. Shaping those encounters are the supervisors, managers, and policy makers who establish the breadth, contours, and particular character of the exchanges.

Behind these scenes are virtual industries of people who share an interest in improving the effectiveness of particular public services. Each street-level bureaucracy has its own corps of university faculty, researchers, federal funding officials, consultants, and interested foundation officers, as well as unions and professional associations at local, state, and national levels that produce research and reform agenda, lobby for favorable outcomes, and keep members informed. These diverse individuals believe in improving the circumstances and performance of street-level occupations.

They also share a paradoxical political environment. The work they perform or support is widely accepted and often highly approved, but the public sector of which they are a part is held in low regard. They experience day-to-day operations as understaffed, and adequate resources seem perpetually remote. This is the current challenge for advocates of these public services: how to balance respect for the individual encounter that is at the heart of street-level service provision, and at the same time negotiate the larger questions of achieving efficiencies, sustaining adequate revenues, and serving as witness for the critical role of these public systems in civic life.

NOTES

Part I: Introduction

Chapter 1

1.   These definitions are analytical. They focus not on nominal occupational roles but on the characteristics of the particular work situations. Thus not every street-level bureaucrat works for a street-level bureaucracy [for example, a relocation specialist (a type of street-level bureaucrat) may work for an urban renewal agency whose employees are mostly planners, builders, and other technicians]. Conversely, not all employees of street-level bureaucracies are street-level bureaucrats (for example, file clerks in a welfare department or police officers on routine clerical assignments).

The conception of street-level bureaucracy was originally proposed in a paper prepared for the Annual Meeting of the American Political Science Association in 1969, "Toward a Theory of Street-Level Bureaucracy." It was later revised and published in Willis Hawley and Michael Lipsky, eds., *Theoretical Perspectives on Urban Politics* (Englewood Cliffs, N.J.: Prentice-Hall, 1977), pp. 196–213.

2.   U.S. Bureau of the Census, Public Employment in 1973, Series GE 73 No. 1 (Washington, D.C.: Government Printing Office, 1974), p. 9. Presented in Alan Baker and Barbara Grouby, "Employment and Payrolls of State and Local Governments, By Function: October 1973," *Municipal Year Book, 1975* (Washington, D.C.: International City Managers Association, 1975), pp. 109–112, table 4/3. Also, Marianne Stein Kah, "City Employment and Payrolls: 1975," *Municipal Year Book, 1977* (Washington, D.C.: International City Managers Association, 1977), pp. 173–179. These figures have been adjusted to represent full-time equivalents. For purposes of assessing public commitments to providing services, full-time equivalents are more appropriate statistics than total employment figures, which count many part-time employees.

3.   Jeffry H. Galper, *The Politics of Social Services* (Englewood Cliffs, N.J.: Prentice-Hall, 1975), p. 56.

4.   Lois Forer, *Death of the Law* (New York: McKay, 1975) p. 191.

5.   *New York Times*, April 4, 1976, p. 22.

6.   Baker and Grouby, "Employment and Payrolls of State and Local Governments."

7.   *New York Times*, July 10, 1977, p. F13.

8.   Of four cities with populations over one million responding to a *Municipal Year Book* survey, the proportion of personnel expenditures to total expenditures in police departments averaged 94 percent and did not go below 86 percent. Cities with smaller populations showed similar tendencies. These observations are derived from David Lewin, "Expenditure, Compensation, and Employment Data in Police, Fire, and Refuse Collection and Disposal Departments," *Municipal Year Book, 1975* pp. 39–98, table 1/21. However, the variation was much greater in the less populous cities because of smaller base figures and the fact that when cities with smaller bases make capital investments, the ratio of personnel to total expenditures changes more precipitously.

That public expenditures for street-level bureaucracies go to individuals primarily as salaries may also be demonstrated in the case of education. For example, more than 73 percent of all noncapital education expenditures inside Standard Metropolitan Statistical Areas goes toward personal services (i.e., salaries). See Government Finances, Number 1, Finances of School Districts, 1972 U.S. Census of Government (Bureau of the Census, Social and Economic Statistics Administration, U.S Department of Commerce), table 4.

Notes

9. Many analysts have discussed the increasing role of services in the economy. See Daniel Bell, *The Coming of the Post-Industrial Society: A Venture in Social Forecasting* (New York: Basic Books, 1973); Alan Gartner and Frank Reissman, *The Service Society and the Consumer Vanguard* (New York: Harper & Row, 1974); Victor Fuchs, *The Service Economy* (New York: Columbia University Press, 1968). On transformations in public welfare, see Gilbert Steiner, *Social Insecurity* (Chicago: Rand McNally, 1966), chap. 1; on public safety, see Allan Silver, "The Demand for Order in Civil Society," in David Bordua, ed., *The Police: Six Sociological Essays* (New York: John Wiley, 1967), pp. 1–24.

10. Charles Reich, "The New Property," *Yale Law Journal*, vol. 72 (April, 1964): 733–787.

11. Carl Hosticka, "Legal Services Lawyers Encounter Clients: A Study in Street-Level Bureaucracy" (Ph.D. diss., Massachusetts Institute of Technology, 1976), pp. 11–13.

12. See Frances Piven's convincing essay in which she argues that social service workers were the major beneficiaries of federal programs concerned with cities and poor people in the 1960s. Piven, "The Urban Crisis: Who Got What and Why," in Richard Cloward and Frances Piven, *The Politics of Turmoil* (New York: Vintage Books, 1972) pp. 314–351.

13. J. Joseph Loewenberg and Michael H. Moskow, eds., *Collective Bargaining in Government* (Englewood Cliffs, N.J.: Prentice-Hall, 1972). A. Laurence Chickering, ed., *Public Employee Unions* (Lexington, Mass., Lexington Books, 1976); and Margaret Levi, *Bureaucratic Insurgency* (Lexington, Mass.: Lexington Books, 1977).

14. The decline is a function of the lower birthrate and periodicity in the size of the school-age population originally resulting from the birth explosion following World War II. See Baker and Grouby, *Municipal Year Book, 1975*, pp. 109ff., on serviceability ratios.

15. This perspective remains applicable in the current period. However, in reaction to this tendency, programs that would eliminate service mediators and service providers, such as negative income taxation and housing allowances, have gained support. Fiscal scarcity has brought to public attention questions concerning the marginal utility of some of these service areas.

16. Consider the New York City policemen who, in October 1976, agreed to work overtime without pay so that a crop of rookie patrolmen would not be eliminated. *New York Times*, October 24, 1976, p. 24.

17. There can be no better illustration of the strength of the organized service workers and their support by relevant interests than the New York State Assembly's overriding of Gov. Hugh Carey's veto of the so-called Stavisky bill. This legislation, written in a period of massive concern for cutting the New York City budget, required the city to spend no less on education in the three years following the fiscal collapse than in the three years before the crisis, thus tying the hands of the city's financial managers even more. *New York Times*, April 4, 1976, p. E6; April 18, 1976, p. E6.

18. The seminal work here is Robert Rosenthal and Lenore Jacobson, *Pygmalion in the Classroom* (New York: Holt, Rinehart and Winston, 1968).

19. Martin Rein, "Welfare and Housing," Joint Center Working Papers Series, no. 4 (Cambridge, Mass.: Joint Center for Urban Studies, Spring, 1971, rev. Feb. 1972).

20. On the alleged importance of bureaucratic detachment in processing clients see Peter Blau, *Exchange and Power in Social Life* (New York: John Wiley, 1964), p. 66.

21. See National Advisory Commission on Civil Disorders, *Report* (New York: Bantam, 1968); Peter Rossi et al., *Roots of Urban Discontent* (New York: John Wiley, 1974).

22. Frances Fox Piven and Richard Cloward, *Poor People's Movements* (New York: Pantheon, 1977), pp. 20–21.

23. Michael Lipsky and Margaret Levi, "Community Organization as a Political Resource," in Harlan Hahn, ed., *People and Places in Urban Society* (Urban Affairs Annual Review, vol. 6) (Beverly Hills, Calif.: Sage Publications, 1972), pp. 175–199.

24. See James O'Connor's discussion of "legitimation" and his general thesis concerning the role of the state service sector, in O'Connor, *The Fiscal Crisis of the State* (New York: St. Martin's, 1973). On social control functions in particular policy sectors see Samuel Bowles and Herbert Gintis, *Schooling in Capitalist America* (New York: Basic Books, 1976); Frances Fox Piven and Richard Cloward, *Regulating the Poor* (New York: Pantheon, 1971); Galper, *The Politics of Social Services;* Richard Quinney, *Criminology* (Boston: Little, Brown, 1975); Ira Katznelson, "Urban Counterrevolution," in Robert P. Wolff, ed., *1984 Revisited* (New York: Alfred Knopf, 1973), pp. 139–164.

Notes

Chapter 2

1. See Chris Argyris, *Integrating the Individual and the Organization* (New York: John Wiley, 1964), pp. 35–41.

2. Frank L. Morris, Sr., "The Advantages and Disadvantages of Black Political Group Activity in Two Northern Maximum Security State Prisons" (Ph.D. diss., Massachusetts Institute of Technology, 1976), p. 40.

3. For some analysts the defining characteristic of professionalism is simply the discretion to make decisions about clients. In this view street-level bureaucrats would unquestionably be professionals. See Albert Reiss, *The Police and the Public* (New Haven: Yale University Press, 1971), p. 122.

4. On rules and the police, see James Q. Wilson, *Varieties of Police Behavior* (Cambridge: Harvard University Press, 1968), p. 31; David Perry, *Police in the Metropolis* (Columbus, Ohio: Charles Merrill, 1975), p. 168. See also Gresham Sykes' discussion of the dilemma of prison guards in being formally required to intervene in all cases of observed infractions, in Sykes, *The Society of Captives* (Princeton, N.J.: Princeton University Press, 1958).

5 For example, the Office of Civil Rights of the Department of Health, Education, and Welfare has responsibility to monitor potential violations as follows: racial discrimination under Title VI of the Civil Rights Act of 1964 in 16,000 public school districts, 2,800 institutions of higher education, and 30,000 institutions of health and social services; in the same areas, discrimination against handicapped people under Section 504 of the Vocational Rehabilitation Act of 1973; sex discrimination under Section 799A of the Public Health Service Act in 1,500 health education institutions, and under Section 745, sex discrimination in nursing schools; sex discrimination under Title IX, Education Amendments of 1972, in 16,000 public school districts; discrimination by federal contractors under Executive Order 11246, innumerable contractors at 863 higher-education campuses, and more than 3,500 additional locations. Virginia Balderama, "The Office of Civil Rights as a Street-Level Bureaucracy," unpublished seminar paper, University of Washington, March, 1976.

6. David Perry and Paula Sornoff report that welfare workers' behavior with clients in California is ruled by 115 pounds of regulations; that the average police officer is obliged to enforce approximately 30,000 federal, state, and local laws. Perry and Sornoff, "Street Level Administration and the Law: The Problem of Police Community Relations," *Criminal Law Bulletin*, vol. 8, no. 1 (January–February, 1972), p. 46.

7. Consider police assertions that they would be less willing to risk intervention if civilian review boards could penalize them for errors of judgment made under hectic and confusing circumstances which civilians might not appreciate.

8. For a discussion of attempts to introduce uniform sentencing for juvenile offenders, see the report of the findings of the Juvenile Justice Standards Project, *New York Times*, November 30, 1975, p. 1; for adult offenders, *New York Times*, October 16, 1977, p. 1.

9. See James Q. Wilson, "The Bureaucracy Problem," *The Public Interest* (Winter, 1967), pp. 3–9.

10. Keith Stevenson and Thomas Willemain, "Analyzing the Process of Screening Calls for Emergency Service" (Cambridge, Mass.: Operations Research Center, Massachusetts Institute of Technology, September, 1974), Technical Report TR-08-74.

11. Interviews with administrative personnel, Veterans Administration hospital, Bedford, Mass., August, 1974.

12. Fred Hechinger, "Where Have All the Innovations Gone?" *New York Times*, November 16, 1975, p. ED30.

13. The emphasis here is on structural explanations. Lower-level participants may also personally disagree with policy objectives. See Donald Van Meter and Carl Van Horn, "The Policy Implementation Process: A Conceptual Framework," *Administration and Society*, vol. 6, no. 4 (1975), pp. 482–483.

14. For this analysis I have drawn on Dahrendorf's observation that assuming ubiquitous conflict among social units helps in understanding some political events better than assuming inclinations toward stability, integration, and interdependence. For Dahrendorf, conflict relations are inevitable since authority relations, which are present in all social units, are necessarily

Notes

relations of subordination and superordination. However, Dahrendorf for general purposes is unable to choose between the two models of social dynamics—the integration or the "coercion" model—although for an analysis of class formation and development he favors the coercion perspective. Similarly, the model stressing conflict outlined here may be applicable under the circumstances outlined here, while the systems-integration model may be appropriate for other aspects of policy analysis. Generally see Ralf Dahrendorf, *Class and Class Conflict in Industrial Society* (Stanford, Calif.: Stanford University Press, 1959), chap. 5.

15. The perspective developed in these paragraphs is elaborated in Michael Lipsky, "Standing the Study of Public Policy Implementation on Its Head," in W. Dean Burnham and Martha Wagner Weinberg, eds., *American Politics and Public Policy* (Cambridge, Mass.: Massachusetts Institute of Technology Press, 1978), pp. 391–402.

16. Argyris, *Integrating the Individual and the Organization,* pp. 59–67.

17. On low motivation of public service workers, see Eric Nordlinger, *Decentralizing the City* (Cambridge, Mass.: Massachusetts Institute of Technology Press, 1972), chap. 3; and E. S. Savas and Sigmund Ginsburg, "The Civil Service—A Meritless System?" *The Public Interest,* no. 32 (Summer, 1973), pp. 70–85.

The problem of maintaining worker participation in organizations is a classic issue of organizational theory. For a significant early analysis, see James March and Herbert Simon, *Organizations* (New York: John Wiley, 1958).

18. Dahrendorf, *Class and Class Conflict in Industrial Society,* p. 178.

19. Donald Van Meter and Carl Van Horn point out that the "disposition of implementors" is critical to policy implementation success. The following discussion elaborates two of the conditions under which, they assert, policy implementors will resist implementation: when the policies to be implemented offend their sense of self-interest, and when the policies threaten features of the organization and procedures they desire to maintain. Van Meter and Van Horn, "The Policy Implementation Process: A Conceptual Framework," pp. 482–483.

20. The discussion is necessarily schematic to a degree. For example, it is an oversimplification to treat street-level bureaucracies as comprised of lower-level workers and managers. In this discussion the term "manager" refers to someone in an immediate supervisory position vis-à-vis street-level bureaucrats (for example, a supervisor in a public welfare agency, a police captain in charge of a precinct sector, or a principal in a nondepartmentalized public school). "Objectives" refers to the goals that the supervisor is charged with realizing. It is necessary to put it this way because the role of supervisor is itself subordinate to other roles in a complex bureaucracy. The focus on the divergence of objectives between the organization and the lowest-level workers could with some modifications be applied to the relations between the lowest-level supervisor and the roles to which this position is subordinate.

21. Argyris, *Integrating the Individual and the Organization,* p. 36.

22. For an extended treatment of the sources of street-level bureaucrats' influence, see Jeffrey Prottas, *People-Processing: The Street-Level Bureaucrat in Public Service Bureaucracies* (Lexington, Mass.: Lexington Books, 1979).

23. This paragraph is based upon personal observations, conversations with court personnel, and sustained discussions with workers in the Boston Court Resources Project.

24. See Jeffrey Prottas, *People-Processing,* chapter 3.

25. See Jon Pynoos, "Breaking the Rules: The Failure to Select and Assign Public Housing Tenants Equitably," (Ph.D. diss., Harvard University, 1974).

26. Internal memo, "Budget Bureau Recommendations for Saving in the Welfare Budget," March 24, 1969, p. IV–6 (author's files).

27. Kuh said he acted under a general provision of the law permitting prosecutors to use discretion to assure humane and rational dispositions. See *New York Times,* June 19, 1974, p. 1. At this date 87 methadone "sellers" were affected by his decision.

28. Pietro Nivola, "Municipal Agency: A Study of the Housing Inspectional Service in Boston," (Ph.D. diss., Harvard University, 1976, chap. 7).

29. David Mechanic, "Sources of Power of Lower Participants in Complex Organizations," *Administrative Science Quarterly,* vol. 7, no. 2 (December, 1962), pp. 349–364.

30. Ibid., p. 352.

31. See Jonathan Rubinstein, *City Police* (New York: Farrar, Strauss, Giroux, 1973), chap. 2.

Notes

32. Thomas Scheff, "Control over Policy by Attendants in a Mental Hospital," *Journal of Health and Human Behavior*, vol. 2 (1961), p. 97, cited in Mechanic, "Sources of Power," p. 363.

Part II: Conditions of Work

Introduction

1. For vivid descriptions of street-level bureaucracies from the client perspective, see Paul Jacobs, *Prelude to Riot* (New York: Vintage, 1968); Joseph Lyford, *The Airtight Cage* (New York: Harper & Row, 1966).

2. Two recent studies of policy making focusing on the importance of the context of decision making, particularly lack of resources and uncertainty, are Martha Wagner Weinberg, *Managing the State* (Cambridge, Mass.: Massachusetts Institute of Technology Press, 1977); Douglas Yates, *The Ungovernable City* (Cambridge, Mass.: Massachusetts Institute of Technology Press, 1977).

3. In this discussion the word "client" is used to refer to the subjects of interactions of street-level bureaucrats. This creates several problems in comparison with common usage. For example, the word "client" commonly is used to refer to people for whom service is performed. In this sense the clients of police are the people (or general public) being protected, rather than the subjects of interaction, which include robbers as well as robbed. Also, there are generic words for the subjects of service which make "client" appear awkward (e.g., doctors' patients, teachers' students or pupils). However, considering all the difficulties it seems less pedantic to refer to "clients" rather than "subjects" and truer to the synthetic objectives of this study to refer often to "clients" rather than to utilize in general discussion the generic words for subjects of study. I trust the reader will bear with me on this point.

  For a discussion of the implications of various terms designating the lowest levels of organizational participation see Amitai Etzioni, *A Comparative Analysis of Complex Organizations* (New York: The Free Press, 1961), pp. 17–21.

Chapter 3

1. Anthony Downs, *Inside Bureaucracy* (Boston: Little, Brown, 1967), p. 3.

2. Sheldon Messinger, "Organizational Transformation: A Case Study of a Declining Social Movement," *American Sociological Review*, vol. 20, no. 2 (1955), pp. 3–10.

3. Carl Hosticka, "Legal Services Lawyers Encounter Clients: A Study in Street-Level Bureaucracy," Unpublished (Ph.D. diss., Massachusetts Institute of Technology, 1976).

4. Don Zimmerman, "The Practical Basis of Work Activities in a Public Assistance Organization," in Donald Hansen, ed., *Explorations in Sociology and Counseling* (New York: Houghton Mifflin, 1969), pp. 245–249, cited in Jeffrey Prottas, *People-Processing: The Street-Level Bureaucrat in Public Service Bureaucracies* (Lexington, Mass.: Lexington Books, 1979), p. 17.

5. Typical case loads per judge per year in selected cities are: Minneapolis District Court, 700; Pittsburgh Common Pleas Court, 1,263; Chicago Preliminary Hearing Court, 2,666 to 7,000. See Martin Levin, "Delay in Five Criminal Courts," *Journal of Legal Studies*, vol. 4, no. 1 (January, 1975), table I, p. 88. Note these figures are for felony cases.

Notes

6. See John H. McNamara, "Uncertainties in Police Work: The Relevance of Police Recruits' Backgrounds and Training," in David Bordua, *The Police: Six Sociological Essays* (New York: John Wiley, 1967), pp. 168–177.

7. Maureen Mileski, "Courtroom Encounters: An Observation Study of a Lower Criminal Court," *Law and Society Review*, vol. 5, no. 5 (May, 1971), p. 479.

8. See Zimmerman, "The Practical Basis of Work Activities in a Public Assistance Organization."

9. Richard Weatherley points out that paperwork also protects workers from clients and provides solace from job pressures. Many workers appreciate the required interruptions from seeing clients, and thus many actually depend upon paperwork routines as job-coping devices that help moderate the work day.

10. For a good discussion of the transition from rookie to veteran, see John Van Maanen, "Working the Street: A Developmental View of Police Behavior," in Herbert Jacob, ed., *The Potential for Reform of Criminal Justice* (Beverly Hills, Calif.: Sage, 1974).

11. See James Q. Wilson, *Thinking About Crime* (New York: Basic Books, 1975), chaps. 3, 8.

12. See Wilson, *Varieties of Police Behavior* (Cambridge, Mass.: Harvard University Press, 1968), pp. 19–20.

13. Carl Werthman and Irving Piliavin, "Gang Members and the Police," in Bordua, ed., *The Police: Six Sociological Essays,* p. 74.

14. See, for example, William A. Westley, "Violence and the Police," *American Journal of Sociology*, vol. 59 (August, 1953), p. 39; Werthman and Piliavin, "Gang Members and the Police," p. 93; Richard Blum, "The Problems of Being a Police Officer," *Police* (January, 1961) p. 12.

15. Gresham Sykes, *The Society of Captives* (Princeton, N.J.: Princeton University Press, 1958).

16. Georgette Bennett-Sandler and Earl Ubell, "Time Bomb in Blue," *New York*, March 21, 1977, p. 47.

17. Alfred M. Bloch, "The Battered Teacher—A New Form of Combat Neurosis," unpublished paper dated March 27, 1976.

18. Howard Becker, "Social Class and Teacher-Pupil Relationships," in Blaine Mercer and Edwin Carr, eds., *Education and the Social Order* (New York: Holt, Rinehart and Winston 1957), pp. 278–279; Bernard Kelner, *How to Teach in Elementary School* (New York: McGraw-Hill, 1958), p. 19.

19. B. L. Margolis et al., "Job Stress: An Unlisted Occupational Hazard," *Journal of Occupational Medicine*, vol. 16, no. 10 (Oct., 1974), pp. 659–661. Interestingly, the most consistent relationships between mental health and working conditions occurred with respect to two other indicators: underutilization of workers' abilities and nonparticipation in decisions affecting one's job.

20. George Kirkham, "What a Professor Learned When He Became a Cop," *U.S. News and World Report*, April 22, 1974, p. 72.

21. In the early 1970s the number of emergency room visits increased at the rate of about 10 percent per year. Thomas Willemain, "The Status of Performance Measures for Emergency Medical Services," Technical Report No. 06-74 (Cambridge, Mass: Operations Research Center, Massachusetts Institute of Technology, July, 1974), p. 3. This figure is clearly too large to be accounted for by increases in population or the absolute number of emergencies experienced. According to a study of Chicago emergency facilities the most important factor in accounting for an increase in utilization of 82 percent per 1,000 population from 1960 to 1969 was the increase in the number of people using the emergency rooms for treatment of nonemergency conditions. Barry Schwartz, *Queuing and Waiting* (Chicago: University of Chicago Press, 1975), p. 127.

22. Catherine Kohler Riessman, "The Supply-Demand Dilemma in Community Mental Health Centers," *American Journal of Orthopsychiatry*, vol. 40, no. 5 (October, 1970), pp. 858–869.

23. This is the hypothesis of Richard A. Posner, "An Economic Approach to Legal Procedure and Judicial Administration," *Journal of Legal Studies*, vol. 2 (1973), pp. 447–448. Cf. Levin, "Delay in Five Criminal Courts," pp. 127—128.

24. Robert Perlman, *Consumers and Social Services* (New York: John Wiley, 1975), p. 70.

25. For discussions of different aspects of changing expectations of the police see Wilson,

Varieties of Police Behavior; Arthur Waskow, *From Race Riot to Sit-in* (Garden City, N.Y.: Doubleday, 1966); James Richardson, "To Control the City: The New York Police in Historical Perspective," in Kenneth T. Jackson and Stanley Schultz, eds., *Cities in American History* (New York, Knopf, 1972), pp. 280–288; Allan Silver, "The Demand for Order in Civil Society: A Review of Some Themes in the History of Urban Crime Police and Riot," in David Bordua, ed., *The Police,* pp. 1–24; Robert Fogelson, *Big City Police* (Cambridge, Mass: Harvard University Press, 1977).

26. C. H. Goodrich et. al., "The New York Hospital—Cornell Medical Center: Progress Report on an Experiment in Welfare Medical Care," *American Journal of Public Health,* vol. 55, no. 1 (1965), pp. 88–93; James Weiss and Merwyn Greenlick, "Determinants of Medical Care Utilization: The Effect of Social Class and Distance on Contacts with the Medical Care System," *Medical Care,* vol. 9 (1970). Cited in Deborah Stone, Institute of Policy Sciences, Duke University, "Professionals and Social Services," unpublished paper (March, 1976).

27. Carol Ruth Silver, "The Imminent Failure of Legal Services for the Poor: Why and How to Limit Caseload," *Journal of Urban Law,* vol. 46 (1969), p. 217.

28. For a similar analysis applied to collective demands see Michael Lipsky and David J. Olson, *Commission Politics: The Processing of Racial Crisis in America* (New Brunswick, N.J.: Transaction Books, 1977), pp. 3–6.

29. Nordlinger makes a well-reasoned argument that out of eighty thousand complaints concerning city services registered in Boston in 1970, fully fifty to sixty thousand would not have been registered in the absence of the Little City Halls program. He estimates that at least half of these calls, representing approximately a third of these service complaints, were legitimate and not crank complaints or trivial. In other words, at least a third of all the service complaints received were new, yet of the kind the city had been receiving under old demand-receiving policies. See Eric Nordlinger *Decentralizing the City: A Study of Boston's Little City Halls* (Cambridge, Mass.: Massachusetts Institute of Technology Press, 1972), p. 286.

30. Reissman, for example, cites the case of an Oklahoma public health clinic that increased tenfold the number of persons brought to the clinic for immunization by relying for outreach on seven paraprofessionals rather than three nurses. Reissman, "The Demand-Supply Dilemma," p. 858.

31. David Kirp, "Schools as Sorters: The Constitutional and Policy Implications of Student Classification," *University of Pennsylvania Law Review,* vol. 121, no. 4 (April, 1973), p. 712.

32. Some of the inactive caseload may consist simply of cases that would not be on the rolls if the worker had had time to find out that they should be eliminated for reasons of changed circumstances. This enrages agency administrators, particularly in welfare or other entitlement programs. For a discussion of these caseload dynamics in legal services see Hosticka, "Legal Services Lawyers Encounter Clients."

33. Here is a concrete if hypothetical illustration. If, on the average, legal service lawyers have formal case loads of eighty and active case loads of twenty, if another lawyer were added to a five-person office, and if no new cases were accepted, then each attorney would have approximately 66 cases (the old case load of the office now divided by six). But each attorney would still have an active case load of twenty. This increases the number of clients actively served, but does not improve the situation qualitatively. The pressure of time remains unchanged since the active case load is a function not of work assigned but of the amount of case pressure that workers can accommodate.

34. Generally, see chap. 11.

35. For example, Milton Heumann has found that a loss of adversary activity in the courts and an increase in plea bargaining apparently are not directly related to case-load pressures. See Heumann, "A Note on Plea Bargaining and Case Pressure," *Law and Society Review,* vol. 9, no. 3 (Spring, 1975), pp. 515–528.

36. Ibid., p. 527.

37. See the discussion in Robert Alford, *Health Care Politics* (Chicago: University of Chicago Press, 1975), p. 222.

38. For a discussion of costs imposed on clients, see chapter 8 herein.

39. See Downs, *Inside Bureaucracy,* p. 188.

Notes

Chapter 4

1. On goal conflicts in police work see James Q. Wilson, *Varieties of Police Behavior* (Cambridge, Mass.: Harvard University Press, 1968); in public education, see Jeffrey Raffel, "Responsiveness in Urban Schools: A Study of Adaptation to Parental Preferences in an Urban Environment," (Ph.D. diss., Massachusetts Institute of Technology, 1972); in public welfare, see Gilbert Steiner, *The State of Welfare* (Washington, D.C.: Brookings, 1971).

2. Willis Hawley, "Dealing with Organizational Rigidity in the Public Schools," (paper presented at the Annual Meeting of the American Political Science Association, September, 1971), p. 22, n. 77. See also Yeheskel Hasenfeld and Richard English, eds., *Human Service Organizations* (Ann Arbor, Mich.: University of Michigan Press, 1974), pp. 9–12.

3. Martin Landau, "On the Concept of a Self-Correcting Organization," *Public Administration Review*, vol. 33, no. 6 (November–December, 1973), p. 536.

4. Daniel P. Moynihan, *Maximum Feasible Misunderstanding* (New York: The Free Press, 1969), chap. 5.

5. Martin Rein, *Social Policy* (New York: Random House, 1970), p. xi.

6. Hasenfeld and English, *Human Service Organizations*, pp. 12–14.

7. See Gary Bellow and Jeanne Kettleson, "From Ethics to Politics: Confronting Scarcity and Fairness in Public Interest Practice," *Boston University Law Review*, vol. 58, no. 3 (May, 1978), pp. 337–390.

8. Amitai Etzioni, *A Comparative Analysis of Complex Organizations* (Glencoe, Ill.: Free Press, 1961).

9. Because teachers, social workers, nurses, and other occupational groups typically display professional characteristics such as length of training, degree of autonomy, etc., to a lesser degree than the professions of medicine and law, some analysts have chosen to call them "semiprofessions" to highlight this distinction. See Amitai Etzioni, ed., *The Semi-Professions and their Organization* (New York: The Free Press, 1969).

10. Martin Levin, "Delay in Five Criminal Courts," *Journal of Legal Studies*, vol. 4, no. 1 (January, 1975), p. 90.

11. On the tendency for organizations to maintain themselves and enhance their position see, notably, Chester Barnard, *The Functions of the Executive* (Cambridge, Mass.: Harvard University Press, 1938).

12. See then President Gerald Ford's statement proposing to reduce the runaway risks of the food-stamp program, *New York Times*, October 10, 1975.

13. Michael Lipsky and Morris Lounds, "Citizen Participation in Health Care: Dilemmas of Government Induced Participation," *Journal of Health Politics, Policy and Law*, vol. 1, no. 1 (Spring, 1976), pp. 85–111.

14. Theodore Sarbin and Vernon Allen, "Role Theory," in Gardner Lindzey and Elliot Aronson, eds., *The Handbook of Social Psychology*, 2d ed. (Reading, Mass.: Addison-Wesley, 1968), pp. 488–567, esp. pp. 498–499, 532.

15. See Wilson, *Varieties of Police Behavior*; Raffel, "Responsiveness in Urban Schools"; and Steiner, *The State of Welfare*.

16. On differences in cities' political cultures see Robert Alford, *Bureaucracy and Participation: Political Culture in Four Wisconsin Cities* (Chicago: Rand-McNally, 1969), and Herbert Jacob, *Debtors in Court: The Consumption of Government Services* (Chicago: Rand McNally, 1969).

17. Wilson discusses the "zone of indifference" in which police administrators are free to act in *Varieties of Police Behavior*, p. 233. The phrase is from Barnard, *The Functions of the Executive*, p. 167.

18. A case in point was provided by Boston policemen charged with preventing white Boston residents from harassing black school children when Boston schools were integrated in 1975. The policemen often grew up in the same neighborhoods as those in the crowds they were trying to control. They were friendly with or lived among neighborhood residents and did not personally approve of school integration as it was being carried out. See John Kifner, "Men in the Middle," *New York Times Magazine* (September 12, 1976), pp. 36ff.

19. The theme of role conflict pervades the literature on police. See, for example, Carl

Werthman and Irving Piliavin, "Gang Members and the Police," Albert Reiss and David Bordua, "Environment and Organization: A Perspective on the Police," and James Q. Wilson, "Police Morale, Reform, and Citizen Respect: The Chicago Case," in Bordua, ed., *The Police;* Herman Goldstein. "Police Discretion: The Ideal Versus the Real," *Public Administration Review,* vol. 23 (September, 1963), p. 142; Arthur Niederhoffer, *Behind the Blue Shield* (New York: Doubleday, 1967).

20. Perhaps the extreme expression of the exclusion of clients as a reference group is found in the courts. As Martin Levin writes, the person "with perhaps the most potential interest in the criminal court—the victim—usually does not even watch its proceedings, and when he does, he does not exercise effective supervision. Indeed, almost all aspects of the court process . . . operate to discourage his effort to watch." Levin, "Delay in Five Criminal Courts," p. 95.

21. See Norman Fainstein and Susan Fainstein, *Urban Political Movements* (Englewood Cliffs, N.J.: Prentice-Hall, 1974).

22. Research findings in this area are summarized in Sarbin and Allen, "Role Theory," pp. 503–506. In their study of job stress Margolis et al. found role ambiguity to be associated with six out of ten measures of job stress. "Job Stress: An Unlisted Occupational Hazard," pp. 659–661.

23. Downs, *Inside Bureaucracy,* chap. 3.

24. For further discussion of problems in measuring performance, see chapter 11. Here the objective is simply to elaborate the proposition that unavailability of performance measures is a common, critical condition of street-level bureaucracy work.

25. Rubinstein, *City Police,* pp. 32–43, 67.

26. John I. Kitsuse and Aaron V. Cicourel, "A Note on the Use of Official Statistics," *Social Problems,* vol. 11 (1963), pp. 131–139.

27. Peter Blau, *The Dynamics of Bureaucracy,* rev. ed. (Chicago: University of Chicago Press, 1963), chap. 3.

28. See Stanton Wheeler, "The Structure of Formally Organized Socialization Settings," in Orville Brim, Jr. and Stanton Wheeler, *Socialization after Childhood: Two Essays* (New York: John Wiley, 1966), pp. 102ff.

We may hypothesize that the willingness of street-level bureaucrats to develop, and the public to accept, these surrogate measures of performance reinforces conservative tendencies. When these reified qualities are accepted as good or significant, or even if they simply determine the reward structure of the agency, the people who display these characteristics remain entrenched. Significantly, it is highly upsetting to the status quo when these surrogate measures are challenged. This is why reform in police departments may be enhanced by insisting that a college degree be a condition of employment. Those who prospered under the old system are disadvantaged by this innovation. But this would only be true in departments that previously had a relatively uneducated staff. To take the point to the extreme, it would also be a destabilizing and possibly advantageous reform in a highly educated department to forbid employment of college graduates. Similarly, it might disrupt the status quo to reward teachers who have previously had outside work experience or to reward teachers who show particular abilities in interacting with a wide range of students, since these are qualities that are not normally rewarded by public school systems.

29. Hawley, "Organizational Rigidity in the Public Schools," p. 13.

30. James G. Anderson, "The Authority Structure of the School: System of Social Exchange," *Educational Administration Quarterly,* vol. 3 (Spring, 1967), p. 136, cited in Hawley, "Organizational Rigidity in the Public Schools," p. 13.

31. David Seidman and Michael Couzens, "Crime, Crime Statistics, and the Great American Anti-Crime Crusade: Police Misreporting of Crime and Political Pressures" (Paper presented at the Annual Meeting of the American Political Science Association, Washington, D.C. 1972).

32. Generally see Pietro Nivola, "Municipal Agency: A Study of the Housing Inspection Service in Boston." (Ph.D. diss., Harvard University, 1976).

33. Albert O. Hirschman, *Exit, Voice and Loyalty* (Cambridge, Mass.: Harvard University Press, 1970).

34. See Hawley, "Organizational Rigidity in the Public Schools," p. 12.

35. Gary Bridges, "Citizen Choice in Public Services: Voucher Systems," in E. S. Savas, ed., *Alternatives for Delivering Public Services* (Boulder, Colo.: Westview Press, 1977), pp.

Notes

51–109; David K. Cohen and Eleanor Farrar, "Power to the Parents?—The Story of Education Vouchers," *Public Interest*, no. 48 (Summer, 1977), pp. 72–97.

Chapter 5

1. Others have commented on the extent to which clients of some organizations are nonvoluntary, and they have attempted to assess the importance of this distinction for treatment and organizational behavior. See Elaine Cumming, *Systems of Social Regulation* (New York: Atherton, 1968). James D. Thompson discusses the extent to which two variables (the extent to which a member of an organization is tightly or loosely controlled by its rules and assumptions and whether the nonmembers, in our case clients, participate in the interaction voluntarily or not) affect the relationship between members and nonmembers of an organization. Thompson's dichotomization of the interaction variable presents the choices in extreme form and does not accommodate gradations. Thompson's two variables when combined yield four organizational types; our analysis draws attention to the probability that, analytically, the participation of most poor people in transactions with public agencies tends to be mandatory. See Thompson, "Organizations and Output Transactions," in Elihu Katz and Brenda Danet, eds., *Bureaucracy and the Public* (New York: Basic Books, 1972), pp. 191–211.

2. The extent to which clients can affect doctors' behavior is the subject of Eliot Freidson's article, "Client and Medical Practice," *American Journal of Sociology*, vol. 65 (January, 1960), 374–382. See also, Amitai Etzioni, "Administration and the Consumer," *American Sociological Quarterly*, vol. 3, no. 2 (September, 1955), pp. 257–264.

3. See Willis Hawley, "Organizational Rigidity in the Public Schools," (paper presented at the Annual Meeting of the American Political Science Association, September, 1971), p. 15.

4. I have found the most accessible discussion of bargaining to be Thomas Schelling, *The Strategy of Conflict* (Cambridge, Mass.: Harvard University Press, 1960).

5. Julius Roth, "Some Contingencies of the Moral Evaluation and Control of Clientele: The Case of the Hospital Emergency Service," in Yeheskel Hasenfeld and Richard English, eds., *Human Service Organizations*, (Ann Arbor, Mich.: University of Michigan Press, 1974), p. 502. For a general orientation to the perspective implicit here see Erving Goffman, *Strategic Interactions* (Philadelphia, Pa.: University of Pennsylvania Press, 1969).

6. Eliot Freidson, *Professional Dominance* (New York: Atherton, 1970).

7. See Gresham Sykes, *Society of Captives* (Princeton, N.J.: Princeton University Press, 1958), pp. 48–58.

8. For a discussion of ways inmates are induced to contribute to their own control in mental hospitals and other institutions that totally circumscribe people's lives see Erving Goffman, *Asylums* (Garden City, N.Y.: Doubleday, 1961), pp. 177–207.

9. Goffman, *Strategic Interactions*.

10. Ira Katznelson, *Black Men, White Cities* (New York: Oxford University Press, 1973), p. 25. On the conceptualization of research on relationships of dominance and subordination, see chap. 2.

11. The title of this section is obviously a paraphrase (apt, I trust) of Peter Berger and Thomas Luckmann, *The Social Construction of Reality* (Garden City, N.Y.: Doubleday, 1976). For a detailed elaboration of the process of client categorization, see Jeffrey Prottas, *People-Processing: The Street-Level Bureaucrat in Public Service Bureaucracies* (Lexington, Mass.: Lexington Books, 1979).

12. For the importance of these distinctions in court processing of juveniles see Robert Emerson, *Judging Delinquents* (New York: Aldine, 1969).

13. On the distinction between structure and behavior see Katznelson, *Black Men, White Cities*, chap. 2.

14. Elihu Katz and S. N. Eisenstadt, "Some Sociological Observations on the Response of

Israeli Organizations to New Immigrants," in Elihu Katz and Brenda Danet, eds., *Bureaucracy and the Public*, p. 79.

15. Reported by Carl Hosticka, "Legal Services Lawyers Encounter Clients. A Study in Street-level Bureaucracy" (Ph.D. diss. Massachusetts Institute of Technology, 1976).

16. Carl Werthman and Irving Piliavin, "Gang Members and the Police," in David Bordua, ed., *The Police: Six Sociological Essays* (New York: John Wiley, 1967), p. 87.

17. Michael Lipsky and Margaret Levi, "Community Organization as a Political Resource," in Harlan Hahn, ed., *People and Politics in Urban Society* (Beverly Hills, Calif.: Sage, 1972), pp. 195–196; Michael Lipsky, *Protest in City Politics* (Chicago, Ill.: Rand McNally, 1970).

18. In coaching the client street-level bureaucrats are only contributing to a process clients otherwise engage in: maneuvering to secure what they think will provide the best chance or the most favorable outcome (getting the best judge, teacher, social worker; phrasing words correctly; having papers ready, etc.).

19. Jon Pynoos, "Breaking the Rules: The Failure to Select and Assign Public Housing Tenants Equitably," (Ph.D. diss., Harvard University, 1974). (See chap. 2, pp. 21–22).

20. Pietro Nivola, "Municipal Agency: A Study of the Housing Inspectional Service in Boston," (Ph.D. diss. Harvard University, 1976), chap. 3.

21. Alan Keith-Lucas, *Decisions about People in Need* (Chapel Hill, N.C.: University of North Carolina Press, 1957), p. 224.

22. Jerome Skolnick describes how defense attorneys instruct clients for best results to express regret and perplexity at their own behavior rather than attempt to explain the behavior away, although this is their inclination. Skolnick, "Social Control in the Adversary System," *Journal of Conflict Resolution*, vol. 11, no. 1 (1967), pp. 59–67, in Jerome Skolnick and Richard Schwartz, eds., *Society and the Legal Order* (New York: Basic Books, 1970), pp. 414–423, citation at p. 418.

23. The tendency of bureaucrats to treat some part of the population specially, in opposition to formal mandates, is explored in Brenda Danet, " 'Giving the Underdog a Break': Latent Particularism Among Customs Officials," in Katz and Danet, *Bureaucracy and the Public*, pp. 329–337. Danet discusses such tendencies in terms of bureaucrats' "latent particularism." From an organizational standpoint "latent particularism" is discussed in terms of "debureaucratization" in Elihu Katz and S. N. Eisenstadt, "Some Sociological Observations on the Response of Israeli Organizations to New Immigrants," in Katz and Danet, pp. 73–88. Coaching the client as discussed here is one form of "debureaucratization." The term is meant to reflect departure from an ideal type of bureaucratic universalism. However, the term is somewhat awkward since it implies a departure from a state of bureaucratic formalism. A bureaucracy which has never achieved the universalism of the ideal type in common terms cannot usefully be described as debureaucratized.

24. For a general treatment of this perspective, see Goffman, *Strategic Interactions*.

25. Joel Handler and Mary Jane Hollingsworth, *The Deserving Poor* (Chicago: Markham, 1971). See also Kenneth Clark, *Dark Ghetto* (New York: Harper & Row, 1965).

26. Goffman, *Asylums*; David Mechanic, *Medical Sociology: A Selective View* (New York: The Free Press, 1968), pp. 115ff.

27. Cf. Murray Edelman's view of the "helping professions" in *Political Language: Words That Succeed and Policies That Fail* (New York: Academic Press, 1977), chap. 4.

28. Robert Rosenthal and Lenore Jacobson, *Pygmalion in the Classroom* (New York: Holt, Rinehart and Winston, 1968); Ray C. Rist, "Student Social Class and Teacher Expectations: The Self-Fulfilling Prophecy in Ghetto Education," *Harvard Educational Review*, vol. 40 (August, 1970), pp. 411–451; see Robert Merton, *Social Theory and Social Structure* (Glencoe, Ill.: The Free Press, 1957), chap. 11. Self-fulfilling prophecies that result from assigning clients to categories without necessarily being affected by the interaction with street-level bureaucrats are discussed in chapter 10.

29. Rist, "Student Social Class and Teacher Expectations."

30. Emerson, *Judging Delinquents*.

31. Richard Weatherley, *Reforming Special Education: Policy Implementation from State Level to Street Level* (Cambridge, Mass.: Massachusetts Institute of Technology Press, 1979).

32. Berger and Luckmann, *The Social Construction of Reality*, p. 30.

33. Eliot Freidson, *Profession of Medicine* (New York: Dodd Mead, 1974), pp. 216ff.

Notes

34. Jerome Skolnick and Richard Schwartz, "Two Studies of Legal Stigma," *Social Problems*, vol. 10 (Fall, 1962), 133–142, cited in Maureen Mileski, "Courtroom Encounters," *Law and Society Review*, vol. 5, no. 5 (May, 1971), p. 496.

35. Handler and Hollingsworth, *The Deserving Poor*; Hosticka, "Legal Servies Lawyers Encounter Clients."

Chapter 6

1. On the role of myth in public policy see Murray Edelman, *Political Language* (New York: Academic Press, 1977), esp. chap. 1.

2. A. Cicourel and J. Kitsuse, *The Educational Decision Makers* (Indianapolis, Ind.: Bobbs-Merrill, 1963), cited in David Kirp, "Schools as Sorters: The Constitutional and Policy Implications of School Classification," *University of Pennsylvania Law Review*, vol. 121, no. 4 (April, 1973), p. 711.

3. Deborah Stone has elaborated the dilemma of physicians who are asked to act as both advocates and overseers of the public purse, in *Controlling the Medical Profession* (Chicago: University of Chicago Press, forthcoming).

4. Richard Weatherley, *Reforming Special Education: Policy Implementation from State Level to Street Level* (Cambridge, Mass.: Massachusetts Institute of Technology Press, 1979).

5. On the tension between supporting and controlling clients see Elaine Cumming, *Systems of Social Regulation* (New York: Atherton, 1968), pp. 6–9.

6. Jerome Skolnick, "Social Control in the Adversary System," in Jerome Skolnick and Richard Schwartz, *Society and the Legal Order* (New York: Basic Books, 1970), pp. 421–422.

7. Peter Blau, *Dynamics of Bureaucracy* (Chicago: University of Chicago Press, 1964).

8. Suggested by Judy Riley, "A Case Study of Street-Level Bureaucracy: Child Protective Services," unpublished seminar paper, University of Washington, 1976.

9. For a review and discussion of political alienation as a psychological construct see Stanley Greenberg, "Political Alienation and Political Action," in Willis Hawley and Michael Lipsky, eds., *Theoretical Perspectives on Urban Politics* (Englewood Cliffs, N.J.: Prentice-Hall, 1976), pp. 176–183.

10. Here I recognize an assumption that, while the subject of considerable debate, remains ultimately unresolvable: self-actualization, particularly tendencies toward creativity, cooperation, and personal growth, is inherently a human quality that people strive to express if given the chance and freed from pursuit of necessities. For a discussion of this orientation in organizational studies see Chris Argyris, "Some Limits of Rational Man Organizational Theory," *Public Administration Review*, vol. 33 (June, 1973), pp. 253–267.

For a summary of how alienation is generally utilized to describe relations of work see Frederick Thayer, *An End to Hierarchy! An End to Competition!* (New York: Franklin Watts, 1973), pp. 47–48; also Amitai Etzioni, *The Active Society* (New York: The Free Press, 1968), chap. 21.

11. Etzioni, *The Active Society*, pp. 618–620.

12. In these paragraphs I have deliberately chosen language to suggest parallels with analyses of the work of industrial workers.

13. On trends in workers' control see *Administration and Society*, vol. 7, no. 1 (May, 1975), an issue devoted to this topic.

14. In response to these work-related problems street-level bureaucracies often do attempt to control the nature of the clientele. This is treated in chapters 7 through 9.

15. Very few studies have concentrated on the dynamics over time of routine treatment of clients by public agencies. See Alan Keith-Lucas, *Decisions about People in Need* (Chapel Hill, N.C.: University of North Carolina Press, 1957) for a study of the treatment of welfare clients in the south in the 1950s. See Waskow, *From Race Riot to Sit-In*, for a study of changes in nonroutine police practice over time. For speculative study of the implications of modernization in police departments see James Q. Wilson, "The Police and the Delinquent in Two Cities," in

Stanton Wheeler, ed., *Controlling Delinquents* (New York: John Wiley, 1968). For a discussion of developments in the bureaucratic treatment of Israeli immigrants over time see Katz and Eisenstadt, "The Response of Israeli Organizations to New Immigrants," in Elihu Katz and Brenda Danet, eds., *Bureaucracy and the Public* (New York: Basic Books, 1972), pp. 73–88.

Part III: Patterns of Practice

Introduction

1. Cf. James Q. Wilson, "The Bureacucracy Problem," *Public Interest*, no. 6 (Winter, 1967), pp. 3–9.

2. For another analysis that assumes people "desire to do a good job," see Downs, *Inside Bureaucracy* (Boston: Little Brown, 1967), p. 198.

3. Lee Rainwater, "The Revolt of the Dirty Workers," *Transaction*, vol. 5, no. 1 (Nov., 1967), pp. 2ff.

4. James March and Herbert Simon, *Organizations* (New York: John Wiley, 1958); Charles Lindblom, "The Science of 'Muddling Through'," *Public Administration Review*, vol. 19 (Spring 1959), pp. 79–88.

5. Useful conceptual distinctions for various phenomena related to coping are provided by Richard Lazarus in *Psychological Stress and the Coping Process* (New York: McGraw-Hill, 1966), chap. 1.

6. Routines are the regularized or habitual patterns by which tasks are performed. Simplifications are symbolic constructs in terms of which decisions about potentially complex phenomena are made, utilizing a smaller set of cues than those presented by the phenomena. Routines are behavioral patterns of response; simplifications are mental patterns of ordering data with which routines may or may not be associated. Peter Berger and Thomas Luckmann discuss the ubiquitous nature of routinization and simplification in *The Politics of Everyday Life* (Garden City, N.Y.: Doubleday, 1976), pp. 28ff and 53ff. They use the terms "habituations" for the former, "typifications" for the latter.

7. See Reinhard Bendix, *Work and Authority in Industry* (New York: John Wiley, 1956), chap. 4. Willis Hawley presents an interesting discussion of the significance of routinization in "The Possibilities of Nonbureaucratic Organization," Willis D. Hawley and David Rogers, eds., *Improving the Quality of Urban Management* (Beverly Hills, Calif.: Sage, 1974), pp. 371–426.

8. See Victor Thompson, *Modern Organization* (New York: Knopf, 1961), p. 14; James March and Herbert Simon, *Organizations* (New York: John Wiley, 1958), p. 142.

9. See the discussion of "Categorization of Data" in Thompson, *Modern Organizations*, p. 17.

10. The importance of routines in developing policy in other areas is well established. For a concise general treatment, see Ira Sharkansky, *The Routines of Politics* (New York: Van Nostrand, 1970).

11. On the meaning of the term "political" see David Easton, *A Framework for Political Analysis* (Englewood Cliffs, N.J.: Prentice-Hall, 1965), p. 50; and Harold Lasswell, *Who Gets What, When, How?* (New York: McGraw Hill, 1936).

12. Karen Orren, *Corporate Power and Social Change* (Baltimore: Johns Hopkins, 1973).

13. James Davis and Kenneth Dolbeare, *Little Groups of Neighbors* (Chicago: Markham, 1968).

14. See Thompson, *Modern Organizations*, pp. 168–169.

15. Julius Roth, "Some Contingencies of the Moral Evaluation and Control of Clientele: The Case of Hospital Emergency Services," in Yeheskel Hasenfeld and Richard English, eds., *Human Service Organizations* (Ann Arbor, Mich.: University of Michigan Press, 1974), p. 500, italics omitted.

Notes

Chapter 7

1. The reactive nature of police work, and police dependence upon citizens in this respect, is stressed in Albert Reiss, *The Police and the Public* (New Haven: Yale University Press, 1971).

2. The latter case is cited by Barry Schwartz, *Queuing and Waiting* (Chicago: University of Chicago Press, 1975), p. 24. This excellent volume provides many insights into issues of priorities in client treatment and the costs of seeking service.

3. See Robert Dahl, "The Analysis of Influence in Local Communities," in Charles Adrian, ed., *Social Science and Community Action* (East Lansing, Mich.: Michigan State University Press, 1960), p. 32.

4. See generally Jonathan Rubinstein, "Suspicions," in *City Police* (New York: Farrar, Straus, 1973).

5. For example, one prosecutor's office that switched from telephone to mail complaint handling in processing white collar crimes experienced a 25 percent reduction in complaints received. Michael Brintnall, "The Allocation of Services in the Local Prosecution of Economic Crime" (Ph.D. diss., Massachusetts Institute of Technology, 1977), chap. 6.

6. See Schwartz, *Queuing and Waiting*, chap. 6.

7. When court clerks use confusing legal language we may call it "bureaucratic language as incantation." Edelman, *Political Language: Words that Succeed and Policies that Fail* (New York: Academic Press, 1977), p. 98. But what shall we call the court clerk's chant that strings words together indistinguishably? Perhaps it should be called "incantation as symbolic language." For attempts to deal positively with the rationing effects of legal language, consider the New York state law requiring consumer contracts to be written in clear, understandable language. See *New York Times*, Aug. 11, 1977, p. B1.

8. This is a paraphrase of the definition of demands in David Easton, *A Framework for Political Analysis* (Englewood Cliffs, N.J.: Prentice-Hall, 1965), p. 120.

9. *New York Times*, September 25, 1977.

10. Leon Mayhew, "Institutions of Representation: Civil Justice and the Public," *Law and Society Review*, vol. 9, no. 3 (Spring, 1975), p. 403. The discrepancy is so great that it would be difficult to attribute it to differences in the nature of the sample.

11. Richard Cloward and Frances Fox Piven, "A Strategy to End Poverty," *The Politics of Turmoil* (New York: Vintage, 1975), pp. 89–106.

12. Gilbert Steiner, *The State of Welfare* (Washington, D.C.: Brookings, 1971).

13. Kitsuse and Cicourel have written that statistics reflect a great deal about the organizations collecting the statistics. John Kitsuse and Aaron Cicourel, "A Note on the Uses of Official Statistics," *Social Problems*, vol. 11 (1963), pp. 131–139. Sometimes the statistics collectors are not the same as those formally charged with providing information about services.

14. Eric Nordlinger, *Decentralizing the City* (Cambridge, Mass.,: Massachusetts Institute of Technology Press, 1972), p. 286.

15. The dynamics of this process are discussed in Michael Lipsky and Morris Lounds, "Citizen Participation and Health Care: Problems of Government Induced Participation," *Journal of Health Politics, Policy and Law*, vol. 1, no. 1 (Spring, 1976), pp. 85–111.

16. See the discussion of the psychological implications of waiting in Schwartz, *Queuing and Waiting*, chaps. 1, 8.

17. Virtually every commentary on welfare practices draws attention to the degradation of clients. See Alan Keith-Lucas, *Decisions about People in Need* (Chapel Hill, N.C.: University of North Carolina, 1957); Steiner, *The State of Welfare* (Washington, D.C.: Brookings, 1971); Piven and Cloward, *Regulating the Poor* (New York: Pantheon, 1971), chaps. 4–5.

18. Jeffrey Prottas, *People-Processing: The Street-Level Bureaucrat in Public Service Bureaucracies* (Lexington, Mass.: Lexington Books, 1979). On the continuing relationships between ghetto fathers who have deserted and their families, see Elliot Liebow, *Tally's Corner* (Boston: Little, Brown, 1967).

19. June Grant Wolf, "The Initial Evaluation at a Walk-In Clinic: Applicant's and Evaluator's Perspectives" (Ph.D. diss., Boston University, 1974), p. 76.

20. First-come, first-served, "constitutes the normative basis for most forms of queueing." Schwartz, *Queuing and Waiting*, p. 93.

21. Ibid., chap. 6.

22. Carl Hosticka, "Legal Services Lawyers Encounter Clients: A Study in Street-Level Bureaucracy" (Ph.D. diss., Massachusetts Institute of Technology, 1976).

23. Catherine Kohler Reissman, "The Supply-Demand Dilemma in Community Mental Health Centers," *American Journal of Orthopsychiatry*, vol. 40, no. 5 (October, 1970), p. 860.

24. See chap. 2.

25. See Jeffry Galper, *The Politics of Social Services* (Englewood Cliffs, N.J.: Prentice-Hall, 1975), pp. 70–71.

26. Reissman, "The Supply-Demand Dilemma," p. 860.

27. See Schwartz, *Queuing and Waiting*, pp. 26–29.

28. Ibid., chap. 5 and fn. 5, p. 201.

29. Robert Perlman, *Consumers and Social Services* (New York: John Wiley, 1975), p. 77.

30. Speaker, Annual Convention of the National Legal Aid and Defenders Association, Seattle, Washington, November, 1975.

31. Nivola, "Municipal Agency: A Study of Housing Inspectional Service in Boston," chap. 3.

32. "Budget Bureau Recommendations for Savings in the Welfare Budget," March 24, 1969. Unpublished document in author's files.

33. Ibid.

34. Ibid.

35. Ibid.

36. *New York Times*, December 21, 1977.

Chapter 8

1. This is developed in Jeffrey Prottas, *People-Processing: The Street-Level Bureaucrat in Public Service Bureaucracies* (Lexington, Mass.: Lexington Books, 1979).

2. The term has come into currency to classify city neighborhoods, arrogantly differentiating among those that are likely to recover if assisted with government funds, those too far deteriorated to save, and those likely to continue to thrive without government assistance.

3. See David Kirp's summary of the evidence in "Schools as Sorters: The Constitutional and Policy Implications of Student Classification," *University of Pennsylvania Law Review*, vol. 121, no. 4 (April, 1973), pp. 705–797.

4. My knowledge of this program was gained over the five-year period in which I served regularly as a project-site visitor.

5. Brenda Danet, " 'Giving the Underdog a Break': Latent Particularism among Customs Officials," in Elihu Katz and Brenda Danet, eds., *Bureaucracy and the Public* (New York: Basic Books, 1973), pp. 329–337.

6. Nicholas Alex, *Black in Blue* (New York: Appleton, 1969).

7. Robert Emerson, *Judging Delinquents* (New York: Aldine, 1969).

8. Barney Glaser and Anselm Strauss, "The Social Loss of Dying Patients," *American Journal of Nursing*, vol. 64 (June, 1964), pp. 119–121.

9. Julius Roth, "Some Contingencies of the Moral Evaluation and Control of Clientele: The Case of the Hospital Emergency Room," in Yeheskel Hasenfeld and Richard English, eds., *Human Service Organizations*, (Ann Arbor, Mich.: University of Michigan Press, 1974), pp. 499–516.

10. David Sudnow, "Normal Crimes: Sociological Features of the Penal Code in a Public Defender's Office," *Social Problems*, vol. 12 no. 3 (Winter, 1965), pp. 255–276; Emerson, *Judging Delinquents*.

Notes

11.   Robert Scott, "The Selection of Clients by Social Welfare Agencies: The Case of the Blind," in Hasenfeld and English, *Human Service Organizations*, pp. 485–498; Donald Schon, "The Blindness System," *Public Interest*, vol. 18 (Winter, 1970), pp. 25–38.

12.   Lois Forer, *Death of the Law* (New York: McKay, 1975).

13.   Sociologist Jules Henry called the tendency of teachers to concentrate on only a few students "partial withdrawal." See Henry, "White Peoples Time, Colored Peoples Time," *Transaction*, vol. 2, no. 3 (March–April, 1965), p. 32.

14.   See *New York Times*, March 3, 1977, p. 33.

15.   Sudnow, "Normal Crimes." See also Erving Goffman, *Relations in Public* (New York: Basic Books, 1971), chap. 6.

16.   Maureen Mileski, "Courtroom Encounters," *Law and Society Review*, vol. 5, no. 5 (May, 1971), p. 513.

17.   Carl Hosticka, "Legal Services Lawyers Encounter Clients: A Study in Street-Level Bureaucracy," (Ph.D. diss., Massachusetts Institute of Technology, 1976).

18.   Mileski, "Courtroom Encounters," p. 503.

19.   Eliot Freidson, *Profession of Medicine* (New York: Dodd, Mead, 1970), p. 257.

20.   Children's Defense Fund, *Children Out of School in America* (Washington, D.C.: Children's Defense Fund, 1974).

21.   Carl Werthman and Irving Piliavin, "Gang Members and the Police," in David Bordua, ed., *The Police* (New York: John Wiley, 1967), p. 76.

22.   Richard Quinney, *Criminology* (Boston: Little, Brown, 1975), chap. 6; Forer, *Death of the Law*, chap. 5.

23.   David Mechanic, *Medical Sociology* (New York: Free Press, 1968), pp. 115ff.

24.   See chap. 5 herein, note 28.

25.   For a convincing discussion of the subjective bases of doctors' views of their work, see Freidson, *Profession of Medicine*, pp. 168–172. The subjectivity of teachers' views of ghetto students is suggested in Peter Rossi et al. *The Roots of Urban Discontent* (New York: John Wiley, 1974), p. 355.

26.   For a balanced discussion of the relationship between racial prejudice and generally biased behavior in judicial sentencing see Willard Gaylin, *Partial Justice: A Study of Bias in Sentencing* (New York: Vintage Books, 1975), chap. 3.

Chapter 9

1.   Settings may also be designed to encourage client penetration of these barriers. Deutscher describes the case of the public-housing applications officer who was pleased to have the receptionist's desk to one side so that prospective applicants would come directly to her desk, bypassing the receptionist. Irwin Deutscher, "The Gatekeeper in Public Housing," in Irwin Deutscher and Elizabeth J. Thompson, eds. *Among the People: Encounters with the Poor* (New York: Basic Books, 1968), p. 49.

2.   See Stanton Wheeler, "The Structure of Formally Organized Socialization Settings," in Orville Brim, Jr. and Stanton Wheeler, *Socialization after Childhood: Two Essays* (New York: John Wiley, 1966), p. 98.

3.   Ibid., p. 98. Wheeler observes that adult socialization agencies *implicitly* conspire to present the client process as benign. Sometimes the conspiracy is not so implicit.

4.   Street-level bureaucracies must continually justify themselves not only to a client public, but also to a public constituency concerned with bureaucratic efficiency and effectiveness. To carry out these tasks street-level bureaucracies expend considerable effort on public relations. On the public relations budgets of police departments, see Lois Forer, *Death of the Law*, (New York: McKay, 1975), p. 176. For an account of police affairs by a New York City deputy commissioner in charge of public relations see Robert Daley, *Target Blue: An Insider's View of the N.Y.P.D.* (New York: Delacorte Press, 1973).

5. Judy Riley, "A Case Study of Street-Level Bureaucracy: Child Protective Services," unpublished seminar paper, University of Washington, 1976; Pietro Nivola, "Municipal Agency: A Study of Housing Inspectional Services in Boston" (Ph.D. diss., Harvard University, 1976).

6. Carl Hosticka, "Legal Services Lawyers Encounter Clients: A Study in Street-Level Bureaucracy," (Ph.D. diss., Massachusetts Institute of Technology, 1976).

7. Joel Handler and Mary Jane Hollingsworth, *The Deserving Poor* (Chicago: Markham, 1971).

8. Howard Becker, "Social Class and Teacher-Pupil Relationships," in Blaine Mercer and Edwin Carr, eds., *Education and the Social Order* (New York: Rinehart, 1957), pp. 278–279.

9. Bernard G. Kelner, *How to Teach in Elementary School* (New York: McGraw-Hill, 1958), p. 19. Also see Willis Hawley, "Dealing with Organizational Rigidity in Public Schools: A Theoretical Perspective" (paper prepared for delivery at the Annual Convention of the American Political Science Association, September, 1971), p. 6.

10. Arthur Niederhoffer, *Behind the Blue Shield* (New York: Doubleday, 1967), p. 53.

11. Jonathan Rubinstein, *City Police* (New York: Farrar, Straus, 1973), pp. 301–316.

12. John Van Maanen, "Working the Street: A Developmental View of Police Behavior," in Herbert Jacob, ed., *The Potential for Reform of the Criminal Justice System* (Beverly Hills, Calif.: Sage, 1974).

13. See Jerome Skolnick, *Justice without Trial* (New York: John Wiley, 1967), pp. 45–46. See also Rubinstein, *City Police*, chap. 6.

14. David Kirp makes this point in an unpublished paper, "The Bureaucratization of Childhood."

15. Hosticka, "Legal Services Lawyers Encounter Clients."

16. Maureen Mileski, "Courtroom Encounters," *Law and Society Review*, vol. 5, no. 5 (May, 1971), p. 503.

17. Dennis Trees, unpublished seminar paper, University of Washington, 1976.

18. Mileski, "Courtroom Encounters," pp. 529–530.

19. James D. Thompson, *Organizations in Action* (New York: McGraw-Hill, 1967), p. 123.

20. Richard Weatherley, *Reforming Special Education: Policy Implementation from State Level to Street Level* (Cambridge, Mass.: Massachusetts Institute of Technology Press, 1979).

21. Nivola, "Municipal Agency."

22. Jeffrey Prottas, *People-Processing: The Street-Level Bureaucrat in Public Service Bureaucracies* (Lexington, Mass.: Lexington Books, 1979), chap. 4.

23. Hosticka, "Legal Services Lawyers Encounter Clients," provides a persuasive discussion of the influence of receptionists. See generally, David Mechanic, "Sources of Power of Lower Participants in Complex Organizations," *Administrative Science Quarterly*, vol. 7, no. 2 (December, 1962), pp. 349–364.

24. Deutscher, "The Gatekeeper in Public Housing."

25. Joel Handler, "The Juvenile Court and the Adversary System: Problems of Function and Form," *Wisconsin Law Review*, vol. 17 (Winter, 1965).

26. Adoption-agency social workers' "nominal function of advocate for the child and advisor to the court on the range of alternatives and possible outcomes relative to a child's development has been transformed into a *de facto* assumption of judicial powers." Thomas E. Nutt and John A. Snyder, *Trans-Racial Adoption* (Study supported under NIMH grant #R03 MH 19805-01), p. 19.

27. Jerome Carlin, "Courts and the Poor" (paper prepared for delivery at the 1966 Annual Meeting of the American Political Science Association, New York, September, 1966), p. 3.

28. See, e.g., *Mental Illness and Due Process* (Ithaca, N.Y.: Cornell University Press, 1962), cited in Carlin, ibid.

29. Ray C. Rist, "Student Social Class and Teacher Expectations: The Self-Fulfilling Prophecy in Ghetto Education," in Yeheskel Hasenfeld and Richard English, eds., *Human Service Organizations* (Ann Arbor, Mich.: University of Michigan Press, 1974), pp. 517–539.

30. David Sudnow, "Normal Crimes: Sociological Features of the Penal Code in a Public Defender's Office," *Social Problems*, vol. 12 (Winter), pp. 255–276.

31. Julius Roth, "Some Contingencies of the Moral Evaluation and Control of Clientele: The Case of the Hospital Emergency Room," in Hasenfeld and English, eds., *Human Service Organizations*, pp. 503–504.

32. Prottas, *People-Processing*.

Notes

33. An opposite practice, which is also consistent with conserving resources, is the tendency to pass the buck for making determinations to other agencies. This is the current complaint of prison reformers who regard indeterminate sentences, originally intended to permit prisoners to demonstrate redeeming characteristics, as functioning to keep them under the control of prison officials who can manipulate the extension or reduction of sentence.

34. Robert Perlman, *Consumers and Social Services* (New York: John Wiley, 1975), p. 67.

35. Jeffry Galper, *The Politics of Social Services* (Englewood Cliffs, N.J.: Prentice-Hall, 1975), p. 70.

36. Rikva Bar-Yosef and E. O. Schild, "Pressures and Defenses in Bureaucratic Roles," in Elihu Katz and Brenda Danet, eds., *Bureaucracy and the Public* (New York: Basic Books, 1973), p. 295.

37. For a useful discussion of the function of appeals in the selective service system see James W. Davis, Jr. and Kenneth Dolbeare, *Little Groups of Neighbors* (Chicago: Markham, 1968), chap. 5.

38. On the difficulty of filing complaints against the police see Walter Gellhorn, *When Americans Complain* (Cambridge, Mass.: Harvard University Press, 1966), pp. 186ff.

39. Frances F. Piven and Richard A. Cloward, *Regulating the Poor: The Functions of Public Welfare* (New York: Pantheon, 1971), p. 173. Piven and Cloward attribute the low number of appeals to the control of the welfare system over clients, resulting in their acquiescence to the system of welfare on its terms, a thesis consistent with earlier arguments in this book.

40. David C. Perry and Paula Sornoff, "Politics at the Street Level: The Select Case of Police Administration and the Community" (rev. version of a paper presented to the Annual Meeting of the American Political Science Association, Washington, D.C., 1972), pp. 62–63.

41. Michael Lipsky, *Protest in City Politics* (Chicago: Rand McNally, 1970), chap. 5.

42. See, for example, David C. Perry and Paula Sornoff, "Street Level Administration and the Law: The Problem of Police-Community Relations," *Criminal Law Bulletin*, vol. 8, no. 1 (January–February, 1972), p. 54.

43. Albert Reiss, Jr., *The Police and the Public* (New Haven: Yale University Press, 1971), p. 125.

44. The word "emergency" is rarely defined in studies of public services except in the specific context in which it is applied. See for example, Morris Schwartz and Charlotte Green Schwartz, *Social Approaches to Mental Patient Care* (New York: Columbia University Press, 1964), p. 50; Egon Bittner, "Police Discretion in Emergency Apprehension of Mentally Ill Persons," *Social Problems*, vol. 14 (1967), pp. 278–292; Freidson, *Profession of Medicine*, p. 118.

45. Lipsky, *Protest in City Politics*, p. 89.

46. Freidson, *Profession of Medicine*, p. 118.

47. See Michael Zubkoff, "Emergency Room Service," in Eli Ginsberg, ed., *Urban Health Services* (New York: Columbia University Press, 1971), pp. 119–124.

Chapter 10

1. For a review of the literature on reconciliation of psychological dissonance, see David Sears and Richard Whitney, *Political Persuasion* (Morristown, N.J.: General Learning Press, 1973).

2. For a discussion of changes in recruits' attitudes toward their jobs over time see John H. McNamara, "Uncertainties in Police Work: The Relevance of Police Recruits' Backgrounds and Training," in David Bordua, ed., *The Police: Six Sociological Essays* (New York: John Wiley, 1967), pp. 163–252. See also Richard Cloward and Irwin Epstein, "Private Social Welfare's Disengagement from the Poor: The Case of Family Adjustment Agencies," in M. Zald, ed., *Social Welfare Institutions* (New York: John Wiley, 1965), pp. 623–643.

3. Eliot Freidson, *Profession of Medicine* (New York: Dodd, Mead, 1974), p. 89.

4. Throughout this study I have focused attention on relationships of street-level bureaucrats to their work. I do not explore here other causes of worker alienation, which include factors outside the work situation. For a brief discussion of absenteeism and other employee behaviors as adaptive responses to work see Chris Argyris, *Integrating the Individual and the Organization* (New York: John Wiley, 1964), chap. 4.

5. The extent to which public employees are protected from being fired and thus may have relatively extreme attitudes of withdrawal from engagement in their work, yet still retain their jobs, is discussed in Eric Nordlinger, *Decentralizing the City* (Cambridge, Mass: Massachusetts Institute of Technology Press, 1972), chap. 3.

6. To some readers it may seem unnecessary to review the reasons that street-level bureaucrats continue to work for organizational objectives to some degree. But in many societies with a less pronounced work ethic, the problem of getting workers to contribute their labor cannot be taken for granted. See, for example, the analysis of public service employment in Judith Chubb, "The Organization of Consensus in a Large Southern Italian City: The Social Bases of an Urban Political Machine" (Ph.D. diss., Massachusetts Institute of Technology), 1978.

For a study that analyzes the problem of organizations from the perspective of obtaining member contributions to organizations, see James March and Herbert Simon, *Organizations* (New York: John Wiley, 1958).

7. Aaron Wildavsky, "The Strategic Retreat on Objectives," in Wildavsky, *Speaking Truth to Power: Policy Analysis as a Problem* (Boston: Little, Brown, 1979).

8. On orientations of judges toward the poor under various circumstances see Jerome Carlin, "Courts and the Poor" (paper prepared for delivery at the 1966 Annual Meeting of the American Political Science Association, New York, September, 1966), p. 7; on teacher orientations see Howard Becker, "Social Class and Teacher-Pupil Relationships," in Blaine Mercer and Edwin Carr, eds., *Education and the Social Order* (New York: Holt, Rinehart and Winston, 1957); on styles of policing, see James Q. Wilson, *Varities of Police Behavior* (Cambridge, Mass.: Harvard University Press, 1968).

9. For an effective description of the dilemmas of a public defender in selecting cases for special attention, see Arthur Rosett and Donald Cressey, *Justice by Consent* (New York: Lippincott, 1976), chap. 6.

10. On other functions of selective recruitment see Anthony Downs, *Inside Bureaucracy* (Boston: Little, Brown, 1967), pp. 228–233.

11. Harold Wilensky and Charles Lebeaux, *Industrial Society and Social Welfare* (New York: Russell Sage, 1958), pp. 233–265.

12. See Richard Weatherley and Michael Lipsky, "Street-Level Bureaucrats and Institutional Innovation: Implementing Special Education Reform," *Harvard Educational Review*, vol. 47, no. 2 (May, 1977), pp. 171–197.

13. Victor Thompson has discussed the extent to which ideology serves as a psychological defense in *Modern Organization* (New York: Knopf, 1961), pp. 114–137.

14. See Donald Cressey, "Achievement of an Unstated Organizational Goal," in Amitai Etzioni, ed., *Complex Organizations* (New York: Holt, Rinehart and Winston, 1961), pp. 168–176.

15. See the discussion of overconformity and other defenses in Rivka Bar-Yosef and E. O. Schild, "Pressures and Defenses in Bureaucratic Roles," in Elihu Katz and Brenda Danet, eds., *Bureaucracy and the Public* (New York: Basic Books, 1973), pp. 288–299.

16. See Michel Crozier, *The Bureaucratic Phenomenon* (Chicago: University of Chicago Press, 1964), pp. 220–224.

17. Carl Hosticka, "Legal Services Lawyers Encounter Clients: A Study in Street-level Bureaucracy," (Ph.D. diss. Massachusetts Institute of Technology, 1976).

18. Robert Perlman, *Consumers and Social Services* (New York: John Wiley, 1975).

19. Anticipation of the consequences of their actions appears to be typical of workers on all levels of the criminal justice system. When New York state passed new drug laws with mandatory sentences in 1973, the New York City police department declined to change enforcement strategies because "it was feared that increasing the number of drug arrests . . . would create intolerable delays in processing cases in the courts." Anthony Japha et. al., "The Effects of the 1973 Drug Laws on the New York State Courts" (New York, 1976), pp. 2–3.

20. William Ryan, *Blaming the Victim* (New York: Random House, 1976).

Notes

21. Jonathan Kozol, *Death at an Early Age* (New York: Bantam, 1967), pp. 10–19.

22. Kenneth Clark has analyzed theories of racial inferiority and cultural deprivation as functional equivalents in *Dark Ghetto* (New York: Harper & Row, 1965), pp. 125ff.

23. See Murray Edelman, *Political Language: Words that Succeed and Policies That Fail* (New York: Academic Press, 1977).

24. Erving Goffman, *Asylums* (Chicago: Aldine, 1961), pp. 86–87.

25. On differences between whites and blacks regarding ghetto residents' capabilities and reasons for failures, see Peter Rossi et al., *Roots of Urban Discontent* (New York: John Wiley, 1974). On some differences in attributions of client responsibility between street-level bureaucrats, see Clarence Stone, "Paternalism Among Social Agency Employees," *Journal of Politics*, vol. 39 (August, 1977), pp. 794–804.

26. Becker, "Social Class and Teacher-Pupil Relationships," pp. 278–299.

27. Judy Riley, "A Case Study of Street-level Bureaucracy: Child Protective Services" (unpublished seminar paper, University of Washington, 1976).

Part IV: The Future of Street-Level Bureaucracy

Chapter 11

1. See Edward Wynne, "Accountable to Whom?" *Society*, vol. 13 no. 2 (January/February, 1976), pp. 30–37.

2. This is not the case with all buffer roles played by people who represent organizations to the public. For example, salespeople are not expected to be responsible to buyers in the same sense that, say, social workers are expected to be responsible to clients. See the discussion of buffer roles in James D. Thompson, "Organizations and Output Transactions," in Elihu Katz and Brenda Danet, eds., *Bureaucracy and the Public* (New York: Basic Books, 1973), pp. 191–211.

3. I am not arguing that discretion never can and never should be reduced. On the contrary, where lower-level workers usurp discretionary powers it is obviously appropriate for management to intervene. [For an example of such usurpation see Irwin Deutscher, "The Gatekeeper in Public Housing," in Deutscher and Elizabeth J. Thompson, eds., *Among the People: Encounters With the Poor* (New York: Basic Books, 1968), pp. 38–52.] However, when instances of appropriately circumscribed discretion are exhausted the basic work of street-level bureaucrats remains.

4. For a discussion of the problems of record keeping and accountability in medicine see Eliot Freidson, "The Development of Administrative Accountability in Health Services," *American Behavioral Scientist*, vol. 19, no. 3 (January/February, 1976), pp. 286–298.

5. The best discussion of the effects of weak management sanctions on developing norms of reciprocity supportive of low levels of effectiveness is Eric Nordlinger, *Decentralizing the City, A Study of Boston's Little City Halls* (Cambridge, Mass.: M.I.T. Press, 1972), chap. 3.

6. Murray Edelman discusses the symbolic implications of administration and bureaucracy for mass democracy in *The Symbolic Uses of Politics* (Urbana, Ill.: University of Illinois Press, 1964), chap. 3.

7. James Q. Wilson describes this tendency for police departments. "The police supervisor . . . would have to judge his patrolmen on the basis of their ability to keep the peace on the beat, and this . . . is necessarily subjective and dependent on close observations and personal familiarity. Those departments that evaluate officers by 'objective' measures (arrests and traffic tickets) work against this ideal. . . ." *Varieties of Police Behavior* (Cambridge, Mass.: Harvard University Press, 1968), p. 291.

8. Peter Blau, *The Dynamics of Bureaucracy*, rev. ed. (Chicago: University of Chicago Press, 1964), pp. 36–56.

9. James D. Thompson, *Organizations in Action* (New York: McGraw-Hill, 1967), p. 123.

10.   David Seidman and Michael Couzens, "Crime, Crime Statistics, and the Great American Anti-Crime Crusade: Police Misreporting of Crime and Political Pressures" (paper presented at the Annual Meeting of the American Political Science Association, Washington, D.C., 1972). Perhaps because they are subject to considerable scrutiny, illustrations of manipulation of statistics by the police are more likely to come to public attention than other public service agencies. See, for example, the criticism of an experiment in Orange County, California, that provided incentive pay increases to police officers for crime reduction. A report on this experiment alluded to the "possibility that the increase in larceny represents a shifting of criminal activities or a reclassification of burglaries into a closely related category which will not harm prospects for an incentive reward," New York Times, November 10, 1974, p. 77. Also, New York Times, May 12, 1972, p. 1.

11.   Significantly, the literature on productivity in public service provision draws its most persuasive examples from these and similar cases of resource deployment, not from the human services area. See, for example, Edward K. Hamilton, "Productivity: The New York City Approach," Public Administration Review (November/December, 1972), pp. 784–795.

12.   A good discussion of these problems of inference is found in Harry Hatry, "Issues in Productivity Measurement for Local Governments," Public Administration Review (November/December, 1972), pp. 776–784.

13.   Hamilton, "Productivity," specifically commends the utilization of quantitative measures ". . . where output is very hard to measure . . . to improve the deployment of resources so as to maximize the probability that our resources will be available at the time and place they are needed most." (p. 787). This may be useful for fire protection where the presence of fire fighters is the critical aspect of service provision. But it cannot be adequate for street-level bureaucracies when resource availability may not be related to service quality.

14.   Consider the following paragraph from a collection of essays on productivity. Mark Holzer, ed., Productivity in Public Organizations (Port Washington, N.Y.: Kennikat Press, 1976), p. 19.

Admittedly, there is an unevenness to productivity measurement. Some measures are relatively sophisticated, others crude. But in the common absence of any yardstick of productivity, even crude information is of value. At least it is a means of introducing systematic quantitative analysis into the decision-making process. Once that precedent is established, incremental refinements will undoubtedly lead to more sophisticated measures. Quantifications should only be attempted, however, if the organization has the qualitative and technical capacity to interpret and apply data meaningfully.

15.   If pay increases for workers and the cost of city services depend on productivity, then productivity measurement and assessment obviously become highly political. For example, New York City workers have sought to measure the size of productivity savings in terms of the net savings or additional income to the city from higher worker output. Fiscal managers, however, argue that productivity savings should be assessed only in terms of lower total wages resulting from the need for a smaller work force to accomplish the job. See the New York Times, March 26, 1977.

16.   For a discussion of these elementary aspects of productivity see Nancy S. Hayward, "The Productivity Challenge," Public Administration Review (September/October, 1976), pp. 544–550.

17.   See New York Times, October 22, 1976, p. A26.

18.   For a discussion of some of these service-rationing practices see Richard Weatherley and Michael Lipsky, "Street-level Bureaucrats and Institutional Innovation: Implementing Special Education Reform," Harvard Educational Review, vol. 47, no. 2 (May, 1977), pp. 171–197.

19.   Similar observations can be made for the apparent desirability of other modern management perspectives. Consider the following view of recent management control developments. "Critics of both sunset and zero-based methods have warned that these seemingly neutral procedures are in fact skewed toward hardware and away from human services. Fighter planes, miles of highway, or water projects are easily quantified; mental health, adequate nutrition, or family welfare are not." Ross Milloy, "Is Carter Serious about Reorganizing the Government? Should He Be?" Working Papers (January/February, 1978), p. 28.

20.   On crisis see Murray Edelman, Political Language: Words that Succeed and Policies that Fail (New York: Academic Press, 1977), chap. 3.

21.   I put "real" in quotes because when a saving is real and when it represents a reduction

Notes

in governmental effort is an empirical and normative question. Sometimes crisis can force management to attend to costs so that real savings are discovered, e.g., energy conservation by reducing unnecessary wattage in bulbs. But at other times a change is simply justified by calling it duplication or waste reduction although it may not be.

22. In part, promotion and retention in street-level bureaucracies are not based on the quality of service provision because service provision is so difficult to measure. Hence surrogates for effective service provision, such as tenure and advanced training, often bearing little relationship to worker effectiveness, are used extensively to reward and promote workers. These are not generally contradicted by more appropriate service delivery measures. On promotion in street-level bureaucracies see John Van Maanen, "Working the Street: A Developmental View of Police Behavior," in Herbert Jacob, ed., *The Potential for Reform of the Criminal Justice System* (Beverly Hills, Calif.: Sage, 1974); David Goodwin, *Delivering Education Services: Urban Schools and Schooling Policy* (New York: Teachers College Press, 1977), pp. 66–67.

23. The phrase is from Donald H. Sweet, *Decruitment: A Guide for Managers* (Reading, Mass.: Addison Wesley, 1975).

24. Letter from Hanna B. Leibowitz to *New York Times*, September 28, 1976, p. 38.

25. "Frozen Means You Don't Move: The Impact of Budget Cuts on People in Massachusetts Institutions" (Massachusetts Advocacy Center, 1978), pp. 46–47.

26. Perhaps the most neglected aspect of the fiscal crisis is the extent to which the firing of public employees represents a reduction in one of the critical functions of big city governments—the provision of relatively secure and decent jobs. After expressing great alarm for many months over the fiscal crisis the *New York Times* eventually recognized this consideration. "The trouble is, the bureaucracy also consists of people. Thus the fiscally sound demand for greater economy and efficiency in the municipal health care bureaucracy could lead to the discharge of thousands of hospital workers. In the absence of alternative job opportunities, the result would be suffering and despair in minority communities—and a sharp increase in welfare rolls." November 9, 1976, p. 36. Frances F. Piven has written presuasively on the redistributive aspects of urban fiscal liberalism and stringency. See an account of her views in the *Boston Globe*, December 9, 1976, p. 8.

27. "Teaching is becoming an old people's profession." See "Levittown Loses Its Younger Teachers in Trims," *New York Times*, May 13, 1978, p. 27.

Chapter 12

1. V. O. Key Jr., "Politics and Administration," in Leonard D. White, ed., *The Future of Government in the United States* (Chicago: University of Chicago Press, 1942), p. 160. Cited in Jesse McCorry, *Marcus Foster and the Oakland Public Schools: Leadership in an Urban Bureaucracy* (Berkeley, Calif.: University of California Press, 1978), chap. 1.

2. The interplay between national culture and the organization of work is explored in Michel Crozier, *The Bureaucratic Phenomenon* (Chicago: University of Chicago Press, 1964), a comparative study of French bureaucracy; Ronald Dore, *British Factory—Japanese Factory: Origins of National Diversity in Industrial Relations* (Berkeley, Calif.: University of California Press, 1973). Arthur Stinchcombe explores the relationship of organizational structures to their environmental origins in "Social Structure and Organization," in James March, ed., *Handbook of Organizations* (Chicago: Rand McNally, 1965), pp. 142–194 (esp. pp. 153–169). I am indebted to Charles Sabel of the Massachusetts Institute of Technology for his thoughtful comments on this topic. See his unpublished essay, "Workers and World Views."

In this chapter I elaborate on the postulate that there is reciprocity between the larger society and bureaucratic institutions. It follows that in different national (or even subnational) cultural settings, there will be manifest differences in bureaucratic organization.

3. These findings are drawn from Gabriel Almond and Sidney Verba, *The Civic Culture*

Notes

(Boston: Little, Brown, 1965); and Michael Banton, *The Policeman in the Community* (London: Tavistock, 1964), cited in Elihu Katz and Brenda Danet, eds., *Bureaucracy and the Public* (New York: Basic Books, 1973), p. 33. See their summary discussion of bureaucracy and culture, pp. 31–42.

4. Katz and Danet, *Bureaucracy and the Public*, p. 34.

5. The dynamics of the dialectic of expansion and contraction in public service benefits are treated in Frances F. Piven and Richard Cloward, *Regulating the Poor* (New York: Pantheon, 1971). See also Michael Lipsky, *Protest in City Politics* (Chicago: Rand McNally, 1970), chap. 2; Murray Edelman, *Political Language* (New York: Academic Press, 1977), chap. 3.

6. To my knowledge few studies have inquired into public agency behavior under conditions varying with agency need to attract clients. For one essay that addresses this consideration, see Michael Lipsky and Morris Lounds, "Citizen Participation and Health Care: Problems of Government Induced Participation," *Journal of Health Politics, Policy and Law*, vol. 1, no. 1 (Spring, 1976), pp. 85–111.

7. For illuminating discussions of the role of social welfare programs, broadly conceived, in contemporary American society, see James O'Connor, *The Fiscal Crisis of the State* (New York: St. Martin's, 1973); Piven and Cloward, *Regulating the Poor;* Ira Katznelson, "The Crisis of the Capitalist City: Urban Politics and Social Control," in Willis Hawley and Michael Lipsky, eds., *Theoretical Perspectives on Urban Politics* (Englewood Cliffs, N.J.: Prentice-Hall, 1976), pp. 214–229.

8. See Jeffry Galper, *The Politics of Social Services* (Englewood Cliffs, N.J.: Prentice-Hall, 1975).

9. Consider also Anthony Downs' discussion in "Why the Government Budget is Too Small in a Democracy," *World Politics*, vol. 12, no. 4 (July, 1960), pp. 541–563.

10. On national variations in welfare benefit levels and administrative organization see Harold Wilensky, *The Welfare State and Equality: Structural and Ideological Roots of Public Expenditures* (Berkeley, Calif.: University of California Press, 1975).

11. On the symbolic significance of public policies see Edelman, *Political Language*.

12. I have stressed throughout the buffer role of street-level bureaucrats, especially in chaps. 5, 6, and 9. For further discussion see Katznelson, "The Crisis of the Capitalist City," and James D. Thompson, "Organizations and Output Transactions," in Katz and Danet, eds., *Bureaucracy and the Public*, pp. 191–211.

13. Morris Janowitz directs attention to ways in which bureaucracies help shape the clients with whom they later interact in *Social Control and the Welfare State* (New York: Elsevier, 1976).

14. Ibid., p. 105. Janowitz asserts that this is generally characteristic of service bureaucracies in welfare states: "Whether one is dealing with the format of public housing or with welfare services associated with family assistance programs and community development, the overall effect on the process of socialization is to separate and in fact isolate the clients from the larger social structure and to seek to treat their needs in a very fragmented fashion. While these programs have eliminated the stark misery of oppressive poverty and the fear of starvation, they contain strong built-in limitations that thwart self-esteem and competence among recipients."

15. For approaches to politics that assume the ubiquity of conflict see Ralf Dahrendorf, *Class and Class Conflict in Industrial Society* (Stanford, Calif.: Stanford University Press, 1969); William Gamson, "Stable Unrepresentation in American Politics," *American Behavioral Scientist* (November–December, 1968), pp. 15–21. See also Lewis Coser, *The Functions of Social Conflict* (New York: Free Press, 1964).

16. Margaret Levi, "Poor People against the State," *Review of Radical Political Economics*, vol. 6 (Spring, 1974), pp. 78–79.

17. For one example of public employees seeking improved services for citizens see the efforts of the Service Employees International Union to obtain better patient care and treatment facilities at Boston City Hospital. *Boston Herald-American*, May 25, 1978, p. 7.

Notes

Chapter 13

1. See Murray Edelman, *Political Language: Words That Succeed and Policies that Fail* (New York: Academic Press, 1977), Chap. 4.

2. For a natural experiment in which, because of a strike in 1967, a city discovered whether it needed the services of a type of street-level bureaucrat, see Arnold Weber, "Paradise Lost: Or Whatever Happened to the Chicago Social Workers?" in Joseph Loewenberg and Michael Moskow, eds., *Collective Bargaining in Government* (Englewood Cliffs, N.J.: Prentice-Hall, 1973).

3. Fred Hechinger, "Smaller Classes Found to Produce Subtle Changes," *New York Times*, April 10, 1979, p. C5. The relationship of class size to achievement may depend on the subject taught. A recent South Carolina experiment found significantly higher reading scores in classes averaging 19.9 students compared to classes averaging 26.7 students. But no appreciable differences were discovered in math scores. See *New York Times*, June 22, 1977, p. 35.

4. *Boston Globe*, September 11, 1977, p. 10.

5. For the argument that work structure is more important than training in determining physicians' attitudes and the character of their practice see Eliot Freidson, *Profession of Medicine* (New York: Dodd, Mead, 1974), chap. 5.
   Richard Weatherley reminds me in a letter that for current workers, training often serves the latent function of providing a break from the job and is a fringe benefit contributing to worker morale, whatever the effect on practice.

6. See John H. McNamara, "Uncertainties in Police Work: The Relevance of Police Recruits' Backgrounds and Training," in David Bordua, ed., *The Police* (New York: John Wiley, 1967), pp. 163–252.

7. See Harold Wilensky, "The Professionalization of Everyone," *American Journal of Sociology*, vol. 70, no. 2 (September, 1964); Amitai Etzioni, *The Semi-Professions and their Organization* (New York: The Free Press, 1969).

8. Usually, increased professionalization is associated with deference of the society toward occupations, discretionary judgment, citizen trust, and reciprocal altruism, as well as the characteristics mentioned here. However, in some cases the term simply denotes an occupational group's increased adherence to accepted occupational norms. Thus increased professionalism among police may mean *less* discretion and greater conformity to legal standards and norms of police conduct.

9. Deborah Stone, "Professionals and Social Services," (unpublished paper, March, 1976); Gideon Sjoberg et al., "Bureaucracy and the Lower Class," in *Sociology and Social Research*, vol. 50 (1966), pp. 325–337.

10. On peer review in medicine see Freidson, *Profession of Medicine*, pp. 137ff.

11. Ronald Gross and Paul Osterman, ed., *The New Professionals* (New York: Simon and Schuster, 1972).

12. For a discussion of increased client participation in service bureaucracies (one generally consistent with the arguments of this chapter), see Alan Gartner and Frank Reissman, *The Service Society and the Consumer Vanguard* (New York: Harper and Row, 1974).

13. On the limitations of group practice in medicine relative to dominant professional norms, see Eliot Freidson, *Doctoring Together: A Study of Professional Social Control* (New York: Elsevier, 1975).

Chapter 14

1.   James W. Davis Jr. and Kenneth Dolbeare, *Little Groups of Neighbors: The Selective Service System* (Chicago: Markham, 1968).

2.   Martha Derthick, *New Towns in-Town* (Washington, D.C.: Urban Institute Press, 1972).

3.   Jeffrey Pressman and Aaron Wildavsky, *Implementation* (Berkeley: University of California Press, 1973). For the first stirrings of the field of implementation studies, see Austin Ranney, "The Study of Policy Content: A Framework for Choice," in Ranney, ed., *Political Science and Public Policy* (Chicago: Markham, 1968), pp. 3–21.

4.   C. Eugene Steurle, "Financing the American State at the Turn of the Century," in W.E. Brownlee, ed., *Funding the Modern American State, 1941–1996: The Rise and Fall of the Era of Easy Finance* (Cambridge: Cambridge University Press, 1996), pp. 409–444.

5.   Iris J. Lav, Elizabeth McNichol, and Robert Zahradnik, "Faulty Foundations: State Structural Budget Problems and How to Fix Them" (Washington, D.C.: Center on Budget and Policy Priorities, May 17, 2005), available at: http://www.cbpp.org/files/5-17-05sfp.pdf (accessed December 10, 2009).

6.   Contracting for services with for-profit agencies may be an entirely different matter. The logic of profit-driven provision of services would predict that management give priority to increasing caseloads and demanding that workers streamline and routinize interactions with clients. See, for example, Janice Johnson Dias and Steven Maynard-Moody, "For Profit Welfare: Contracts, Conflicts, and the Performance Paradox," *Journal of Public Administration Research and Theory*, vol. 17, no. 2 (2007), pp. 189–211. Such pressures exist in the public sector, to be sure, but perhaps not so overtly or legitimized by the rationale of the market. The discussion of contracting for services draws on Steven Rathgeb Smith and Michael Lipsky, *Nonprofits for Hire: The Welfare State in the Age of Contracting* (Cambridge, Mass.: Harvard University Press, 1993).

7.   For a discussion on professionalism as an autonomous source of accountability in organizations, see Carolyn J. Hill and Laurence E. Lynn Jr., *Public Management: A Three-Dimensional Approach* (Washington, D.C.: CQ Press, 2009), pp. 322–325.

8.   This section draws on Michael Lipsky, "Revenues and Access to Public Benefit," in Jorrit de Jong and Gowher Rizvi, eds., *The State of Access: Success and Failure of Democracies to Create Equal Opportunities* (Washington, D.C.: Brookings Institution Press, 2008), pp. 137–147.

9.   Elizabeth McNichol and Nicholas Johnson, "Recession Continues to Batter State Budgets; State Responses Could Slow Recovery" (Washington, D.C.: Center on Budget and Policy Priorities, 2009), available at: http://www.cbpp.org/files/9-8-08sfp.pdf (accessed December 10, 2009).

10.   Jon Honeck, "The Governor's Announcement on Taxes" (Cleveland, Ohio: The Center for Community Solutions, October 1, 2009), available at: http://www.communitysolutions.com/images/upload/resources/IncomeTaxStatement100109.pdf (accessed December 19, 2009).

11.   *New York Times*, October 9, 2009, p. A25.

12.   A staple of public opinion research is that people generally like what government does, but tend to have a poor opinion of government as such. See, for example, Meg Bostrom, "By, or for, the People? A Meta-analysis of Public Opinion of Government," (New York: Demos, 2005), available at: http://www.demos.org/pubs/ByOrForthePeople20050426.pdf (accessed December 10, 2009).

13.   Paul Pierson, "From Expansion to Austerity: The New Politics of Taxing and Spending," in Martin Levin et al., eds., *Seeking the Center: Politics and Policymaking at the New Century* (Washington, D.C.: Georgetown University Press, 2001), p. 66.

14.   The primary exception in the United States has been the transformation of the basic welfare program for dependent children from an entitlement program to a time-limited assistance program emphasizing work effort.

Notes

15. "Kaiser/Harvard Consumer Protection in Managed Care Survey, December, 1997," *Caring*, vol. 17, no. 3 (March, 1998), pp. 12–20, available at: http://www.ncbi.nlm.nih.gov/pubmed/10179020 (accessed December 10, 2009). Generally, support for government initiatives to solve social and economic problems has been on the rise since 2001, as has skepticism toward elected officials. For a review before developments associated with the election of President Obama and the economic collapse, see *Trends in Political Values and Core Attitudes: 1987–2007* (Washington, D.C.: Pew Research Center for the Public & the Press, March 22, 2007), available at: http://people-press.org/report/312/trends-in-political-values-and-core-attitudes-1987-2007 (accessed November 22, 2009).

16. Among other works, see Murray Edelman, *The Symbolic Uses of Politics* (Urbana: University of Illinois Press, 1964).

17. For example, one can test whether providing a low income family with a housing voucher improves its members' life chances. See James Rosenbaum and Stephanie DeLuca, "Is Housing Mobility the Key to Welfare Reform?" (Washington, D.C.: Center on Urban and Metropolitan Policy, The Brookings Institution, September, 2000), available at: http://www.brookings.edu/~/media/Files/rc/reports/2000/09metropolitanpolicy_rosenbaum/rosenbaum.pdf (accessed October 23, 2009).

18. See Lizbeth Schorr, "Charities' Work Demands Flexible Evaluation," *Chronicle of Philanthropy*, August 20, 2009, pp. 33ff.; also Michael Edwards, *Small Change: Why Business Won't Save the World* (San Francisco: Barrett-Koehler, 2009).

19. In his inaugural address, President Obama emphasized that the role of government should be approached pragmatically, and that government accountability is of the highest priority. "The question we ask today is not whether our government is too big or too small, but whether it works—whether it helps families find jobs at a decent wage, care they can afford, a retirement that is dignified. . . . [T]hose of us who manage the public's dollars will be held to account—to spend wisely, reform bad habits, and do our business in the light of day—because only then can we restore the vital trust between a people and their government." Obama Inaugural Speeches, January 20, 2009, available at: http://obamaspeeches.com (accessed December 10, 2009).

20. For a discussion that begins to treat the complexity of generalizing about accountability over the range of occupational roles and work environments that are encompassed by the term street-level bureaucracy, see Peter Hupe and Michael Hill, "Street-Level Bureaucracy and Public Accountability," *Public Administration* vol. 85, no. 2 (2007), pp. 279–299.

21. See pp. 3, xii, this volume. Some have even suggested that the book may be read as unequivocally endorsing the discretionary behavior street-level bureaucrats exhibit. See, for example, Janet Coble Vinzant and Lane Crothers, *Street-Level Leadership: Discretion and Legitimacy in Front Line Public Service* (Washington, D.C.: Georgetown University Press, 2007), p. 9.

22. Evelyn Brodkin, "Bureaucracy Redux: Management Reformism and the Welfare State," *Journal of Public Administration Research and Theory*, vol. 17, no. 1 (2007), pp. 1–17.

23. *New York Times*, April 29, 2009, p. A19.

24. See pp. 196–198, this volume.

25. But even clerks can exercise discretion. See Saul Weiner et al., "Rationing Access to Care to the Medically Uninsured: The Role of Bureaucratic Front-Line Discretion at Large Healthcare Institutions," *Medical Care*, vol. 42, no. 4 (April, 2004), pp. 306–312.

26. See Ian Taylor, "Discretion and Control in Education: The Teacher as Street-level Bureaucrat," *Educational Management Administration & Leadership*, vol. 35, no. 4 (2007), pp. 555–572; Tony Evans and John Harris, "Street-Level Bureaucracy, Social Work and the (Exaggerated) Death of Discretion," *British Journal of Social Work*, vol. 34 (2004), pp. 871–895.

27. Virginia Department of Motor Vehicles, "Virginia Performs," available at: http://vaperforms.virginia.gov/agencylevel/src/ViewAgency.cfm?agencycode=154 (accessed October 24, 2009).

28. Celia Hagert, "Updating and Outsourcing Enrollment in Public Benefits: The Texas Experience" (Austin, Tex.: Center for Public Policy Priorities, November, 2006), available at: http://www.cppp.org/files/3/CPPP_PrivReport_%28FS%29.pdf (accessed October 11, 2009).

29. On the hidden costs to citizens of efforts to save money through what are advertized as essentially administrative reform, see Michael Lipsky, "Bureaucratic Disentitlement in Social Welfare Programs," *Social Service Review*, vol. 58 (1984), pp. 1–17.

30. Greg Marston, "Employment Services in an Age of E-Government," *Information, Communication & Society*, vol. 9, no. 1 (February 2006), pp. 83–103.

31. David Landsbergen, "Screen Level Bureaucracy: Databases as Public Records," *Government Information Quarterly*, vol. 21 (2004), p. 25.

32. In this section I draw on Michael Lipsky, "The Paradox of Managing Discretionary Workers in Social Welfare Policy," in Michael Adler et al., eds., *The Sociology of Social Security* (Edinburgh: Edinburgh University Press, 1991), pp. 212–228.

33. Evelyn Brodkin, *The False Promise of Administrative Reform* (Philadelphia: Temple University Press, 1986).

34. Jerry Mashaw, *Bureaucratic Justice: Managing Social Security Disability Claims* (New Haven, Conn.: Yale University Press, 1983).

35. Robert Behn, *Leadership Counts: Lessons for Public Managers from the Massachusetts Welfare, Training, and Employment Program* (Cambridge, Mass.: Harvard University Press, 1991). This account also draws on my experiences as a consultant with the Massachusetts Department of Public Welfare from 1983 to 1988.

The department leaders resisted evaluation through random assignment, despite considerable pressure to do so, primarily for two reasons. First, they believed in placing people in jobs, and thus considered it wrong to deny some citizens access to important services. Second, they believed that it would not be possible to isolate a true control group, because so many ET activities consisted of statewide publicity and collective efforts to assist welfare recipients. See Behn's extensive discussion of ET's fit with the standards of random assignment experimentation, chap. 9.

36. Ibid., chap. 1.

37. For an account of a welfare agency that did not put comparable management tools in place and failed in transforming workers' orientations, see Marcia K. Meyers et al., "On the Front Lines of Welfare Delivery: Are Workers Implementing Policy Reforms?" *Journal of Policy Analysis and Management*, vol. 17, no. 1 (1998), pp. 1–22. Soeren Winter and colleagues in many papers have explored on an empirical basis the contributions of management initiatives, public policy dictates, and other interventions to bringing street-level bureaucrats' performance in line with policy directives in Denmark. See, for example, Peter J. May and Soeren Winter, "Politicians, Managers, and Street-Level Bureaucrats: Influences on Policy Implementation," *Journal of Public Administration Research and Theory*, vol. 19, no. 3 (2009), pp. 453–476.

38. For the origins of CompSTAT, see Jack Maple, *The Crime Fighter: Putting the Bad Guys Out of Business* (New York: Random House, 2000).

39. In many articles Robert Behn seeks to identify the core elements of the CompSTAT approach for a range of public management reforms that purport to build on the model. See, e.g., "Designing PerformanceStat," *Public Performance and Management Review*, vol. 32, no. 2 (December, 2008), pp. 206–235.

40. For another instance of shaping workers' behavior in the direction of generosity, see Robert Garot, "Bias Forged through Suspicion: The Housing Gatekeeper Reconsidered," in Stacy Burns, ed., *Sociology of Crime, Law, and Deviance*, vol. 6 (Greenwich, Conn.: JAI Press, 2005), pp. 77–104.

41. See p. 15, this volume.

42. Lisa Dodson, *The Moral Underground: How Ordinary Americans Subvert the Unfair Economy* (New York: New Press, 2009). This behavior has been described as "sabotage" of agency policy in John Brehm and Scott Gates, *Working, Shirking, and Sabotage: Bureaucratic Response to a Democratic Public* (Ann Arbor: University of Michigan Press, 1997).

43. Steven Maynard-Moody and Michael Musheno, *Cops, Teachers, Counselors: Stories from the Front Lines of Public Service* (Ann Arbor: University of Michigan Press, 2003), p. 24.

44. Michael Hill and Peter Hupe, *Implementing Public Policy* (London: Sage Publications, 2002), p. 27.

Notes

45. "The law's emphasis needs to shift from applying sanctions for failing to raise test scores to holding states and localities accountable for making the systemic changes that improve student achievement." "Joint Organizational Statement on No Child Left Behind (NCLB) Act" (Boston, Mass.: FairTest, 2004), available at: http://www.fairtest.org/joint%20 statement%20civil%20rights%20grps%2010-21-04.html (accessed December 10, 2009).

46. To take an example with significant implications, in some schools serving Native American students study units focusing on the history and culture of Native Americans—subjects critical to helping native youth understand and appreciate their heritage—have been dropped by schools giving priority to test results. Presentation by Hon. Ernie St. Germaine, Honoring Nations Symposium, Cambridge, Mass., September 18, 2009.

47. Gerald Grant and Christine E. Murray, *Teaching in America: The Slow Revolution* (Cambridge, Mass.: Harvard University Press, 1999), p. 215.

48. Dorothy Anagnostopoulos uses a street-level bureaucracy perspective to analyze Chicago teachers' responses to a new accountability agenda in "The New Accountability, Student Failure, and Teachers' Work in Urban High Schools," *Educational Policy* vol. 17, no. 3 (July 2003), pp. 291–316.

49. Linda Darling-Hammond and Milbrey Wallin McLaughlin, "Investing in Teaching as a Learning Profession," in Darling-Hammond and Gary Sykes, eds., *Teaching as the Learning Profession* (San Francisco: Jossey-Bass, 1999), pp. 376–411; see also Ron Haskins and Susanna Loeb, "A Plan to Improve the Quality of Teaching in American Schools" (policy brief, The Brookings Institution, Spring, 2007), available at: http://www.brookings.edu/~/media/Files/rc/papers/2007/spring_childrenfamilies_haskins/spring_childrenfamilies_haskins.pdf (accessed November 29, 2009).

50. Mary E. Dilworth and Joseph A. Aguerrebere, "NCLB's Highly Qualified Teacher: A Placeholder Definition," *National Journal of Urban Education and Practice*, vol. 1, no. 2 (Fall, 2007), pp. 111–135.

51. See Dilworth and Aguerrebere, p. 127.

52. Dilworth and Aguerrebere, p. 119.

53. See chap. 4.

54. Letter to the legislature, Lewis H. Spence, Commissioner of the Department of Social Services, April 24, 2002, p. 3.

55. Lewis H. Spence, Letter to Fellow Employees, January 21, 2005, p. 2.

56. Linda T. Kohn et al., eds., *To Err Is Human: Building a Safer Health System*, Committee on Quality of Health Care in America (Washington, D.C.: National Academy Press, 2000), available at: http://www.nap.edu/openbook.php?isbn=0309068371 (accessed October 19, 2009). See pp. 209–210, this volume.

57. On the relationship of citizen trust and experiences with street-level policy, see Bo Rothstein, "The State and Social Capital: An Institutional Theory of Generalized Trust," *Comparative Politics* (July 2008), pp. 441–459.

58. See Margaret Levi, "A State of Trust," in Valerie Braithwaite and Levi, eds., *Trust and Governance* (New York: Russell Sage Foundation, 1998), pp. 77–101.

59. Murray Edelman, *Constructing the Political Spectacle* (Chicago: University of Chicago Press, 1988).

60. See p. 5, this volume, and "U.S. Census of Government Employment by Geography and by Government Function," March, 2007.

INDEX

Absenteeism, 17, 80, 143, 257n
Accountability, 159–165; and client
organization, 189; in education, 233;
increasing, 195; in medicine, 258n; and
performance measures, 165–169; and
policy making by street-level bureaucrats,
221–223; and productivity, 170–172; and
professionalism, 203; and responsiveness,
230–231
Administrative law judges (ALJs), 226
Adoption agency workers, 130
Adult continuing education, 92
Advocacy, 72–75, 99; discouragement of, 185;
in the professions, 203
Affirmative action, 135–136
Aguerrebere, Joseph A., 232–233
Aid to Families with Dependent Children, 94
Alcoholism, 18, 20, 102, 112; among police,
32; and the ideology of benign
intervention, 119
Alex, Nicholas, 253n
Alford, Robert, 245n
Alienation, 17, 75–80
Allen, Vernon, 246n–247n
Almond, Gabriel, 260n
Alternatives to incarceration, 19–20, 43
Altruism, 71–73, 144, 185; and
professionalism, 201, 204
Ambulance services, 16, 136, 167
Anderson, James G., 247n
Antigovernment perspective, 217–221, 264
Apathy, 17
Appeals, 134–136
Appointments, 96, 98
Argyris, Chris, 241–242n, 250n, 257n
Aronson, Elliot, 246n
Arrest rates, 51–52, 114
Atkins, Charles, 226
Attrition, 174–175
Automated service systems, 224–225
Autonomy of street-level bureaucrats, 221–
225

Baker, Alan, 239n–240n
Banton, Michael, 261n
Barnard, Chester, 246n
Bar-Yosef, Rivka, 256n–257n
Becker, Howard, 155, 244n, 255n, 257n–258n
Behn, Robert, 227

Bell, Daniel, 240n
Bellow, Gary, 246n
Bendix, Reinhard, 251n
Bennett-Sandler, Georgette, 244n
Berger, Peter, 248n–249n, 251n
Bias, 141–142, 155–156; and bureaucratic
work settings, 85; and client
differentiation, 108–116; media emphasis
on government failures over successes,
218; racial, 111, 115, 181–182
Bittner, Egon, 256n
Blau, Peter, 51, 166, 240n, 247n, 250n, 258n
Blind, the, 109
Bloch, Alfred M., 32, 244n
Blum, Richard, 244n
Bordua, David, 240n, 244n–245n, 247n,
249n, 254n, 256n
Boston, 10, 127–128, 135, 261n; Little City
Halls program in, 35, 92; police in, 246n;
pretrial diversion programs in, 20; public
housing in, 21–22, 65, 96, 101, 108
Boston City Hospital, 261n
Boston Housing Authority (BHA), 21–22, 108
Bowles, Samuel, 240n
Bridges, Gary, 247n
Brim, Orville, 247n, Jr.
Brintnall, Michael, 252n
Brodkin, Evelyn, 222
Budgetary constraints, 214, 216–217
Building inspectors, 120, 204; see also
Housing inspectors
Bureaucracies: reform of, 192–211; and
societal values, 180–188; see also
Organizations; Public service workers;
Street-level bureaucrats
Bush, George W., 231

Carey, Hugh, 240n
Carlin, Jerome, 130, 255n, 257n
Carr, Edwin, 244n, 255n, 257n
Cheating, 17
Chicago, 5, 99
Chickering, A. Lawrence, 240n
Child abuse and neglect, 155
Child Protective Services (CPS), 74–75, 233–
236
Cicourel, Aaron V., 247n, 250n, 252n
Citizen patrols, 194
Citizen review boards, 124

Index

Civil-rights compliance officers, 14
Civil rights movement, 212–213
Civil service system, 17, 23–24, 79, 82, 143, 206
Clark, Kenneth, 249n, 258n
Clerks, 14, 128–130, 239n
Clients, 83, 243n; championed by organized public employees, 190–191; conceptions of, held by public service workers, 141–142, 151–156; control of, with procedural routines, 117–128, 185; differentiation of, 105–116; and emergency procedures, 136–139; impact of contact with, 190; increasing autonomy of, 193–196; increasing participation of, 208; informal selection of, 102–103; nonvoluntary, 54–59; organization by, 119, 189; psychological burdens borne by, 93–94, 104; referrals of, 132; screening of, 128–131; social construction of, 59–70
Cloward, Richard, 10, 240n, 252n, 256n–257n
Cohen, David K., 248n
Collective bargaining, 80, 206; for client needs, 190–191; see also Unions
Community action agencies, 10–11, 92
Community dispute resolution, 194
Community relations officers, 135–136, 146
Comprehensive Employment and Training Act (CETA), 178
CompSTAT initiative, 228–229
Computers, 198
Conservative movement, 215, 217–221
Contracting for public services, 215–216, 224, 263n
Coping behavior: client differentiation as, 151–156; and client-processing mentality, 140–156; necessity of, 187; procedural, 121–125; routines as, 85; see also Routines
Correctional facilities, 12–13, 15, 147; contradictory goals of, 41–42, 165; the medical model in, 148; work conditions in, 31–32; see also Prisons
Corruption, 63
Coser, Lewis, 261n
Court clerks, 90, 94, 252n
Courts, 3, 5, 203; access to, 102; as agents of social control, 11; bias in, 113–114; case priorities in, 135; function of setting in, 117–118; goal conflicts in, 42; rubberstamping of recommendations to, 129–131; service rationing by, 90; waiting imposed by, 97–98; see also Judges
Couzens, Michael, 247n, 259n
CPS (Child Protective Services), 74–75, 233–236
Creaming, 49, 107–108, 166
Creativity, 250n

Cressey, Donald, 257n
Criminal justice system, 15; see also Correctional facilities; Courts; Prisons
Criticism of public services, 217–221
Crozier, Michel, 257n, 260n
Cumming, Eleanor, 248n, 250n
Cynicism, 78

Dahl, Robert, 252n, 254n
Dahrendorf, Ralf, 241n–2242n, 261n
Danet, Brenda, 248n–249n, 251n, 253n, 256n–258n, 261n
Davis, James W., 214, 256n
Davis, Karen, 251n
Decentralization, 116, 207–208
Recruitment practices, 176–177
Demonstration projects, 187
Denver Plan, 200
Department of Health, Education, and Welfare, 164, 241n
Department of Housing and Urban Development, 21
Derelicts, 18
Deutscher, Irwin, 254n–255n, 258n
Diagnostic related groups (DRGs), 225
Dilworth, Mary E., 232–233
Direct service provision, abandonment of, 215–216
Disability insurance determinations, 226
Discretion in policy implementation, 13–25, 84–85, 149–150, 221–229, 233–236
District attorney, 22–23
Doctors, 73–74, 110, 254n; appointments with, 98; emergency room, 130; and home visits, 120; and the medicalization of social problems, 148; Medicare claims by, 45; as policy makers, 19–21, 25; practice standards of, 202–203; role conflicts of, 162; use of emergency procedures by, 138; in the VA hospital system, 20–21, 23; see also Medical practice
Dodson, Lisa, 230
Dolbeare, Kenneth, 214, 251n, 256n
Domestic relations courts, 130
Downs, Anthony, 243n, 245n, 251n, 257n, 261n
Draft boards, 84, 256n
Drug laws, 22
Drug treatment centers, 43, 93, 152

Easton, David, 251n–252n
Economic Opportunity Act of 1964, 41
Edelman, Murray, 219, 236, 249n–250n, 252n, 258n–259n, 261n–262n
Education, 5, 77, 206, 231–233; see also Schools; Special education; Teachers
Educational vouchers, 93, 104

Index

Index

Index